Armchair Traveller
at the bookHaus

November 1925: in search of health and sun, DH Lawrence arrives on the Italian Riviera with his wife Frieda and is exhilarated by the view of the sparkling Mediterranean from his rented villa. But over the next six months Frieda will be fatally attracted to their landlord, a dashing Italian army officer, and Lawrence will write two stories prefiguring *Lady Chatterley's Lover*: *Sun* and *The Virgin and the Gipsy*, both tales of women drawn to earthy, muscular men. Drawing for the first time of the unpublished letters and diaries of Rina Secker, the wife of Lawrence's publisher, Owen reconstructs the drama leading up to the creation of one of the most controversial novels of all time, and explores Lawrence's passion for all things Italian.

Lady Chatterley's Villa

DH Lawrence on the Italian Riviera

Richard Owen

Armchair Traveller
at the bookHaus

First published in Great Britain in 2014 by
The Armchair Traveller at the bookHaus
70 Cadogan Place
London SW1X 9AH
www.thearmchairtraveller.com

A CIP record for this book is available from the British Library

The moral right of the author has been asserted

Print ISBN: 978-1-907973-98-7
ebook ISBN: 978-1-907973-99-4

Typeset in Garamond by MacGuru Ltd
info@macguru.org.uk

Printed and bound in China by 1010 Printing International Ltd

Cover image: Lawrence and Rina Secker at the Villa Bernarda, 1926

With thanks to Pollinger Ltd for their kind permission to reproduce
material copyright © The Estate of Frieda Lawrence Ravagli

Quotation from *Footsteps: The Adventures of a Romantic Biographer*
reprinted by kind permission of HarperCollins Publishers Ltd, copyright ©
Richard Holmes 1985

'"Biography" meant a book about someone's life. Only for me it was to become a kind of pursuit, a tracking of the physical trail of someone's path through the past, a following of footsteps.'

Richard Holmes, *Footsteps: Adventures of a Romantic Biographer*

Contents

Acknowledgements

I am indebted to a number of people in England and Italy who helped me to trace Rina Secker and her connection to DH Lawrence. None of them, however, is responsible for any errors, which are my own.

I owe thanks first of all to Anthea Secker, Rina and Martin Secker's daughter-in-law, who first drew my attention to the story of Rina and the Lawrences on the Riviera, generously made material available to me from the family archives, and encouraged the project throughout. Her daughter Alice Briggs has also been unfailingly helpful, tracking down further letters, notes and photographs at Bridgefoot. Alice has taken a close interest in the emerging picture, together with her sister Kitty Cox and (in the United States) Adrienne Dion, the granddaughter of Rina's sister Anna Marie.

Among DH Lawrence scholars I thank above all John Worthen, Emeritus Professor of DH Lawrence Studies at Nottingham University, who read the original manuscript and offered invaluable advice. Others who commented on the manuscript and to whom I am most grateful include Claire Tomalin, Brenda Maddox, Isobel Colegate and John Woodhouse, Professor Emeritus of Italian at Oxford University.

At Bene Vagienna several residents were generous with their time and hospitality: Giacomo Borra, the mayor, Sergio Gazzera, Rina's cousin (and former mayor) and Michelangelo Fessia, head of the Bene Vagienna Cultural Association and a descendant of the Capelleros through his grandmother Giuseppina, Luigi Capellero's sister.

At Spotorno I am indebted to Giuliano Cerutti, the former town archivist, and Domenico Astengo, the Savona-based poet and literary scholar, both of whom have made life-long studies of DH Lawrence's stay in Spotorno and generously shared their memories and expertise with me.

On the Italian Riviera I also thank my parents-in-law, Ray and Edythe Crosse, to whom I owe many happy stays in Alassio; Alessandro Bartoli; Jacqueline Rosadoni née Poole, the English librarian at Alassio; Maura Muratorio; Valerie Falchi, née Wadsworth; and Massimo Bacigalupo of Genoa University. Between them they have shown admirable dedication in preserving the memory of the British heyday on the Italian Riviera.

Alessandro and Cristina Mirenda were kind enough to show us round Villa Mirenda at Scandicci. At Fiascherino and Lerici I am indebted to Silvio Vallero and Pietro Ferrari, to Carla Sanguineti, and to Simonetta and Giovanna Fiori of the Hotel Fiascherino. At Monaco I thank the État Civil office of the Mairie, the Bibliothèque Louis Notari, and the office of the *Journal de Monaco* at the Ministere d'État.

My thanks to Andrew Harrison, director of the DH Lawrence Research Centre at Nottingham University; Jayne Amat and the staff of the Manuscripts and Special Collections archive at the Kings Meadow campus of Nottingham University; and the staff of the Bodleian Library in Oxford, Gloucestershire Libraries and Westminster Libraries and Archives. I am indebted to Barbara Schwepcke, Ellie Shillito and all at Haus Publishing.

Last, but very much not least, I thank my wife, Julia, my companion in over 30 years of travels, who joined me in following the footsteps of Lawrence, Frieda and Rina.

Introduction

'Italy was Lawrence's true home, the Mediterranean his only sea, the gods of vine and olive the only ones that did not let him down.'

Anthony Burgess

'The English need this Italian *physical* way of approaching life.'
Frieda Lawrence to Rina Secker from Florence, 13 May 1926

I WAS FIRST drawn to DH Lawrence while at Nottingham University in the Sixties, not long after the 1960 *Lady Chatterley* trial. I even had, I remember, a poster-sized photograph of him on the wall of my room. And I fell under the spell of the Italian Riviera and the history of its English (and Scottish) colonies over three decades of family holidays on the Ligurian coast. The two came together – quite unexpectedly – when I was offered access to the unpublished letters of Rina Secker, with their vivid eyewitness descriptions of Lawrence's stay in the Riviera seaside town of Spotorno.

DH Lawrence is not often associated with the Italian Riviera. In *Lady Chatterley's Lover* Lady Connie makes love to the virile gamekeeper Oliver Mellors in the woods while her impotent husband Sir Clifford, shattered by the First World War, is cared for up at Wragby Hall by his nurse and housekeeper, Mrs Bolton. The setting is the Midlands, the background is industrial unrest and the post-war decline of the upper classes in their grand houses. What could be more English?

Yet Lawrence wrote what he would later call his '*very improper novel*' not in England but in Italy, the country where he spent a third of his adult life. He loved – and wrote lyrically about – all the things the British have loved about Italy for centuries: the sunshine, the flavours, the landscape, the people. For a miner's son from Nottingham the impact of Italy – and he lived in some of the most delectable Italian spots of natural beauty – was tremendous: '[it is] so beautiful, it almost hurts' as he wrote at Lerici. *Lady Chatterley* was written, as Lawrence's wife Frieda points out, 'in the Tuscan hills in an umbrella pinewood', just after she and Lawrence had spent six months at a villa above the resort of Spotorno, beneath the ruins of a medieval castle, amid vines and orange trees. This period had brought back to Lawrence all the Italian sensuality and 'blood conscious' love of life which had had such an impact on him during his first encounter with Italy 13 years before.

Frieda said that Lawrence had wanted to write *Lady Chatterley* 'all his life', adding that 'only an Englishman or a New Englander could have written it' since it was – paradoxically – 'the last word in Puritanism'. He still had in his mind vivid impressions of his last visit to his native Midlands, just before he left for Spotorno, when he was appalled by the 'dismal' industrial landscape which forms the backdrop to the novel.

It was at Spotorno in November 1925 that the dapper Lieutenant Angelo Ravagli of the Bersaglieri Regiment showed Frieda around the Villa Bernarda. She walked ahead of him in a clinging skirt with 'well-calculated movements of her body', as Ravagli later remembered. She then sat on a bed and remarked provocatively that it was 'perfect for making love', while looking into Ravagli's eyes.

In the novel, later banned because of its frank portrayal of sex, Lawrence drew on his wife's affair with Lieutenant (later Captain) Ravagli to create the story of Connie's attraction to Mellors, formerly Lieutenant Mellors of the Indian Army, 'with a very fair chance of being a captain'. It was also at the Villa Bernarda that Lawrence sat writing two stories which prefigure his novel of love and sex across the class divide – *The Virgin and the Gipsy* and *Sun*, which are based on the woman who brought him to Spotorno in the first place: Rina Secker, née Capellero, the bright, attractive and strong-minded Anglo-Italian wife of Lawrence's London publisher, Martin Secker.

In most accounts of DH Lawrence's life Rina is mentioned only briefly – largely, I suspect, because she kept herself in the shadows. This book brings her into the light. She even contributed to the character of Connie herself: Frieda once startled a literary party in London by declaring 'Rrrina my dear, Lady Chatterley is you', and sounded her out about appearing as Lady Chatterley in a film version of the story.

ALTHOUGH I DID NOT HAVE TIME to research and write this book until I left *The Times* in 2010, my interest in Lawrence and Rina began with an article on a scheme by FAI (Fondo per L'Ambiente Italiano), the Italian equivalent of the National Trust or English Heritage, to offer visitors guided tours of places in Italy associated with British writers. The piece described the period Percy Bysshe Shelley, his wife Mary and her half-sister Claire Clairmont spent at Casa Magni, in the seaside hamlet of San Terenzo near Lerici on the Gulf of the Poets, shortly before Shelley's death by drowning off the coast near Viareggio. There was also a tour dedicated to Byron's passionate love affair with Countess Teresa Guiccioli at the Villa Saluzzo Mongiardino in Albaro, a suburb of Genoa, before he set off to fight for Greek independence and die of fever at Missolonghi; and sites at Spotorno, between Alassio and Genoa on the Italian Riviera, associated with DH Lawrence.

I thought no more about it, until I received a letter from

Anthea Secker, whose late husband, the Reuters, *Daily Telegraph* and *Financial Times* journalist Adrian Secker, was the son of Martin and Rina Secker. She had, she said, letters and memorabilia relating to Rina, her Anglo-Italian mother-in-law, who as a young wife and mother had taken Adrian to the Italian Riviera, thereby attracting Lawrence and Frieda to Spotorno and unwittingly sparking off one of the most tempestuous and creative periods in the great writer's life. Rina's letters home to Martin, Mrs Secker said, contained eyewitness accounts of the Lawrences which had never been published.

Anthea Secker lives, as her parents-in-law Martin and Rina Secker did before her, at Bridgefoot, a three-storey early-18th-century Queen Anne dower house with gardens and out-houses at Iver in Buckinghamshire. Two celebrated architects, ES Prior and GF Bodley, lived there successively before Martin Secker took it over in 1912: Bodley restored the house, created a corridor between the main house and an adjoining cottage, and laid out the formal gardens with their clipped yews and walkways of pollarded fruit trees leading down to the bridge over the stream from which the house gets its name.

I went to Bridgefoot while on leave from Rome, and was astonished to find a time capsule: in an age when many fine houses have been mercilessly gutted and irreparably 'made over', Bridgefoot remains much as it must have been when the Secker family first moved in over a hundred years ago, with its book-lined corridors, family portraits, and elegant morning and drawing rooms. Martin Secker was the hands-on editor of a small publishing house, which despite its modest size, published some of the most important and innovative books of the early 20th century. He brought his authors to the house, they came to stay there, and even wrote their books in Bridgefoot's tranquil atmosphere. Secker did much of his work from home, brought his letters and papers back there, and left them there when he died in 1978.

Rina's papers were also brought to the house when she

died at Iver a decade earlier: they too were untouched. Anthea Secker showed me the letters written by Rina during a period in the 1920s when Rina and the young Adrian were living in Italy, right next door to DH Lawrence and Frieda. For a variety of reasons Rina spent much of her married life away from Martin, and wrote to him almost daily in a careful and educated hand. The letters are informative, witty and extremely observant: she noticed everything and passed on an engaging commentary to her publisher husband back at Bridgefoot of the doings and sayings of his most important – and most difficult and temperamental – author.

Going through the family papers, I found an envelope in the hand of DH Lawrence himself. Inside was an unpublished letter to Rina from Lawrence, offering her advice on writing. Then another letter came out of the trunk, in which Lawrence told Rina he looked forward to spending time with her on the Riviera, 'down there by the sea'. I found another familiar hand too – the looping, Germanic script of Frieda, who wrote a series of unpublished letters to Rina from New Mexico and Florence.

More letters, diaries and photographs came to light in the attics and outhouses, the letters neatly bundled together and tied up with ribbon or string, and in some cases with elastic bands which had perished. Some dated from the time of Rina's marriage to Martin Secker, others from her second marriage, to a Swiss-Italian banker named Carlo Lovioz. Some of the letters were in a leather attaché case bearing the initials 'RS' for Rina Secker, others in a tin trunk initialled 'CML' – Caterina Maria Lovioz – and lined with a copy of *The Times* from 1962, six years before Rina's death.

I made a pilgrimage to Spotorno to find out what had happened to the Villa Bernarda – and found that instead of being kept as an historic site and tourist attraction it had been converted into flats. After a period as a small hotel, the Pensione Chateau, it had fallen into decline and was 're-developed' in 2002. The then mayor, Giancarlo Zulino, described the development of Lawrence's former villa as a 'reconstruction', with some of its walls retained: others called it 'an act of barbarism'.

But the street – or rather walled alleyway – on which it stood, beneath the ruined castle high above the sparkling waters of the Mediterranean, had been renamed Via David Herbert Lawrence. The Hotel Miramare from which Rina observed Lawrence and Frieda – and which her father Luigi Capellero owned – was still on the seafront below, as was the Hotel Ligure, where the Lawrences stayed before moving into the villa up the hill.

'We got here yesterday,' Lawrence wrote to the agent Curtis Brown, 'it is lovely and sunny, with a blue sea, and I'm sitting out on the balcony just above the sands, to write.' A memorial on the wall of Via Lawrence put up by the local council in September 1986 reads: 'The eternally young Mediterranean, the shining moon, the lights of the village, brought peace to the unquiet heart of DH Lawrence, who stayed here with Frieda in the winter of 1925–1926.'

Rina's letters from Spotorno, I noticed, were written from the Villa Maria. I set out to find it. It turned out – after a long search, with much local scratching of heads – to be not near the Villa Bernarda up on the hill, but down on the seafront, a charming sugar-pink stuccoed villa set behind high wrought-iron railings and guarded by magnificent palm trees. The Villa Maria was right next to the Hotel Miramare, indeed part of it: it served – and still serves – as the private quarters of the hotel proprietors, who in Rina's day were her mother and father. The hotel itself has acquired an extra storey and a lift since the 1920s but – rather like Bridgefoot back in Iver – is essentially much as it must have been when the Lawrences and the Capelleros admired the spectacular sheltered bay and wide sandy beach.

This book is not a biography of DH Lawrence: it is an attempt to recreate his relationship with Italy by bringing the world of the Villa Bernarda, the Villa Maria, the Hotel Miramare and the Hotel Ligure back to life. It is the story of how

Italy, especially the Riviera with its sun, olive groves, villas and sparkling sea, gave new life to a great writer tormented by tuberculosis, and in the process inspired works which continue to exercise power over us nearly a hundred years later. It is also the story of a lost paradise of British expats in the 1920s, the Jazz Age, a world of tennis clubs, fancy dress balls, flirtations and affairs on the sandy beaches and in English tea rooms and libraries.

Rina Secker never published a memoir of her time with the Lawrences, even though Frieda assured her she had a gift for writing and Lawrence himself offered her advice on a writing career. In 1944, when she was in Merano during the Second World War, the Irish diplomat Charles Bewley suggested she should write her 'literary reminiscences'. 'I expect you ought to publish your Lawrentian memoirs', her journalist son Adrian told her in 1962, the year she began to put her archives in order. He advised her to broach the idea with Frieda's daughter Barby, by then Barbara Barr, with whom Rina had shared those extraordinary days in Spotorno. As far as we know, she never did. In a sense, however, she did indeed leave us her memoirs. They are in the letters which she so carefully tied up in ribbon and placed in a trunk 50 years ago at Bridgefoot.

I

Nottingham to Lake Garda

O N ONE OF THOSE SUNLIT, almost 'summery' days the
Riviera can offer even in November, a train carrying
DH Lawrence and his German wife Frieda pulled in with a
hiss of steam at the resort of Spotorno.

So elated was the thin, red-bearded Lawrence to be back
in Italy that he leant eagerly out of the carriage window as
the train drew – 10 minutes late – into Spotorno station,
within sight of the sparkling sea, the hotel-lined prom-
enade and the beach. Rushing up the platform in a whirl
of excitement came the woman he was looking out for:
Rina Secker, the Italian wife of Martin Secker, Lawrence's
publisher, who had found them a villa overlooking the
Mediterranean.

After a lifetime of restless travelling – New Mexico,
Ceylon, Australia – intermittent 'bronchial' troubles (in
reality, tuberculosis), and endless battles with censorship
and prudery, Lawrence could breath a sigh of relief. He felt
instantly at home. Rina embraced 'DH' while her parents,
Luigi and Caterina, hung back shyly with the pram containing Rina's baby son, Adrian.

Lawrence and Frieda's luggage was collected and the party
walked down to the seafront to enjoy a welcome glass of vermouth at the Capellero's seaside hotel, the Miramare. A light
breeze rippled the blue Mediterranean as the new arrivals

admired the sand, the promontory and the island of Bergeggi just off the coast.

Up above them on the hill stood the Villa Bernarda, where Lawrence and Frieda would spend the next six months. They could have had little idea of the drama awaiting them. 'It's a nice old house sticking up from the little hill, under the castle, just above the village and the sea', Lawrence wrote when he saw the villa shortly after arriving. It was 1925, Lawrence had just turned 40, and he was in a state of rare bliss.

'The sun shines, the eternal Mediterranean is blue and young, the last leaves are falling from the vines in the garden. The peasant people are nice, I've got my little stock of red and white wine – from the garden of this house – we eat fried chicken and pasta and smell rosemary and basilica in the cooking once more – and somebody's always roasting coffee – and the oranges are already yellow on the orange trees. It's Italy, the same forever, whether it's Mussolini or Octavian Augustus.'

Sunshine, sparkling sea, abundant wine, pasta with herbs, and someone 'always roasting coffee' – it is a picture you can almost smell. It is also a picture you can see today: like many of the Italian Riviera towns, Spotorno is much as it was when Lawrence was there. The railway has been moved to the back of the town from the centre, and there are high-rise flats where the local quarry once was, but Spotorno retains its charming medieval centre, with the delicious smell of cooking from family-run trattorias, geraniums tumbling from window boxes and washing flapping from balconies. Some of the houses in its narrow alleys still have faded frescoes; those on the front of the parish church of the Santissima Annunziata, by contrast, have been recently restored to their original bright colours.

Lawrence was still nostalgic for New Mexico; in an essay written at Spotorno, 'A Little Moonshine with Lemon', he compared the view from the balcony of his bedroom on the top floor of the Villa Bernarda with that from the ranch at

Kiowa which he had just left behind. He recalled with nostalgia the fir tree in front of the cabin at the ranch, and the horses he and Frieda rode there. But he also remembered how cold it was in winter, with snow on the ground.

In Spotorno there was no snow, and he was drinking vermouth to celebrate St Catherine's Day (25 November) – the name day of Rina Secker. At Kiowa, by contrast, he would have been drinking moonshine, because of Prohibition – 'not very good moonshine, but still warming: with hot water and lemon, and sugar, and a bit of cinnamon'. Just before moving into the villa, Lawrence had written a review of a book called *The Origins of Prohibition*, in which he celebrated the 'healthy' human appetite for beer and wine and condemned the hypocrisy of those who banned alcohol for others while allowing themselves 'the occasional drink'.

In a second essay, 'Europe v. America', he now spelt out his 'relief' at being back in Europe. The view from his balcony, he wrote in a poem entitled 'Mediterranean in January', 'persuades me to stay'. He would not go back to New York, the city of bank clerks, until the Mediterranean turned 'shoddy and dead' and the sun 'ceases shining overhead'. The contrast with America, in other words, was in Europe's – and Italy's – favour. 'The sea goes in and out its bays, and glitters very bright' he wrote. 'There is something forever cheerful and happy about the Mediterranean: I feel at home beside it'. In *Etruscan Places* he would observe that it was 'a relief to be by the Mediterranean, and gradually let the tight coils inside oneself come slack'. He preferred the 'deep insouciance' of Italy to the 'frenzy' which was 'characteristic of our civilisation but which is at its worst, or at least its intensest, in America.' Italy felt 'very familiar', Lawrence told his American friends on Capri, Earl and Achsah Brewster, 'almost too familiar, like the ghost of one's own self. But I am very glad to be by the Mediterranean again for a while. It seems so versatile and so young, after America, which is everywhere tense. I wish we were all richer, and could loiter around the coasts of the old world, Dalmatia, Isles of Greece, Constantinople, Egypt. But it's no good: we've got to go *piano-piano*'.

'Almost too familiar': the phrase will strike a chord with anyone who has become involved with Italy and cannot escape its seductive spell – and Lawrence was very involved indeed, to the point where he was nicknamed 'Lorenzo'. His decision to accept Rina and Martin's advice and go to Spotorno did not exactly come out of the blue. Although he is more often associated with the Midlands and New Mexico, he had a life-long passionate attachment to Italy, starting in 1912, when as a young man he fell in love with Frieda Weekley, the aristocratic German wife of a Nottingham professor.

BORN BARONESS Emma Maria Frieda Johanna von Richthofen at Metz, one of three von Richthofen sisters, she was a force of nature, distantly related to Manfred von Richthofen, the First World War fighter pilot known as the Red Baron. Her father, also a Baron, was governor of Metz: her mother too was an aristocrat by birth. Lawrence found Frieda – at 32, six years older than himself – uninhibited, direct and sensual, the 'woman of a lifetime'.

Frieda had a comfortable domestic life with Professor Weekley – but had secretly already had a series of lovers, both in Nottingham and on trips back to her native Germany when her husband thought she was visiting relatives. She was pretty and voluptuous: only later did she fill out into the large, dumpy and rather unkempt woman she became, making it more difficult to imagine her as a Teutonic temptress.

Frieda certainly believed in her right to free love. She believed too that it was the role of a woman to nurture a man's talent or genius: one of her lovers was Otto Gross, the psychiatrist, whom she admired as 'a remarkable disciple of Freud'; another was Ernst Frick, a painter and anarchist. Frieda's choice of Weekley as a husband might therefore seem out of character. On the other hand, although conventional (certainly compared to Gross or Frick), he was no dry, dusty professor. Author of *The Romance of Words*, Ernest Weekley was good-looking, witty, even passionate. He taught modern languages at Nottingham, and spent a year as a lecturer at the University of Freiburg – and when he met Frieda and proposed to her in the Black Forest, she accepted. They were married in 1899.

But Weekley was 34 at the time of their marriage, and Frieda was 20. Although she had three children in swift succession – Montague (1900), known as Monty, Elsa (1902) and Barbara (1904), known as Barby, who would later play a key role in the drama at Spotorno – Frieda began to feel trapped. She was lively and mischievous, while the professor was more reserved, and their sex life was, by her own account, less than satisfactory. As she puts it in her memoir *Not I, But the Wind* (the title is taken from a DH Lawrence poem), 'I was living like a somnambulist in a conventional set life'.

The young man who woke her from her sleep was from a very different background. David Herbert Lawrence, known to his friends as Bert, was the fourth of five children of Arthur Lawrence, a miner, and his wife Lydia, who lived in the coalmining district of Eastwood in Nottinghamshire. Arthur had been a handsome man and an accomplished dancer, a gregarious figure and a 'lively talker' with blue eyes and a curly black beard – but he drank too much, and Lydia came to feel she had married beneath her. Their often violent rows are reproduced in *Paul Morel* – later re-named *Sons and Lovers* – together with Lawrence's close, intense relationship with his possessive mother and the trauma of her death from cancer in 1910.

Lawrence was a frail youth, subject to bouts of pneumonia. He attended the local Congregational Chapel, won a scholarship to Nottingham High School and – after a short period as a clerk in a surgical appliances factory – studied for a teacher's certificate at what was then University College, Nottingham, teaching first in Nottingham itself and then in

Croydon. But he knew he was destined for something more: he once startled his boyhood friend Willie Hopkin by declaring he was going to be an author, adding 'I have genius! I know I have.'

Ford Madox Ford later recalled that all his life, Lawrence 'considered that he had a "mission".' He began to write stories and poems, drafting a novel which would become *The White Peacock*, published in 1910. With his pale face, lean, lanky figure, excitable high-pitched Midlands-accented voice and penetrating blue eyes (the red beard came later), he already had what Katherine Mansfield would later call a 'passionate eagerness for life'. He was delicate and sensitive, and given to sudden rages, his Nottingham friends later recalled, but also capable of impetuous acts of kindness and generosity.

His first love, Jessie Chambers, lived at Haggs Farm in the countryside near Eastwood, where Lawrence spent much of his spare time. Some of his love affairs were sexual, some platonic. Although Jessie shared his love of literature and was the model for Miriam in *Sons and Lovers*, her apparently frigid and 'sacrificial' reaction when he finally persuaded her to have sex with him led to their break-up. Other women in his life in the early days included Alice Dax, a married woman, and Louie Burrows, a fellow student teacher who Lawrence described as 'a glorious girl ... bright and vital as a pitcher of wine' and to whom he was engaged for just over a year (though he later said he had not really meant to propose to her).

By the time he went to the Weekleys' house for lunch at his former professor's invitation early in March 1912, Lawrence was making his way in the world. Nothing, however, prepared him for Frieda. That fateful encounter in the sitting room in the middle class suburb of Mapperley would change his life – and hers. Lawrence had gone to seek Weekley's advice about his idea of going to Germany to teach. But the professor was not there at first, and so Lawrence and Frieda had a fateful half hour alone together, talking about

Oedipus and the dichotomy in women between 'body and spirit'. Many years later Frieda recalled 'the red velvet curtains blowing out of the French windows' as they talked, and Lawrence's long, thin figure and 'quick straight legs, light, sure movements. He seemed so obviously simple. Yet he arrested my attention. There was something more than met the eye'. Lawrence reported excitedly to the literary critic and editor Edward Garnett that Frieda was 'splendid', 'the finest woman I've ever met'.

Frieda, it seems, at first just wanted an affair – she and Lawrence crossed the Channel together and travelled to Metz in May 1912. But before leaving for Germany she had confessed to her husband about her affairs with Gross and Frick, and Lawrence was the last straw. Weekley sent a telegram to Frieda to say their marriage was at an end, with no possibility either of reconciliation or of access to the children. Frieda was to suffer terribly from being deprived of her son and daughters, yet later claimed she had been determined to marry Lawrence from the first, writing that 'I had to be his wife if the skies fell, and they nearly did.'

And so Lawrence and Frieda began a union which lasted until Lawrence's death 18 years later – beginning it in earnest not in Germany, but in Italy. However, it was a union in which Frieda continued to believe in 'free love', while Lawrence hankered after a solid marriage and a family, though he and Frieda never did have children. 'The best thing I have known', he wrote much later in *Fantasia of the Unconscious*, 'is the stillness of accomplished marriage, when one possesses one's own soul in silence, side by side with the amiable spouse, and has left off craving and raving and being only half of one's self.' Frieda was not much of a Hausfrau; on the contrary, she was careless and slovenly, and it was the tidier Lawrence who throughout their life together did all the housework, cleaning, cooking and maintenance. They quarrelled incessantly. But he saw her always as the Frieda he had fallen for in Nottingham.

They stayed at first at an inn in the Isar Valley, then at a flat in Icking made available to them by Frieda's married sister Else, who used it as her own 'love nest' for affairs. Frieda made clear to Lawrence from the start that she too was still a free spirit by going to bed with a German army officer in Metz, and then by swimming across the chilly Isar River at Icking and offering herself to a no doubt startled woodcutter (shades of Mellors the gamekeeper). As they made their way over the mountains toward the Italian border in August 1912 with knapsacks and just £23 in cash, she made love to Harold Hobson, a student who had joined them on the trek together with Garnett's son David, while Lawrence was out picking Alpine flowers. According to Lawrence's autobiographical novel *Mr Noon*, Frieda told Lawrence bluntly that Hobson 'had me in the hay hut', her motive being that 'he told me he wanted me so badly'.

Averaging ten miles a day, they trudged over the mountains in the rain, past the roadside crucifixes which gave Lawrence the subject for his essay 'The Crucifix Across the Mountains', which begins 'The imperial road to Italy goes from Munich across the Tyrol, through Innsbruck and Bozen to Verona, over the mountains.' He saw the crucifixes and statues of Christ as beautiful monuments to an 'obsession with the fact of physical pain, accident, and sudden death.'

Lawrence's mood darkened further when he misread the map and he and Frieda became hopelessly lost. Somehow they got by train to Bolzano (then still in Austria and called Bozen), but were turned away when they tried to get a room because of their filthy appearance. They did find a room in Trent, but it was infested with bugs and the toilets were 'indescribable'. With Frieda in floods of tears, they took a train to Riva on Lake Garda, largely because a station travel poster had caught their eye, portraying what they hoped would turn out to be the Italy they had dreamed of: a purple and emerald green lake lined with roses, oleanders and vineyards full of black grapes.

It was. At Riva, just (at that time) on the Austrian side of the border, but thoroughly Italian in character, they stayed in a pensione, the Villa Leonardi. They were so poor they had to cook in their room (to the annoyance of the maid). But Lawrence was ecstatic. It was 'quite beautiful, and perfectly Italian', he wrote to Edward Garnett. 'The water of the lake is of the most beautiful dark blue colour you can imagine' and 'wonderful to swim in'. 'Out here seems so much freer than England,' he wrote to his former fiancée in Nottingham, Louie Burrows. 'The lake is dark blue, a beautiful colour, and so sunny. Here we have only had one shower in a fortnight. It is beautiful weather, and warm.' The figs were 'just ripe – 2d a lb – and grapes – miles and miles of vineyards – and peaches. They are also just getting the maize. It's fearfully nice.'

2

Gargnano to Lerici

LAWRENCE'S LOVE AFFAIR with Italy now began. Everything was 'beautiful'. 'I am here on the border of Italy,' Lawrence wrote to his former married lover in Nottingham, Alice Dax, from Riva in September 1912. 'It is a beautiful place. Figs and peaches and grapes are just ripe. Grapes are hanging everywhere, tons of them, very beautiful.' The lake was dark blue and 'clear as crystal. It is very beautiful indeed.' He and Frieda were planning to spend the winter at Gargnano, 20 miles further down the lake, in Italy proper. Gargnano, Lawrence told Louie Burrows, was 'a funny place, rather decayed', but 'fearfully pretty, backed with olive woods and lemon gardens and vineyards. I think I shall be happy there, and do some good work.'

At Gargnano, noted for its red wines and home to a detachment of the Bersaglieri regiment with their elaborate uniforms and plumed helmets, Lawrence and Frieda took rooms on the first floor of the Villa Igea overlooking the lake. The Bersaglieri were – and still are – famed for running in formation instead of marching. As the historian GM Trevelyan wrote in 1919, they were 'the noblest Italian types'. Watching them from her window, Frieda wrote to David Garnett, 'They are beautiful creatures. The men so loose and soldiers with *such* hats, a foam of cockfeathers on them I long for one, a hat not a soldier.' Some 13 years later she did long for the soldier as much as the hat, in the form of Angelo Ravagli, the Bersaglieri officer who was their landlord in Spotorno. In 1912 Lawrence too was struck by the Bersaglieri, telling Edward Garnett in October that the soldiers were 'so good looking and animal' – not, of course, anticipating that one such good-looking animal would become his wife's lover.

The garden of the Villa Igea – situated in a lakeside continuation of Gargnano called, rather confusingly, Villa – had roses, oranges and persimmons, which Lawrence was much taken with: at Spotorno 13 years later Rina would describe him trying (and failing) to make persimmon jam. There were scorpions in Eden – literally so: he found one in the spittoon which Frieda kept at their bedside as an ashtray because she smoked so much. But even so, 'I live in sunshine and happiness, in exile and poverty, here in this pretty hole', Lawrence wrote to the illustrator Ernest Collings. Even a surprise visit from Harold Hobson in December did not spoil the idyll: evidently sure of his welcome, Hobson turned up without warning and stayed for three weeks, his roll in the hay hut with Frieda apparently overlooked.

The local tourist association today offers a guide to Lawrence's Gargnano, including the lemon groves, the yellow-fronted Villa Igea, where his room faced the lake – 'in the morning I often lie in bed and watch the sunrise' – and the walk he described through the labyrinthine 'tiny, chaotic backways of the village' and up a 'broken staircase' to the church of San Tommaso, perched above the village and bathed in 'tremendous sunshine' but dark and cool inside. 'I went into the church. It was very dark, and impregnated with centuries of incense. It affected me like the lair of some enormous creature. My senses were roused, they sprang awake in the hot, spiced darkness.'

Below the church he could see – as you can still see – the 'confused, tiled roofs of the village' and the pale blue water beyond. The lake lay 'dim and milky, the mountains are dark blue at the back, while over them the sky gushes and glistens with light. At a certain place, on the mountain ridge, the light burns gold.' He encountered a woman in an apron and kerchief spinning a blue-checked cloth on the parapet, and she seemed to him 'like a fragment of earth' or a 'living stone of the terrace, sun-bleached'. On the way back down, in search of primroses, he could hear 'the water tittle-tattling away, in the deep shadows below' as he watched a steamer down on the lake 'in the warm stillness of the transcendent afternoon'.

In the same sketch he gives a memorable description of two monks deep in conversation as they walk among the vines: 'They marched with the peculiar march of monks, a long, loping stride, their heads together, their skirts swaying slowly, two brown monks with hidden hands, sliding under the bony vines and beside the cabbages, their heads always together in hidden converse'. He watches night fall: 'The day was gone, the twilight was gone, and the snow was invisible as I came down to the side of the lake. Only the moon, white and shining, was in the sky, like a woman glorying in her own loveliness as she loiters superbly to the gaze of all the world, looking sometimes through the fringe of dark olive leaves, sometimes looking at her own superb, quivering body, wholly naked in the water of the lake'.

'Considering the wandering nature of Lawrence, known as a restless globetrotter, why did he choose Gargnano?' the visitor's guide asks. It also ventures an answer: Lawrence found a refuge there from the mechanised and money-dominated world he detested, and saw in Gargnano's residents the guardians of an archaic world 'not overwhelmed by the turmoil of modern life'. Garda was 'beautiful as paradise', he wrote, a world away from the great mass of London and the 'black, fuming, laborious Midlands and north-country', from an England which was 'conquering the world with her machines and her horrible destruction of natural life'. Italians, by contrast, believed in the flesh, the senses; like William Blake's tiger 'burning bright, in the forests of the night'.

Lake Garda now has many more tourists than a hundred

years ago, and is a popular holiday destination for sailing and water-sports, not least for Germans, Swiss and Austrians. But Gargnano, now spruced up instead of 'rather decayed', has somehow remained a charming lakeside village: its pink and yellow houses still perch on the western shore of the lake, their lights twinkling in the clear water as night falls, the lake steamers still come and go, and although many of the lemon houses which Lawrence described have disappeared, some are still there, with their 'rows of naked pillars rising out of the green foliage like ruins of temples'.

To climb up to the church of San Tommaso you now have to cross a busy main road which was not there in Lawrence's day, and the adjoining Franciscan convent is now a 'European Peace Centre'. But the pergola shaded by olive trees where Lawrence sat is still there, the garden of the Villa Igea (now divided into apartments) is scented with roses, lemon trees and bougainvillea, and Gargnano still offers the fish, olive oil, lemons and capers which gave the runaways from Nottingham their first taste of Italy – and of freedom.

At Gargnano Lawrence was enormously productive: he transformed *Paul Morel* into *Sons and Lovers*; wrote *The Fight for Barbara*, a play about a couple living in Italy who are confronted by the woman's husband and her parents; sketched out *The Sisters*, which would become *The Rainbow* and *Women in Love*; and wrote both his play *The Daughter in Law* and the travel essays of *Twilight in Italy*. He was, Frieda said, a 'writing machine', with Italy providing the stimulation. Lawrence was not always dewy-eyed about Italy: it often irritated him profoundly, as it irritates many an expatriate resident. 'The older I get, the angrier I become, generally', he said later, when he and Frieda were living in Sicily. 'And Italy is a country to keep you in a temper from day to day: the people, I mean.'

But Italy, Lawrence found, confirmed his growing belief in the Southern power of the senses – 'blood consciousness', or 'phallic consciousness' – rather than the mechanical coldness of Northern intellect. He was, he realised, 'just as emotional and impulsive' as the Italians were, and finally free of cold, puritanical England. 'My great religion is a belief in the blood, the flesh, as being wiser than the intellect,' he told Ernest Collings. 'We can go wrong in our minds. But what our blood feels and believes and says is always true. That is why I like to live in Italy. The people are so unconscious. They only feel and want: they don't know.'

This was the sensuality and earthiness he had reacted to viscerally in the journey across the Alps, where 'everything is of the blood, of the senses' and where he had watched a peasant clasping hay to his chest with his shirt clinging to his 'hot, firm skin' as the rain trickled down to his loins in a 'hot welter of physical sensation'. This insight remained with Lawrence all his life: years later, in 1928, he would 'explode with rage' when hearing Aldous Huxley and his biologist brother Julian suggest mankind was capable of genetic improvement. The answer to the world's troubles, Lawrence insisted, did not lie in science but rather in 'the dark loins of man', in greater freedom for human instincts and intuitions.

He was starting to acquire fairly good Italian. 'I don't know any Italian, but it doesn't matter', he told Louie Burrows from Riva. He told Edward Garnett at about the same time that he and Frieda knew 'about 10 words of Italian'. He recounted a conversation with an olive farmer who failed to understand him trying to say 'It's a late harvest' in Italian. 'I feel like saying to him, "Don't be a pig, I've done my best".' At Gargnano, however, he began taking Italian lessons from the local schoolmistress, a stern lady with black gloves and a slight squint, and was evidently a quick learner. By the time of his later visits to Italy he was fluent, if not always strictly grammatical, and delighted in inserting Italian phrases into his letters.

In April 1913 he and Frieda moved up to a farm at San Gaudenzio overlooking the lake, owned by a family called Capelli (changed to Fiori in *Twilight in Italy*). Here Lawrence sat and wrote in the loft of a deserted lemon house 'high up, far, far from the ground, the open front giving across the lake and the mountain snow opposite flush with twilight'. He also painted the view along the road from Gargnano to San Gaudenzio. But he sensed that even here the 'lemon culture' was giving way to an economy dominated more by money than by honest toil; Giovanni, the son of a local innkeeper, was known as 'John', Lawrence discovered, because he had worked in America and was planning to go back there even though some Americans had called him a 'damn Dago'.

Later that year Lawrence and Frieda left Italy for a while for Bavaria, and then travelled back to England, Lawrence to attend his sister Ada's wedding in Eastwood to William Clarke, a tailor, and Frieda to try and see her children, a disastrous move which only resulted in a court order forbidding her access. They rented a seaside flat near Broadstairs, where they met the critic John Middleton Murry, his partner, the writer Katherine Mansfield, and Lady Cynthia Asquith, daughter-in-law of the Prime Minister, Herbert Asquith.

But Italy tugged them back. They returned to Bavaria and then Italy in September 1913: this time though they travelled separately, with Frieda calling on her family at Baden-Baden and Lawrence travelling through Switzerland to Como. It was a 'sad and gloomy thing' to walk from Italy to France, he wrote, but 'a joy' to do the opposite and walk south to Italy. 'I walked all the way from Schaffhausen to Zurich, Lucerne, over the Gotthard to Cirolo, Bellinzona, Lugano, Como', he told Edward Garnett with evident pride. He admits in *Twilight in Italy* that he occasionally took trams, trains and steamers, but it was still quite an achievement. 'It was beautiful – Switzerland too touristy however – spoilt', he wrote. In Milan Lawrence drank a Campari on the Piazza Duomo while waiting for Frieda and reflected on his encounter with emigré Italian workers in Switzerland, their nostalgia for home, and his own relief on reaching Italy again.

Their destination this time was not Lake Garda, but

the Gulf of the Poets near La Spezia, where the poet Percy Bysshe Shelley – who Lawrence greatly admired – had once lived in the small seaside village of San Terenzo, near Lerici, with his pregnant wife Mary and her half-sister Claire Clairmont, who was Byron's mistress. He and Frieda were thinking of Lerici, Lawrence wrote to Lady Cynthia Asquith from Irschenhausen in August 1913, '[in the] Shelley and Byron tradition'.

After a week at a hotel in Lerici, the Albergo delle Palme ('jolly good food, wine, and all included – a big bedroom with a balcony just over the sea'), they found a cottage nearby at Fiascherino, an isolated cove of breathtaking beauty where the maritime pines still cling precariously to the rocks above the water. They had to wait before moving in, but Lawrence was soon scrubbing the floors with his braces tied round his waist while Frieda played Beethoven on a piano delivered to them by boat – at the time there was no access to the cottage by road. The piano had to be hauled up the beach by local fishermen, an event still talked about a hundred years on: it was a scene, as the literary critic Laura Guglielmi has observed, straight out of Jane Campion's film *The Piano*. Silvio Vallero, grandson of Ezechiele Azzarini, a local fisherman whom Lawrence befriended, remembers his grandfather remarking that it was clearly Frieda who 'wore the trousers' ('*porteva i cazon*' in local dialect). 'Frieda *will* hire a piano, not a hurdy-gurdy', Lawrence complained to Lady Cynthia Asquith. He complained too about the workmen who had made a fuss about bringing it by steamer and rowing boat – 'I loathe and detest the Italians'. The locals deferred to him and Frieda as 'Signoria', or gentry, which he claimed to find embarrassing given his humble origins ('How's that for grandeur! Shades of my poor father!').

In fact, he was blissfully content: the area was 'so beautiful, it almost hurts'. 'I am so happy with the place we have at last discovered, I must write smack off to tell you'. Lawrence told Edward Garnett at the end of September 1913. 'There is a little tiny bay half shut in by rocks, and smothered by olive woods that slope down swiftly'. There was 'a four roomed pink cottage among vine gardens, just over the water and under the olive woods'. The cottage, the Villino Ettore Gambrosier, would 'D.V.' (Deo Volente, or God willing), be his next home, he said, though it was not available for another eight days. 'I feel I can't wait.' Like Gargnano, it was a refuge for a couple escaping scandal and still not married.

Today tiny Fiascherino and the village of Tellaro on the next headland, 20 minutes walk away, are no longer undiscovered: they offer hotels and holiday apartments with swimming pools, tennis courts, bars and restaurants. The four-roomed pink cottage or *villino* where Lawrence and Frieda lived is no longer there: it was incorporated into a grand grey-painted turn-of-the-century villa, which at the time of writing is dilapidated and awaiting re-development.

But the three-storey beach-side Casetta Rosa ('Pink House') where the local fishermen once lived just below ('awfully nice people') survives, next to the charming pink-painted Hotel Fiascherino, and a slightly incongruous wartime pillbox, its gun loopholes filled with flowers. The olive groves, fig trees, rocky coves and crystalline waters are still there, and you can still sense the 'exquisite' peace Lawrence found at Fiascherino, as he told Garnett: 'One gets by rail from Genoa or from Parma to Spezia, by steamer across the gulf to Lerici, and by rowing boat round the headlands to Fiascherino ... You run out of the gate into the sea, which washes among the rocks at the mouth of the bay. The garden is all vines and fig trees, and great woods on the hills all round.' There were wild yellow crocuses, and 'the Mediterranean washes softly and nicely, with just a bit of white against the rocks. Figs and grapes are ripe.'

When Lawrence tried to swim, Frieda yelled to him from the shore 'If you can't be a real poet you'll drown like one, anyhow.' Lawrence was indeed conscious of the danger of drowning like Shelley: the cottage was 'an hour's walk from

San Terenzo, Shelley's place', he wrote to Sir Edward Marsh, the sponsor of the English 'Georgian poets' and an adviser to Churchill and Asquith. 'The full moon shines on the sea, which moves about all glittering among black rocks. I go down and bathe and enjoy myself. You never saw such clear, buoyant water.' He did not swim more than a dozen yards, he admitted, but 'I am always trying to follow the starry Shelley ... I don't work much, and don't want to work. If I'd got the smallest income I should be delighted to loaf forever'. 'I think Shelley a million thousand times more beautiful than Milton', he wrote to Marsh two months later.

There was a sole orange tree in the garden, but it was 'a beauty', he wrote to his old Eastwood friend Willie Hopkin, with the big, heavy oranges 'swinging gold in their dark green leaves' as the wind blew down from the Apennines. The beauty of the olives, 'so grey, so delicately sad' put him in mind of the New Testament: 'I am always expecting when I go to Tellaro for the letters to meet Jesus gossiping with his disciples as he goes along above the sea, under the grey, light trees'.

He was 'very fond of the Italians' (the incident over the piano was apparently forgotten). 'The hills are full of voices, the peasant women and children all day long and day after day, in the faint shadow of the olives.' They picked the fallen fruit, 'pannier after pannier full'. The church at Tellaro overlooked the water, he wrote, and there was a local story that the villagers were once woken by the tolling of the bell at night to find that the rope was being pulled by an octopus warning them of the threat of Saracen pirates. Lawrence found this feat 'quite possible': the local octopuses were large, after all, six or seven pounds, caught by fishermen using long spears, 'and you never saw anything so fiendishly ugly'.

The Mediterranean, however, was 'quite wonderful – and when the sun sets beyond the islands of Porto Venere, and all the sea is like heaving white milk with a street of fire across it, and amethyst islands away back, it is too beautiful.' Lawrence acted as a witness at the wedding of his neighbour and friend Ezechiele Azzarini, even putting on his best suit and patent leather boots for the occasion, and walking with the wedding party from the church at Tellaro to register the marriage at Ameglia in the hinterland, 'three hours there and back', the bride in 'white silk and orange blossom'. He much enjoyed the feast afterwards, washed down with Ligurian wine – though he avoided the freshly caught octopus or *polpo*, still a local speciality cooked in olive oil and lemon juice. 'I can eat snails all right,' Lawrence told Willie Hopkin, 'but octopus – no.'

Lawrence and Frieda stayed for nine months: Lawrence improved his Italian further by taking lessons with a young teacher and aspiring poetess, Eoa Rainusso, the sister-in-law of Ezechiele the fisherman. On the whole they preferred the locals to British expats, but were taken up by a well connected couple, the Waterfields – Aubrey, a painter, and his wife Lina, who later became the *Observer* correspondent in Fascist Italy – and visited their castle at Aulla 16 miles inland from La Spezia, beneath the mountains of Carrara, where Michelangelo had once obtained the marble for his sculptures. The Lerici idyll did not last, however: in June 1914 Frieda went to Metz to see her family, while Lawrence walked part of the way over the Swiss mountains. They met up again in Heidelberg, and then went to London, where Lawrence published *The Prussian Officer and Other Stories*.

He also married Frieda at Kensington Register Office, her divorce from Weekley having come through. War with Germany was declared in August while Lawrence was on a walking tour of the Lake District: he later recalled 'the amazing, vivid, visionary beauty of everything' as a world came to an end. Frieda's German nationality was now problematic: they were even suspected by suspicious neighbours of poisoning the blackberry bushes.

Through friends, Lawrence and Frieda found a cottage in an overgrown orchard at Chesham in what Lawrence would later call 'damp and dismal Bucks'. Lawrence was unwell: although he never admitted it, his bouts of pneumonia were tubercular, and he was increasingly frail. It was now that he was visited for the first time by Martin Secker, accompanied by Compton Mackenzie, who was staying at Bridgefoot to finish *Sinister Street*, his most celebrated novel. Lawrence had first written to Secker in 1911, writing from Croydon, 'I am very much flattered by your offer to publish a volume of my short stories, to tell the truth I sit in doubt and wonder because of it', but regretting that his second novel was promised to Heinemann even though it was 'erotic'.

'I first made the acquaintance of DH Lawrence one afternoon during the hot, dry August of 1914', Secker later wrote. He was visiting Gilbert Cannan, one of his novelists, and Cannan's wife Mary at their converted windmill between Chesham and Tring. Mackenzie and Lawrence had an interesting discussion about Dostoevsky, Secker recalled, while Frieda 'provided us with cups of tea'. Lawrence was impressed at having married into the 'ancient and famous house of Richthofen', Mackenzie thought, and his 'rage at the war was fed by his having a German wife. I hardly exaggerate when I say that one might have supposed we had gone to war with Germany solely for the purpose of annoying Lawrence personally.' When Lawrence told Frieda 'we must get down somewhere to the sea', Mackenzie invited them to stay with him on Capri, where he had a villa.

Once again, Italy beckoned. For the time being, however, they were confined to England: it was now that Lawrence grew his beard, 'behind which I shall take as much cover henceforth as I can.' In 1915 Lawrence and Frieda moved to a cottage at Greatham near Pulborough in Sussex, lent to them by Viola Meynell, daughter of the poet Alice Meynell and fiancée (for the time being) of Martin Secker, before going on to Hampstead. Lawrence now acquired further influential friends and admirers including the Hon. Dorothy Brett, the partially-deaf daughter of the second Viscount Esher, and moved in high social and literary circles at Garsington, the Oxfordshire estate of the exotic society hostess Lady Ottoline Morrell (caricatured in *Women In Love* as Hermione Roddice).

Lawrence was furious over the banning of *The Rainbow* as obscene, and planned to leave for Florida. Instead he and Frieda went to Cornwall, where Lawrence promptly fell ill: he claimed it was a 'cold', but pains in his arms and legs suggested something more serious. Tuberculosis was suspected after he spat blood, but a doctor diagnosed only 'nervous exhaustion' with accompanying 'bronchial mucus'. Lawrence underwent a medical examination for military service at Bodmin, but was exempted on health grounds. He was medically examined again later in the war, this time in Derby, and classed fit for non-military service – though in the end he was never called up.

Frieda constantly feared internment as an enemy alien, and was suspected by neighbours in Cornwall of signalling to German submarines attacking Atlantic convoys off the Cornish coast, especially when three British ships were sunk in the Bristol Channel. In October 1917 their cottage was searched, and they were served with an order forbidding them to reside in Cornwall or any other coastal area. For two years they scraped by, thanks to the generosity of friends and relations (including Lawrence's sister Ada, now Ada Clarke) in London, Berkshire and the Midlands.

Lawrence began a new novel, *Aaron's Rod*, about a man who walks out on a conventional marriage to seek a new life. He also published *New Poems*, this time with a new publisher who would stay with him for the rest of his life: Martin Secker. When the war ended in 1918 Lawrence predicted – correctly – that Germany would rise again, and that there would be another global conflict. He survived a bad bout of flu in the epidemic which killed millions in Britain and Europe at the end of the war, and again made plans to go to America.

But he and Frieda had one of their many rows, and she left for Baden-Baden to see her mother. It was very nearly the end of the marriage. Lawrence, the poet Richard Aldington recorded, 'seemed not to care if he never saw her again'. They had agreed to meet in Italy, however, and Lawrence sailed from Dover to France in November 1919. His destination this time was not Gargnano, or Lerici, but another Italian jewel: the island of Capri.

3

Capri to Sicily

L AWRENCE WAS ON HIS WAY BACK to the 'blazing, blazing sun' and the 'lapping Mediterranean', as he wrote to Lady Cynthia Asquith. His first stop was Turin, where he stayed at the palatial villa of Sir Walter Becker, a wealthy shipowner who was a patron of the British Red Cross in Italy and who had just been given his knighthood for founding a wartime hospital for British troops.

Lawrence took the train to Genoa 'beside a lovely sunset sea' to La Spezia, and headed down the Italian coast to Florence via Lerici, where he called briefly at Fiascherino to see his fishermen friends from the pre-war days. He was aware of the gathering political storm in Italy: the November 1919 election saw the beginning of the end for the ruling Liberals, and the rise of the Socialists, shortly to be swept aside in turn by an emerging force, the Fascists, led by a ruthless and ambitious new leader, Benito Mussolini. But Lawrence brushed politics aside. 'Italy is still gay – does all her weeping in the press – takes her politics with her wine, and enjoys them,' he reported to Lady Cynthia. 'Great excitement over the elections – but lively and amused excitement – nothing tragic or serious.'

In Florence he walked from the Santa Maria Novella railway station to Thomas Cooks on Via Tornabuoni to collect his mail. There he found a note from the writer

Norman Douglas – who had fled England to avoid prosecution after propositioning a boy in the Natural History Museum – to say he had found him a room in the Pensione Balestri, close to the Ponte Vecchio. It was raining, the Arno was swollen, and Lawrence lost much of what little money he had on him in Florence when his wallet was stolen while he was getting onto a crowded train at Fiesole – an incident which, like a number of other details of his journey, found its way into *Aaron's Rod*. But he enjoyed Florence like any other tourist, admiring Giotto's tower as 'a lily stem', the jewellers' windows 'blazing with light' on the Ponte Vecchio and the huge copy of Michelangelo's David, 'white and stripped in the wet', which stood – and indeed still stands – in front of the imposing Palazzo Vecchio.

'Here am I on my lonely-o, waiting for Frieda', Lawrence wrote towards the end of November 1919 to Gertrude Cooper, a childhood friend. 'Italy is very nice, sunny and gay still, with good red wine'. When Frieda finally arrived by train at four in the morning, he met her and took her for a moonlit drive around Florence in an open horse-drawn carriage. After that night, Frieda later wrote, Florence became 'the most beautiful town to me, the lily town, delicate and flowery'.

They headed at first not for the Mediterranean but for Abruzzo, a mountainous region 50 miles east of Rome dotted with castles and medieval hilltop towns. In Berkshire Lawrence had got to know – and admire – Rosalind Baynes, the wife of a Cambridge doctor who was hardly ever at home. Lawrence was struck by Rosalind's Pre-Raphaelite beauty, and had long conversations with her about Italy. Rosalind suggested to Lawrence that he should go to stay at a mountain village called Picinisco: it had been recommended to her father, the celebrated sculptor Sir Hamo Thornycroft – creator of the statue of Oliver Cromwell outside Parliament at Westminster – by Orazio Cervi, an Italian emigré to Britain from Picinisco who became a noted artist's model because of his physique and looks, and posed for Millais and Lord Leighton as well as Thornycroft.

Cervi offered them the use of his house. So now, after a week in Florence, Lawrence and Frieda travelled via Rome (which he disliked – 'tawdry and so crowded'), and then southwards by train to Monte Cassino and finally by bus to Picinisco, high on a ridge in the mountainous Comino Valley. This was the landscape of the second part of *The Lost Girl*, the tale of a Midlands girl who falls for an Italian and leaves the safety of England for the wilds of Italy, in which Picinisco becomes Pescocalascio, a village reached by pony and trap and then on foot – a 'sheer scramble – no road whatever'. Access is now rather easier, and the restored house, Casa Lawrence, with its wrought iron balconies and walled garden, is part DH Lawrence museum, part comfortable country B&B (*agiturismo*) set in the lush landscape of the Lazio-Abruzzo border, with local restaurants offering hearty Abruzzo fare such as egg-rich *chitarra* (guitar) pasta, ricotta cheese with honey and saffron, rich meat sauces and the local red wine, Montepulciano d'Abruzzo.

There were few such comforts in 1919 however – Lawrence even complained that there was hardly any wine – and Abruzzo was not quite the idyll they were looking for. For a start Orazio Cervi's house was two miles from Picinisco itself, and it was all 'a bit staggeringly primitive ... You cross a great stony river bed, then an icy river on a plank, then climb unfootable paths, while the ass struggles behind you with your luggage'. Downstairs, Lawrence reported back to Rosalind, was a 'cave-like kitchen' with one teaspoon, two cups, one saucer, one plate and two glasses. Upstairs were three bedrooms with bare floors and 'a semi barn for maize cobs'. They cooked on a wood fire with chickens wandering in and out and the donkey tied to the doorpost, 'making his droppings on the doorstep'.

The nearest market was at Atina five miles away, there was no bath, and the bedrooms were unheated. The snowy mountain peaks were beautiful (they still are – Picinisco is now in the National Park of Abruzzo, Lazio and Molise), and local shepherds played the traditional, haunting Abruzzo bagpipes as Christmas approached (they still do). But – understandably – the Lawrences only lasted a week. They got up at 5.30 in the morning, walked the five miles to Atina, caught a bus back to Cassino, the nearest railway station, and reached Naples by train in time to catch the 3pm boat to Capri, which they eventually reached in a 'little iron tub of a steamer' after first being turned back to Sorrento in high seas with 'a lot of spewing Italians'.

They had been brought to the island by Compton Mackenzie's offer of lodgings: at the end of 1919 Mackenzie made good his promise and found them 'two large well-furnished rooms and a kitchen' on the top floor of a palazzo, with a charcoal stove and a view of the Bay of Naples. There was a noisy cafe beneath, and the maid was discovered to be wearing Frieda's clothes and jewels when they weren't there, but it didn't matter. Lawrence had the company of a congenial Romanian neighbour with whom he cooked and talked philosophy.

Capri was 'almost operatic', Norman Douglas wrote in *South Wind*, a best-selling novel published by Martin Secker in 1917 in which Capri appears as the fictional island of Nepenthe. It was 'full of surprises – of unexpected glimpses upon a group of slender palms, some gleaming precipice, or the distant sea. Gardens appeared to be toppling over the houses; green vines festooned the doorways and gaily coloured porches; streets climbed up and down, noisy with rattling carriages and cries of fruit-vendors who exposed their wares of brightest hues on the pavement ... The houses, when not whitewashed, showed their building stone of red volcanic tufa; windows were aflame with cacti and carnations; slumberous oranges glowed in courtyards.'

All in all, a rather different Italy from Abruzzo. 'Picinisco was too icy-mountainous – we escaped here', Lawrence wrote to Secker from Capri just after Christmas 1919. 'I had your letter with the offer for *The Rainbow* and *Women in Love*,' he wrote a month later. 'I should like to be with you, because you really care about books.' On Capri Lawrence put fiction aside for a moment, writing instead *Psychoanalysis and the Unconscious*, in which he discussed the ideas of Freud. He wrote it on a portable typewriter lent to him by Compton Mackenzie, undeterred by the fact that the black on the ribbon had disintegrated and only the red was usable. Lawrence declared this to be 'helpful', Mackenzie later recalled. 'I never grasped why.'

Lawrence later returned the typewriter, together with a bottle of Benedictine for Mackenzie's birthday, carrying both for a mile and half in a walk which ended in a steep cliff path down to the villa. 'Anybody but Lawrence would have hired a *facchino* (porter),' Mackenzie observed. 'This was Lawrence when for an hour or two he was at peace with life.' Lawrence discussed Greek philosophy in the main piazza with Mackenzie, who remembered how Lawrence 'suddenly stopped and began to argue that men must give up thinking with their minds. "What we have to learn is to think here," he affirmed solemnly in that high-pitched voice of his with its slight Midlands accent. As he said this he bent over to point a finger at his fly-buttons, to my embarrassment and the obvious surprise of other people strolling on the piazza.' On Capri Lawrence went 'on and on' about 'the need for people to think with their genital organs instead of their minds', as well as 'on and on' about the Etruscans, until 'at last I had to stop what was turning into too long a sermon'.

They also discussed a projected joint expedition to the South Sea islands to 're-colonise the Kermadec Islands' in the South Pacific, which never came off (the islands are now part of New Zealand). Instead they sang 'Sally in Our Alley' and other music-hall songs at the piano at Mackenzie's villa, Casa Solitaria, though 'in different keys'. The two men got on well, though Mackenzie was pained by the way Lawrence poked fun at his silk pyjamas. Mackenzie was also pained by

Lawrence's tendency to put unkind portraits of his friends into his books and conversation: 'I used to regret the way Frieda was forever encouraging her Lorenzo with boisterous laughter to pull people to pieces.'

Lawrence was always quick to take offence, once complaining that at a New Year's Eve party on Capri that Mackenzie had come into the room and 'merely waved' at Lawrence and Frieda instead of immediately going over to them. He could also be dismissive of fellow writers, including James Joyce. 'I sent Lawrence the copies of *The Little Review* I was receiving from Chicago with the serialisation of James Joyce's *Ulysses*,' Mackenzie recalled. 'He was horrified by it. I see now a gloomy Lawrence walking along that cliff path to Casa Solitaria. He is wearing a covert coat, only the top button of which is fastened; he is carrying a string bag in which there is an orange and a banana, and under his arm are the copies of *The Little Review* I had lent him. "This *Ulysses* muck is more disgusting than Casanova," he proclaimed. "I *must* show that it can be done without muck".'

Mackenzie suggests that this was perhaps the moment when the concept of *Lady Chatterley's Lover* began to lodge in Lawrence's mind. Lawrence, he says, was much exercised by his inability to achieve orgasm simultaneously with Frieda, 'which according to him must mean their marriage was still imperfect in spite of all they had both gone through'. Mackenzie assured him that 'such a happy coincidence was always rare', adding that if he really intended to 'convert the world to proper reverence for the sexual act by writing about it in a novel', he should remember that – as the Greek poets had acknowledged – 'except to the two people who are indulging in it, the sexual act is a comic operation'.

Lawrence went pale 'and hurried off with his string bag to eat his lunch in solitude'. The next day he 'came into my room and said abruptly "Perhaps you're right. And if you're right …" He made a gesture of despair for the future of the human race'. He did, however, concede the point later in *Lady*

Chatterley, in which while making love to Mellors Connie muses that God must have a 'sinister sense of humour' to make men and women engage in this 'ridiculous performance ... The butting of his haunches seemed ridiculous to her, and the sort of anxiety of his penis to come to its little evacuating crisis seemed farcical.'

Lawrence's mood would not have been improved by Secker's foot-dragging over the publication of *Women in Love* (a title Secker found 'provocative'), and re-publication of *The Rainbow*: Secker told Mackenzie he was thinking of offering Lawrence £300 for the first and £200 for the second, on which Lawrence could 'live comfortably in Italy for a year' and finish another book. But Secker was worried about lawsuits; he told Mackenzie – 'I am a little tired of the whole thing ... Lawrence's books are not worth competing for from a money making point of view.' However, Secker did publish them, saying 'I feel instinctively that anything to do with DHL is rather dangerous, but I am prepared to take risks.' This showed a degree of courage on Secker's part, Mackenzie observes, which he had not seen recognised anywhere.

Capri, once a haven for writers, from Lawrence to Graham Greene, tends nowadays to be crowded with day trippers attracted by the Blue Grotto, the debauched Emperor Tiberius's clifftop retreat, the Villa Jovis, and the (often pricey) open-air cafes. However, in 1920 tourism was in its infancy: what put Lawrence off was the 'snobbish' Capri expat society, much as he would later take against Alassio on the Riviera. He took to referring to Capri as 'Cranford', after Elizabeth Gaskell's fictional gossip-ridden town, and complained that he also found Capri too rocky and 'arid'.

In February 1920 Lawrence set off from Naples for another island, Sicily, to see the Greek temples at Agrigentum. For the time being he had had enough of Capri: he wrote to Catherine Carswell in February 1920 that he had grown 'very sick' of an island which was little more than a 'stewpot of semi-literary cats'. 'Petty gossip', Compton

Mackenzie comments tartly, was no doubt as rife in Capri as in any English village, but 'if Lawrence and Frieda had not themselves always encouraged that gossip they would not have taken it so seriously.'

Lawrence was not at first impressed by Sicily – though his travelling companion, the doctor and novelist Francis Brett Young, claimed this was largely because Lawrence's hat had blown off while he was admiring the temples. He nonetheless decided to settle in Taormina, perched above the warm Ionian Sea, with its spectacular Greek amphitheatre, Saracen castle and medieval and Renaissance palaces. He found a villa just outside the town, the Villa Fontana Vecchia, and rented the upper floors, with views over the Strait of Messina; the owner and his extended family lived downstairs.

Lawrence and Frieda moved in on 8 March 1920, and felt immediately at home in Sicily, absorbing the Moorish, Greek and Norman cultures of the island's tumultuous and colourful past. 'I like Sicily – oh, so much better than Capri,' Lawrence wrote to his German uncle by marriage, Fritz Krenkow. 'It is so green and living'. He was enchanted by 'the undying beauty of Sicily and the Greek world, a morning beauty that has something miraculous in it, of purple anemones and cyclamens, and sumach and olive trees and the place where Persephone came above-world, bringing back Spring.'

The villa is still there, perched above the road with its green shutters, verandas, thick stone walls and arched Norman windows, in what was then a dusty road into the mountains and is now Via David Herbert Lawrence. It was here that Lawrence wrote one of his most famous poems, 'Snake': 'A snake came to my water-trough on a hot, hot day, and I in pyjamas for the heat, to drink there.' He describes coming down the steps with his pitcher, beneath the 'deep, strange-scented shade of the great dark carob tree', and throwing a log at the snake, which disappears into a fissure in the wall – an act the poet regrets as a petty and mean assault on 'one of the lords of life'.

Lawrence wrote to Rosalind Baynes: 'We've got a nice big house, with fine rooms and a handy kitchen, set in a big garden, mostly vegetables, green with almond trees, on a steep slope at some distance from the sea. It is beautiful, and green, green, and full of flowers.' Mount Etna, 'witch-like under heaven, slowly rolling her orange-coloured smoke', was far lovelier than Vesuvius, and although there were a good many English people around, 'one needn't know them'.

Lawrence was irritated at being overcharged and 'diddled' – 'the Sicilians are the greatest swindlers and extortionists' – he had rows with Frieda, overheard by their landlord, and Sicily was 'sweltering'. But the villa was ten minutes out of town and 'lovely and cool', the sea was 'pale and shimmery', the prickly pears were in yellow blossom, and life at the Fontana Vecchia was 'very easy, indolent and devil-may-care'. He felt he had lived there for 'a hundred thousand years'.

Lawrence was still musing about a trip to the South Seas, writing in high excitement to Mackenzie – who had heard of a suitable ketch with a large saloon, four cabins and a smoking lounge – that he looked forward to learning 'all about sloops, yachts, clippers and frigates, clewlines and bowlines and topsle gallants, ensigns and mizzens, forepeaks and so on'. He would not pray when sailing 'because I believe Jesus is no good at sea' – an odd remark given that Jesus famously walked on water – but would invoke 'Aphrodite and Poseidon and Dionysus.'

Instead Mackenzie was persuaded by Secker – who naturally enough opposed the South Sea venture – to take a 60-year lease on the tiny, almost uninhabited islands of Herm and Jethou in the Channel Islands. Lawrence and Frieda meanwhile settled for a trip to Malta – but by the summer of 1920 they were ready for a break from each other. Frieda left for Baden-Baden, while Lawrence headed for Florence, where he had a passionate and – for him – rare adulterous affair.

The main attraction in Florence for Lawrence was the

brown-eyed beauty of Rosalind Baynes, who after recommending Abruzzo to him had now moved to Italy herself and was living near Fiesole with her baby daughter. By her own account (written as Rosalind Thornycroft, her maiden name) they went to bed at his suggestion after having lunch and dinner together and then sitting outside in the dark holding hands. Lawrence had just turned 35.

Lawrence was nothing if not direct: he asked her if she missed having sex, and she replied that she did but was 'fastidious'. He then suggested she have sex with him, adding that she was of course free to say no. 'Yes indeed, I want it,' she told him. He made no move until the following Sunday, when they cooked a typical English lunch of roast beef and Yorkshire pudding together, walked into Fiesole afterwards to buy sorb-apples, and returned to the villa to sit outside as night fell. 'We sit there until it is quite dark, our hands held together in union,' Rosalind wrote in her diary, using the present tense for immediacy. 'And so to bed.' Frieda found out, of course: she later told Mabel Luhan in New Mexico that when she came back from Baden-Baden she sensed something 'in the air' and forced Lawrence to confess. He wrote to Rosalind over the years, but never saw her again.

He left Florence earlier than he needed to and waited for Frieda in Venice before they returned to Sicily together. Lawrence found Venice 'melancholic with its dreary bygone lagoons'. 'I expect Frieda here today – then we shall go almost at once to Taormina,' he wrote to Compton Mackenzie at the beginning of October 1920. 'I can't do anything in Venice. Italy feels awfully shakey [*sic*] and nasty, and for the first time my unconscious is uneasy of the Italians.'

Women in Love now appeared in the US, and was published in England by Secker – though with cuts, toning down its sexual content in an edition which Lawrence found 'shoddy'. The reviews were discouraging: the magazine *John Bull* said it was 'a book the police should ban'. 'We got back here last week,' he wrote to Mackenzie from Taormina later in October. 'Peace and stillness and *cleanness*, flowers, rain, streams, bird singing, sea dim and hoarse: valley full of cyclamens ... We are quite alone at Taormina. I haven't been out to see who, English, is here. Feel I don't want. Prefer to be quite alone this winter, rather than that sort of well-to-do riff-raff.' The answer lay in escape to another Mediterranean island with a colourful history of independence: Sardinia.

4

Sardinia to Spotorno

LAWRENCE AND FRIEDA'S visit to Sardinia was brief – barely ten days – but it produced his meticulously observed and often hilarious account of the island, *Sea and Sardinia*, published two years later, with its famous opening lines on eternal restlessness: 'Comes over one an absolute necessity to move. And what is more, to move in some particular direction ... Why can't one sit still?'

And so in January 1921 they filled their *kitchenino* or travelling food bag at dawn with bacon sandwiches – 'good English bacon from Malta, a god-send indeed' – locked the doors of the Fontana Vecchia and shut the windows on the verandas (though one was warped and would not fasten), and set off past the carob tree, mimosa and jasmine for Palermo. Here they took the steamer to Cagliari, the Sardinian capital, which an enchanted Lawrence found 'golden-looking' like Jerusalem, rising into the sky 'like a town in a monkish, illuminated missal' with its sandstone fortress at the top. What Lawrence was after was the old, 'uncaptured Sardinia' buried beneath the modern Italy with its trains and 'motor omnibuses', the Sardinia of the Phoenicians, the Arabs and the Byzantines. Lawrence was fascinated to find in Sardinia an enclosed 'medieval' outlook, with 'no interest in the world outside', but feared – rightly – that modern life would eventually make inroads.

Today most tourists head for the stunning if often packed coastline of sandy beaches and turquoise sea, while the rich show off their yachts on the Costa Smeralda in a display of ostentatious wealth. But the interior still has the rugged beauty Lawrence found there, with its wooded slopes and ravines and a population of fiercely independent Sardinians proud of their heritage as a country 'lost between Europe and Africa', as Lawrence put it. Today a train dubbed the *Trenino Verde* (Little Green Train) chugs the 100 miles from Arbatax to Mandas and a nature reserve of cork trees and wild horses, through the great wild, 'scrubby and uninabited' heath and moorland which reminded Lawrence of Cornwall or Derbyshire and which he found quite unlike the 'romantic eighteenth century' landscapes of mainland Italy.

Sea and Sardinia has some of Lawrence's most rhapsodic descriptions of landscapes, of the people with their colourful costumes and 'dark velvet eyes' – and of vegetables and fruit. His account of a Sardinian market still makes the mouth water, with the deep green spinach, white and purple cauliflowers, crimson radishes, scarlet peppers, white succulent fennel, shining oranges, dangling clusters of dates and baskets of almonds and walnuts.

It was not all idyllic however: there was often nothing to do, especially in the evening ('One goes to bed when it's dark, like a chicken,' one railwayman told Frieda at Mandas) and the food and hospitality left much to be desired. Their route took Lawrence and Frieda – who appears in the book as the 'queen bee', abbreviated to 'q-b' – by train (third class) to Mandas, with its strangely familiar small houses 'like a row of railway-men's dwellings', and up into the mountains of the Gennargentu massif to Sogorno, which Lawrence had imagined to be a 'magic little town' but which prompted one of his black rages when the inn turned out to be sordid, with a 'filthy bedroom'.

From Sogorno they travelled by bus on a 'precipitous road' – Lawrence greatly admired Italian road and rail engineering

– to Nuoro and down to the coast at Siniscola, a 'crude, stony place, hot in the sun, cold in the shade', and the port of Terranova (Olbia), where a steamer took them (and a picnic of sardines, bread and chocolate) to Civitavecchia for the journey back to Sicily via Rome and Naples. On the ship back to Palermo Lawrence was irritated by a loud and cocky 'bounder' from Milan who accused the English of lording it over Europe and living cheaply in Italy, to which Lawrence – fuelled by whisky – retorted that the English in Italy were overcharged in hotels and insulted by waiters, shop assistants and railway porters. Sardinia had been cold, and the inns and food (even the wild boar stew) had been dismal.

Yet for all that, Sardinia, Lawrence wrote, had brought home to him 'how old the real Italy is ... Wherever one is in Italy, either one is conscious of the present, or of the medieval influences, or of the far, mysterious gods of the early Mediterranean.' To penetrate Italy awoke 'strange and mysterious chords' in the traveller. It was 'like a most fascinating act of self-discovery, back, back down the old ways of time.'

After another interlude in Germany Lawrence and Frieda returned to Sicily via Florence and then Capri, where they encountered Earl and Achsah Brewster, eccentric American Buddhists and artists who would play a key part in Lawrence's life, and who planted the idea of a trip to Ceylon (Sri Lanka). Lawrence had now finished *Aaron's Rod*, in which Aaron, after his affair with the Marchesa, finds not only that adultery involves guilt, but also that from the male point of view sex and orgasm are so overwhelming that they leave the man feeling 'withered and blasted' and not wanting to be touched by women who tend to 'cling' after lovemaking. The novel ends with Aaron symbolically throwing his flute – the 'rod' of the title – into the River Arno from a bridge.

The man who in 1912 – the year he met Frieda – had proclaimed himself 'the priest of love' now wanted 'the sex-idea burned out of one, cauterised bit by bit', preferring 'the stillness of an accomplished marriage'. 'I here and now, finally and forever give up knowing anything about love, or wanting to know,' he wrote to the Brewsters. 'I believe it doesn't exist, save as a word.' Whether this reflects the way Lawrence felt after the Rosalind Baynes affair, and whether he now ceased to make love to Frieda, is an open question. It is likely, however, that from this point on he became less sexually active, even if he did not actually become impotent. In Baden-Baden, during a crisis over Frieda's mother's illness, they had separate bedrooms.

Back in Sicily Lawrence finished a volume of novellas, *The Ladybird*, *The Fox* and *The Captain's Doll*. As ever, he was restless. 'If I hadn't my own stories to amuse myself with I should die, chiefly of spleen,' he wrote to Earl Brewster from Taormina. He was going through one of his periods of irritation with Italy, which throughout his life alternated with periods of enchantment. The Italians were 'really rather low-bred swine nowadays, so different from what they were,' while the natives of Taormina were 'as mean and creeping as ever.' Italy was turning 'rancid in my mouth'. He even told Catherine Carswell he was 'done with Italy': Lawrence 'loved Italy as much as any English poet ever did, and he got from it more than most,' she wrote later, but there were times when he wanted something more than 'the easy and eminently workable Latin compromise with life.'

His mood was partly caused by the unrest and strikes which formed the backdrop to Mussolini's seizure of dictatorial power in 1922: 'The country is sickening, and such a muddle ever increasing,' he wrote to Mary Cannan in December 1921. 'I am tired of it ... I shall be glad to go.' He was also running short of cash: 'My stock of English money is almost gone,' he told Brewster. 'I feel at the moment I don't care where I live.' The Brewsters had gone to Ceylon and wanted him to join them.

There was an alternative offer from Mabel Dodge Sterne, a wealthy and neurotic American arts lover and socialite who was on her third husband and would later become Mabel

Luhan after her fourth marriage, to Tony Luhan, a Pueblo Indian. 'A woman wrote and said we could have a house and all we want in Taos, New Mexico, one of the southern states of the USA,' Lawrence told Mary Cannan. Taos, he explained, was a little town near the Arizona desert with a tribe of aboriginal Indians, 6,000 feet high and 25 miles from the nearest railway station. 'There is a little colony of American artists there, and that may be horrible. But we are going.'

Lawrence at first postponed America, saying that 'at the eleventh hour' he had realised he couldn't face it. Instead in February 1922 he and Frieda sailed for Ceylon from Naples, carrying with them, bizarrely, the painted side of a Sicilian cart portraying St Genevieve and a medieval jousting scene, in addition to two steamer trunks, a hat box and five pieces of luggage. He did not take to Ceylon, however, and in August 1922 Lawrence and Frieda sailed again, this time for San Francisco by way of Australia (which produced *Kangaroo*) and Tahiti. Less than a week after arriving in San Francisco they set off by train and car for Taos.

If there is a rival for Italy in the places which inspired Lawrence, it is New Mexico. 'The moment I saw the brilliant, proud morning shine high up over the deserts of Santa Fe, something stood still in my soul,' he wrote. He found Mabel Luhan irksome and domineering, as did Frieda, who – rightly – suspected Mabel of plotting to supplant her. They stayed at first in Mabel's guest house, but not wanting to be dependent on her, they rented cabins on a ranch she owned called the Del Monte, 17 miles north of Taos, together with two Danish painters.

A visit to Mexico – as opposed to New Mexico – in March 1923 alerted Lawrence to Mexican traditions and gods: he was much taken with the figure of Quetzalcoatl, which inspired him to write *The Plumed Serpent*, the story of Kate Forrester, an Anglo-Irish widow seduced by Mexico and its Aztec rituals. There are various accounts of tensions between Lawrence and Frieda in Mexico, and when Frieda left for

England to see her children, who were now old enough to decide whether to meet her, Lawrence refused to go with her. 'I feel so cross with Lawrence, when I hear him talk about loyalty', Frieda wrote to Adele Seltzer, the wife of Lawrence's American publisher, as she sailed alone from New York. 'Pah, he only thinks of himself ... He can go to blazes, I have had enough.'

Lawrence did eventually join her, in November 1923, but found he hated being back in England – 'an island no bigger than a back garden, chock-full of people who never realise there is anything outside their back garden, pretending to direct the destinies of the world.' His mood was not improved by his suspicion that Frieda was having an affair with John Middleton Murry, whose wife Katherine Mansfield had died the previous year of tuberculosis. According to his own account, Murry held back out of loyalty to Lawrence, telling Frieda 'No my darling, I mustn't let Lorenzo down.' But Lawrence did not believe Murry had resisted temptation, and the simmering tensions boiled over when Lawrence held a dinner shortly before Christmas 1923 for some of his closest friends amid the gilt and red plush of the Cafe Royal in Regent Street.

Lawrence invited them all to join him and Frieda in Taos. It all went badly awry, however. Everyone drank too much claret, and Lawrence went white in the face after drinking port, which did not agree with him. He had apparently hinted 'very gently' that port was not a good idea, but nobody heard him. The last straw, according to Catherine Carswell, was Murry going up to Lawrence and kissing him effusively. Murry admitted he had 'betrayed' Lawrence 'in the past' but vowed he would never do so again – or so Catherine remembered. Murry later rather lamely insisted in his own account that what he had actually said was 'I love you, Lorenzo, but I won't promise not to betray you.' 'Women can't understand this,' Murry told Catherine across the table. 'This is an affair between men.' She retorted that 'it wasn't a woman who betrayed Jesus with a kiss.' At this point Lawrence, looking 'pale and frightfully ill', was sick over the table and passed out. The dinner came to be referred to by the Lawrence circle as 'The Last Supper'. 'Well, Catherine, I made a fool of myself last night,' a chastened Lawrence told Carswell the following morning. 'We must all of us fall at times. It does no harm so long as we first admit and then forget it.' In the end the only one who came with them to New Mexico was Dorothy Brett.

It was at this point that Italy again entered Lawrence's life – this time in the form of Rina Capellero. Rina – by now Mrs Martin Secker – was not among the guests at 'The Last Supper', but she was by now getting to know Frieda and Lawrence well. She visited them in Hampstead at the end of 1923, and made a good impression on the Lawrences' circle of literary and artistic friends. She was six months pregnant, and during her pregnancy had suffered a mysterious haemorrhage which must have given rise to fears of a miscarriage. She evidently kept this from the Lawrences, however, giving the impression that she was under the weather without being specific.

'I am so sorry you aren't well!' Frieda wrote to Rina at Bridgefoot from Hampstead. 'You will so hate it I know, and such a strain on your patience!' Lawrence was 'grumbling dreadfully at this England weather and all', and had caught a cold which Frieda had also caught, 'if not so bad.' 'You mustn't get the hump,' Frieda told Rina, 'I always think one feels low with the dying year and when the days get longer one cheers up!' She hoped Martin and Rina would at least have 'a jolly Xmas. We will come to lunch with you when you are better. Don't get bored whatever you do. All the people who met you here said very flattering things about you.'

In March 1924 Lawrence and Frieda set sail with Brett for New York and returned to Taos, this time to a 160-acre ranch provided for them by Mabel Luhan on Lobo (Wolf) mountain, which they named Kiowa, after a local Indian trail. Mabel made the ranch over to Frieda as her property, in exchange for the manuscript of *Sons and Lovers*. As usual Lawrence set about repairing, painting and re-roofing the dilapidated ranch cabins.

'We have worked so hard on the ranch with six Indians and two Mexicans,' Frieda wrote to Rina at distant Bridgefoot in June 1924, on notepaper decorated with a coloured drawing of the Indian pueblo at Taos. 'It's very rough and simple but I love it – some day you must come, there's a little guest house. Today there's a big forest fire, one of the dangers of this dry country and these huge pines. We ride a lot, have to – if we want to get about.' She was enclosing a small pair of moccasins for Rina's new baby. 'They'll be too big, but I wanted to be on the safe side.'

In August 1924 Lawrence suffered a bronchial haemorrhage, and he was further downcast by the death of his father Arthur in September at the age of 78. In October 1924 he, Frieda and Brett went to Oaxaca in Mexico – the background to *Mornings in Mexico* – and here at the end of January 1925 Lawrence suffered a disastrous collapse which nearly killed him. In Mexico City, where Lawrence suffered a relapse, a doctor diagnosed 'tuberculosis in the third stage', according to Frieda, adding that he had only 'a year or two' to live at most. 'We have left the ranch for the winter, it's 9,000 feet high so it's cold in the winter but *always* sunny in the daytime and I love it,' Frieda wrote to Rina at Bridgefoot from Mexico City. 'But now we go down to a semi-tropical place and I almost feel mean to tell you that we have had sunshine always since we left England, and *such* sunshine.' Despite his illness Lawrence was attending a dinner laid on in his honour with a hundred guests, 'with readings in Spanish from his books'. He had wanted to cancel, 'but I would not let him ... After all they mean well.' Rina had sent Frieda a bag of lavender 'which smells good in my bag, thank you very much for sending it ... How are you and the boy? How different the house must be! Did you ever get a little pair of moccasins I sent for him?'

Brett had returned to Taos from Mexico earlier than the

Lawrences, after Frieda jealously accused her of spending too much time with her husband. Lawrence and Frieda now came back to Taos too, and Lawrence appeared to recover. He wrote a play, *David*, his take on the Biblical story of David and Saul, and the essay *Reflections on the Death of a Porcupine*, with Brett continuing to type up the manuscripts despite Frieda's outbursts of jealousy. When the Lawrences left the Kiowa ranch for New York and then England in September 1925 – Lawrence had just turned 40 – Brett stayed behind. But she would shortly join them again in Italy, the country to which Lawrence and Frieda now returned yet again – this time, thanks to Rina, starting in Spotorno.

They sailed first for England on 22 September. He wrote to his mother-in-law, 'I am quite glad to be out of America for a time, it's so tough and wearing, with the iron springs poking out through the padding.' He was, he admitted 'homesick' for Europe: America was 'too savage' 'The Europeans still have a vague idea that the universe is greater than they are, and isn't going to change very radically,' he wrote to Nancy Pearn at Curtis Brown, 'But the Americans are tense ... as if they felt that once they slackened, the world would really collapse. It wouldn't.' He was not 'crazy about the Riviera, as the Americans say', but he expected to 'go south – Italy, or Sicily, or Egypt – for the winter'.

Lawrence and Frieda arrived at Southampton at the end of September and went to London. Lawrence visited Martin and Rina Secker at Bridgefoot, and was appalled that despite high unemployment Secker could not find anyone to cut '16 acres of good thick hay still standing' because local workers preferred the dole. It must have been on this occasion that Rina planted the idea of the Riviera and Spotorno. Lawrence hated the English weather, complaining to Secker in October after travelling back to Nottingham, 'Of course I'm in bed with a cold, the moment I come here'. He felt 'foreign' in his own land, where people were like fish in an aquarium. 'No doubt about it, England is the most fantastic Alice in

Wonderland country'. The return to Nottingham did not help: 'I can't look at the body of my past, the spirit seems to have flown'.

Frieda was happier: two years earlier she had made it up with her son Monty, who was by then 23 and working at the V&A, but who at this stage still sided with his father and refused to acknowledge Frieda and Lawrence as a couple. Her daughters Elsa, now a secretary, and Barbara (Barby), who had just finished studying at the Slade, were more friendly. Barby visited her mother and Lawrence in Ripley at the house of Lawrence's married sister Ada, and noted Ada's hostility toward Frieda for having 'gone off with her favourite brother' – an animosity which was to explode later at Spotorno.

After a week in London, where they met Murry and Cynthia Asquith – who was compiling a book of ghost stories and asked Lawrence to contribute – the Lawrences left for Baden Baden at the end of October 1925. Lawrence wanted 'space and sun'. They toyed with the idea of going to Paris or Dalmatia, but pondering Rina Secker's talk at Bridgefoot of sun and sea at Spotorno, where her father Luigi Capellero had bought a hotel, they once again gravitated toward Italy. Lawrence wrote to Brett: 'We may stay on the Italian Riviera for a while.'

5

The Lure of the Italian Riviera

T HE WORD 'RIVIERA' tends nowadays to evoke the French Riviera. As for Italy, if foreigners think of Liguria they tend to think of Portofino and the Cinque Terre. The Italian Riviera has been overshadowed by Tuscany and Umbria, where the hill towns and villas echo to the sound of British and other foreign tourists and second home owners.

Yet not so long ago it was the Riviera coast of Italy which was the favourite playground of the middle classes, and which attracted British visitors long before the arrival of the Lawrences in the 1920s. The Ligurian landscape of blue sea backed by mountain ranges, with the smell of herbs and pines and the sound of church bells, entranced writers from Byron and Shelley to Dickens and Edward Lear. The Italian Riviera was a lost paradise combining the exotic – olive trees, Ligurian wines, fishing villages – with the comforts of British expat life: tennis clubs, libraries, dances, Huntley and Palmer biscuits, Gordon's Gin.

And above all, the sun. In Victorian times – long before skin cancer scares – the idea of 'heliotherapy' took root in the form of sun cures for various complaints and diseases, such as tuberculosis. British visitors and other Northerners were also lured South by sex and the freedom to indulge in lax morals. As the Italian writer Alessandro Bartoli points out, Italy was seen as the land of spontaneity and escape from 'Victorian society's morals and aversion to sex. Many Victorian authors and intellectuals believed that the Southern sun wiped away the hypocrisies and false conformism of north European Protestant and Evangelical society.'

The idea that the warm South was a hotbed of immorality was not new: as early as 1830 Dr James Johnson, a Royal physician who made a tour of the Riviera, declared that 'Where climate provides constant stimulation for the senses, passion will predominate over reason.' Excess could even lead to death, the doctor warned his fellow countrymen, since 'where the passions are indulged, the range of existence will be curtailed.' Many of the British residents on the Riviera were respectable church-going pillars of society – but as Pamela Cooper, the daughter of the English chaplain at San Remo in the 1920s noted, they also included 'alcoholics of both sexes who spent the winter in their luxurious villas on the waterfront', 'good time' aristocrats who were ostracised by clubs in London, 'and divorcees'.

The Riviera, Baedeker informed its readers in 1931, was 'an Italian word meaning a strip of land between the mountains and the sea', and was 'the name given to that part of the Mediterranean coast that extends in a beautiful curve from Marseilles to Pisa between the Ligurian Sea and the precipitous Maritime Alps'. It added: 'Nowhere else in the Mediterranean does Nature display her beauty with such lavishness. In winter and spring this world-famous coast is the resort of thousands of invalids and pleasure seekers of every nationality, and in summer it has recently become popular for sea-bathing.' Small towns were 'picturesquely perched on the hill slopes and heights', and all along the coast, 'on romantic cliffs washed by the sea', were ruined Saracen Towers which had once kept a lookout for sudden incursions by pirates from the North African coast.

By the time of the Grand Tours, the Italian stretch of the Riviera was gaining a reputation for cultural wonders, sunshine, and the healthy Mediterranean diet, as fashionable in the 18th and 19th centuries as it is now. There followed, as Giovanni Assereto of Genoa University, has observed, a 'polite invasion by elite tourism', consolidated by the completion of the coastal railway linking Genoa to Nice in 1864. Queen Victoria became a frequent visitor: she found the Riviera a comforting change of scene after the death of her husband Prince Albert in 1861. The Riviera, Michael Nelson notes, 'had been a backwater until the British started to settle there in the eighteenth century. At the time of the Queen's death a century and half later, it was one of the most developed parts of France and Europe'.

By 1861 the British Medical Journal was declaring San Remo to be 'the most beautiful and healthiest place with the mildest climate to be found on the Mediterranean coast', adding that it was ideal for people with 'a delicate constitution' or chest ailments. In the early 20th century the idea that the Southern sun had a therapeutic effect was reinforced by a fashionable Swiss doctor, Auguste Rollier. 'The sun cure for tuberculosis and undernourished children is becoming a recognized part of modern treatment for these conditions,' said *Time* magazine in 1923. The British government recommended sun cures for victims of the 1918–19 Spanish flu epidemic, which killed 200,000 people in England alone, with posters at English railway stations declaring 'Sunshine is Life – Come to the Riviera'.

At the time of the Lawrences' stay the magnet was a resort with an English church, an English library, and streets with English (or Scottish) names: Alassio. Alassio already had a thriving British colony founded by wealthy English and Scottish families – the McMurdos, the Gibbs, the Hanburys. It offered a superb three-mile-long sandy bay with the snail-shaped island of Gallinara just offshore, and picturesque tumbledown houses hung with lobster pots and washing lines.

'Alassio has the most temperate climate in summer and the highest temperature in winter of any European resort,' proclaimed a 1929 Illustrated Guide which Rina Secker used at

Alassio when she moved there after Spotorno, and which she kept in her archive. It was 'not we who affirm this', the guide said, but well known experts who recommended Alassio for cures of rheumatism, arthritis and bronchitis which 'appear miraculous'.

'Every year numerous foreigners of all nationalities, especially English, leave their own country to come and sojourn on the Italian Riviera, particularly that part of it which lies between Genoa and Ventimiglia and is called the Riviera di Ponente, or Western Riviera,' wrote Rina's landlord at Alassio, the engineer and architect Count Francesco Vergerio di Cesana. Its mild winters and abundant sunshine, the Count declared in the January 1927 edition of *The Italian Riviera Illustrated Magazine*, widely read by British expats, 'entice and attract those who live in northern climes, who, fleeing from the fogs and frosts of those regions, are able on the blue shores of the Mediterranean to change those gloomy days of the North into others full of light and life, thus procuring for themselves the means of keeping or restoring their health'.

The English, the Count said, generally arrived in November – as indeed the Lawrences did – to pass the winter on the Riviera, and many stayed until June. But some were starting to stay throughout the summer 'in those localities where, like Alassio, the shore is so marvellously adapted for sea-bathing and where the hot months can be passed so delightfully in congenial surroundings full of comfort and amusements'. Some became so enamoured of the sky, the sea, the climate and the kindness and hospitality of the inhabitants, Count Vergerio observed, that they built their own villas 'overlooking the sapphire sea and surrounded by dark green orange trees and golden mimosas'.

In 1926 – when the Lawrences were at Spotorno and Frieda's daughter Barby, then 21, was at Alassio – the travel writer Gordon Home described the delights of Alassio in lyrical terms in his *Along the Rivieras of France and Italy* – the wide golden sand and gleaming white waves at the edge of a blue sea, 'that exquisite blue one remembers always in association with the broken shade of olive groves and long, fresh grass starred with wild flowers'. He regretted that the municipality was modernising the town despite 'appeals from the English who appreciate the charm of old Alassio'. But the new villas and hotels were hidden by the trees on the town's slopes, 'and down below among the pink and cream stuccoed buildings can be seen evidence of the English life of the town in the church, the reading room and tennis club'.

The potential of Alassio for villas had been spotted as early as 1867 by Thomas Hanbury, a Quaker tea and cloth merchant who made a fortune in China as a young man by developing property. Hanbury, who had become the largest private landowner in Shanghai, returned to Europe and bought the seaside estate of La Mortola at Ventimiglia in his thirties, creating a celebrated botanical garden. Alassio's first English doctor arrived in 1878, and three years later a neo-Gothic Anglican church arose beside the railway line, along with a meeting hall and tea rooms.

Soon these pioneers were joined by other expats attracted to the sun, including Charles Lamport, a shipping magnate whose formidable daughter Hilda founded the English Library, and Edward Elgar, who in 1904 rented a villa and composed his overture *In the South – Alassio* after the theme had come into his head during an afternoon walk up to the village of Moglio in the hills above the resort. As the English community grew, the first church was replaced in 1927 by a much larger one up the hill on the other side of the railway line. The growing library was housed, together with the tea room, first in Hanbury Hall, the British club, and then in a building adjoining the new church called The Octagon.

Nowadays most visitors arrive in the summer, when the beaches are packed: in former times, the attraction was the promise of sun in the winter, even if the promise was not always kept. It was, the travel writer Cecil Roberts noted in his 1955 account of Alassio, 'an illusion of visitors from the north that the winter on the Riviera coast is warm and sunny'. It was very warm during the day, Roberts wrote, when 'the sun shone, the sea sparkled and the air was balmy', but come nightfall, as icy winds blew from the mountains behind, the Riviera villas and apartments – not built for cold – needed stoves and fires (as Rina Secker and DH Lawrence both note with feeling in their letters).

On the other hand, he records, letters from home described a wintry Britain 'wrapped in a thick fog or saturated with rain, where it was dark at three o'clock' – and reading such letters 'at a cafe in front of a sparkling sea, where the light was so great that sunglasses had to be worn or the awning lowered' made the expats realise their good fortune. 'It is safe to say that out of the three hundred and sixty-five days, three hundred of them are as perfect as any that God has designed for this world of tribulation,' Roberts declared. 'Sleet, snow, fog and damp are unknown to us. When it rains, it rains in a fierce downpour that performs its refreshing business quickly and thoroughly. The next day the sky is blue again, the pavements dry.' The 'dark, sodden days' of an English winter were 'unknown here.'

Alassio, as modern travel writer Lee Marshall has observed, was the pearl in 'a carefree world of winter expatriate colonies between Bordighera and Rapallo that reached its high-water mark between the two world wars, and disappeared almost overnight in 1939 … It's difficult to understand why when Nice, Cannes and Antibes are still very much on our radar, the resorts of the Italian Riviera – whose sun is just as reliable, sea equally inviting, and back country full of undiscovered little gems – no longer figure in the British tourist imagination. Inland from Alassio and Albenga are a series of stone-hewn Ligurian villages as pretty as anything Tuscany has to offer.'

The villas the British built, Giovanni Assereto suggests, showed 'a high degree of respect for the natural and human landscape', with a 'use of traditional materials, the restoration of old buildings and the love for parks that tastefully blend exotic plans with the local flora'. If the drawback was that the British visitors tended to live 'withdrawn in their exclusive clubs, libraries, churches and tennis clubs' as if Italy were another British colony, even teaching their Ligurian servants 'the scarcely exciting art of English cuisine', the advantage was that they made Italians on the Riviera less provincial and more aware of the region's potential at a time 'when tourism was a byword for elegance'.

By the mid-1920s there were about 100 important British-owned villas in Alassio and 3,000 British residents and visitors. In 1925 Alfred Hitchcock chose Alassio as the backdrop for his first film, a silent movie called *The Pleasure Garden*, set on the beach and at the Villa della Pergola, built by General McMurdo and later taken over by the Hanburys. This was the 'Jazz Age', the 'Roaring Twenties', with fun and frivolity taking centre stage in a reaction to the horrors and deprivations of the First World War. The shady mile-long narrow lane which runs between high-sided houses parallel to the beach and contains the town's main shops and restaurants was – and still is – affectionately dubbed 'Il Budello', literally 'the intestine', or as the English called it, with Anglo-Saxon humour, 'The Drain'. In her study of the British colony at Alassio, Maura Muratorio notes that the arrival of the English was also a boon for a seaside village which had until then eked a living from fishing and olive groves: 'The arrival of a great number of foreign guests was the solution to many economic problems. Many village men chose to abandon the hard labour of fishermen and farmers and go to work as coachmen or gardeners for the English families. The women were hired as maids, nannies and cooks'.

Today most of the English have gone, replaced by second home owners from Milan, Turin and Switzerland. But the stuccoed, turreted villas are still there – many built on extensive land acquired at Alassio in the 1880s and 1890s by

Thomas Hanbury and his son Daniel, with their scented terraces, palm trees, eucalyptus trees, geraniums, nasturtiums, marigolds and irises. The Anglican church, which still held occasional services for a dwindling congregation when I first started going to Alassio in the 1980s, was de-consecrated in 1998 and turned into an exhibition and cultural events centre. The Hotel Norfolk on the winding road up to Moglio, above Elgar's villa, became the local hospital.

Down at the seaside the Cafe Vairo, where most expats gathered, has disappeared, as has the Casino and the Home and Colonial Stores. The Casa Bianca, home of the painter Richard West, is now a hotel, and the English school by the sea, the Villa delle Palme, has long been a private house. The first English Church by the railway line has been converted into flats.

But the 'English Pharmacy', or Farmacia Inglese, is still there, opposite the town hall gardens, with its original carved and gilded shelves, as is the Anglo-American travel agency. The Villa della Pergola has been saved from developers and survives as an exclusive hotel, with exotic restored gardens and a display in the hall of English memorabilia – Lear's watercolours, Elgar's sheet music, tennis balls from the club, a model of Daniel Hanbury's Silver Ghost Rolls Royce, and Kenneth Grahame's *The Wind in The Willows*, in which the Sea Rat beguiles Ratty with romantic tales of sailing to Alassio from Corsica.

The Hanbury Tennis Club is still going strong, and despite a temporary ban during the Fascist period when English names were obliterated, Alassio still boasts a Via Elgar, a Viale Gibb and a Viale Hanbury in its centre. Much of Miss Lamport's English Library has survived, and its books are still available for reading and borrowing.

On the whole DH Lawrence did not much take to Alassio: he disliked the rather snobbish atmosphere of upper class expat colonialism and the genteel tea parties and tennis club gatherings. 'Went to Alassio yesterday to see F's daughter Barby,' Lawrence wrote to Dorothy Brett from Spotorno in December 1925. 'Alassio well begins "Alas", for it's a chronic hole, awful!' He longed for the sun, and adored the Ligurian landscape, but preferred Spotorno, which Martin Secker assured him did not get as many visitors as its rivals along the coast.

Spotorno had 'a sandy beach at the mouth of a short and very steep valley' with a 'fragment of a castle or tower', Gordon Home noted in his travel guide – unaware, evidently, that just beneath the castle DH Lawrence was busy writing. Spotorno offered 'a beautiful view of the coast as far as the Portofino promontory, with Genoa's shimmering opalescence showing above the distant amethyst sea and the little island of Bergeggi, close at hand, where the heaving waters are deep peacock blue'.

Spotorno was not as well known as Alassio – though in January 1927 the *Alassio News* noted that 60 British visitors were registered at its hotels, and the same month the Municipio or town hall of Spotorno placed an advertisement in *The Times* informing readers that there were 'quiet, sunny residences' in the form of apartments and villas to be had for a rent of '£8 to £16 per season', as well as 'comfortable hotels and pensions' for '25 shillings to 2 guineas weekly, including taxes'.

The corniche road to Spotorno, perched between cliffs netted against landslides on one side and a vertiginous drop to the sea on the other, still today sweeps down to a sandy bay and the walled seaside town of Noli, Spotorno's picturesque neighbour. Once an episcopal see and independent maritime republic – as Lawrence notes in his letters – Noli still has its medieval castle on the hill above the bay, with a miraculously intact wall winding up to it.

After the First World War the 2,000 or so annual visitors to Spotorno could also enjoy the benefits of electric street lighting for the first time. There were other delights: on 9 January 1926, according to the *Alassio News*, the Grand Hotel

Palace at Spotorno hosted a concert for harp and piano by performers from Milan and Savona.

Lawrence and Frieda may well have attended. But the real reason they were in Spotorno was the Hotel Miramare. Inaugurated on 3 July 1910, the hotel had 20 rooms, augmented by an adjoining villa, the Villa Maria, and it had (and still has) its own beach. What mattered to Lawrence was not so much the beach, or the concerts, or even the amaretto biscuits he enjoyed, but the fact that by the time he went to the Riviera the Hotel Miramare was owned by Luigi Capellero, Rina's father.

6

Rina and Martin

Frieda Lawrence once claimed that Rina Secker had inspired the character of Lady Chatterley. According to Adrian Secker his mother, who was good at imitating Frieda's 'booming voice', with its rolling Teutonic rs, used to tell the story of Frieda 'once electrifying a staid literary party they were at, apropos *Lady Chatterley* when it was still a scandal', by roaring 'Rrrina my dear, you must read it, she is you, you will see.'

One striking photograph from the Spotorno period shows Lawrence staring at the camera with his hat nonchalantly placed on a wall while Rina sits at his shoulder, her hands folded on her lap, gazing dreamily into the distance on Lawrence's right, her face averted from the camera. Another photograph Lawrence sent to his friend and admirer Dorothy Brett from Spotorno on 25 January 1926 showed 'Rina's posterior' – or so Lawrence claimed.

'They were obviously very close, my mother and the Lawrences,' Adrian wrote on another occasion. When Frieda sold the film rights to *Lady Chatterley's Lover* in the 1930s to a Swiss film producer in Paris called JE Siebenhaar, he approached Rina and asked her to supply him with her 'personal reminiscences' of Lawrence as background material. Frieda wrote to Rina to reassure her that Siebenhaar hoped to make 'a good film' which would be 'very English' – and suggested that the part of Lady Chatterley could be played either by Frieda's daughter Barby or by Rina herself. 'You go and try! If you can't be Lady C you might have another part to begin with.'

The film was never made. Connie Chatterley is a composite figure, and draws – among others – on Frieda herself. But what Frieda clearly meant was that Rina had an impact on Lawrence quite apart from her role, as her son Adrian later recalled, in 'installing the Lawrences with the Ravaglis – with the outcome we all know'.

She did not (as far as we know) have an affair with a gamekeeper. But Rina was attractive to men (her letters to Martin from Alassio in the 1930s refer rather tauntingly to her many admirers at club dances and balls), and was always conscious of her appearance; in photographs of her at Iver proudly showing off her newborn baby just before leaving for Spotorno she has the fashionable hair style known in the 1920s as 'earphones', with braided hair coiled into two buns, one behind each ear. Later photographs show her with shorter, bobbed hair, as the Jazz Age hairstyle fashions changed: Lawrence, who was clearly taken with her, complimented Rina on her 'bangs', or fringe. She had 'wonderful eyes', high cheek bones, a winning smile, a strong personality and – something which would have impressed Lawrence as much as her femininity – a way with words.

Her letters to Martin from the Riviera reveal a descriptive power, with some odd turns of phrase but also a remarkable command of English given that she was brought up in an immigrant Italian family in London. 'Why don't you write?' Frieda asked her in 1926. 'On all sorts of things! The Italian way of looking at things ... Of course I am not certain, but I think you have some force that would carry, and you know I am not such a fool as people think me.' Lawrence evidently agreed: in a hitherto unpublished letter to Rina in 1927 – the year after the Spotorno interlude – he offered her advice on how to get into print. He thought she might do well as a society or woman's columnist. Lawrence wrote to Rina at Bridgefoot from the Villa Mirenda near Florence. A news correspondent had to be 'an expert journalist of considerable experience', whereas Rina was more suited to the role of social observer – the kind of thing, he suggested, that was done by Iris Tree, daughter of the actor Sir Herbert Beerbohm Tree.

The only problem, Lawrence warned Rina, was that to be a society gossip writer meant that 'you have to run round seeing people and seeing shows, garden parties etc – and you don't get a *vast* salary. But it might be worth it.' She should 'write a few snappy little "interviews" or "reports" to show you can do them: then see if you can get onto some paper like *Vanity Fair*, or *Harpers Bazaar* or *Good Housekeeping*: they pay pretty well. If there's anything I can do, I'll do it. But what can I do?' He added: 'I do think it would be good for you to be doing some work of your own ... Make a start somehow, and you'll get somewhere.' Rina was *nervosa*, Lawrence wrote from Spotorno, even 'a living block of discontent – why, I don't know, for she's not so perfect. But I think she's ill.' This was blunt – but he was rather kinder in his 1927 letter to Rina herself, suggesting she was simply '*désoeuvrée* to a degree', that is adrift, at a loose end.

At the time she was close to Lawrence and Frieda in Spotorno Rina was indeed given to mood swings after giving birth to her son Adrian. She had clearly come to sunny Spotorno as much to lift her spirits as to benefit her (or little Adrian's) health: the change from 'silent Bridgefoot' to the Mediterranean would do her good, Lawrence thought, and she would be 'perfectly all right' if she could just leave the boy with her mother and 'get a good walk in the hills with us all'. One of her favourite words in her letters is 'neurasthenia', applied both to herself and to her mother Caterina: nervous exhaustion, involving headaches, anxiety attacks and depression. But she was also vibrant, observant, mischievous, flirtatious and coquettishly aware of her charms. This is strikingly similar to Lawrence's description of the 'feminine' and 'womanly' Connie Chatterley, with the 'growing restlessness' and sense of 'disconnexion' which drives her into the arms of Mellors.

Rina was not originally from Spotorno: although her parents were Italian, she was born in Monte Carlo and brought to London as a baby, thus becoming both Italian (by parentage) and English (by upbringing). Her parents were from Piedmont, in the mountains of northern Italy: Luigi Capellero, Rina's father, was from a family of bakers in the medieval hilltop town of Fossano. The Capelleros moved to the charming nearby former Roman town of Bene Vagienna, on a fertile plain beneath the foothills of the Maritime Alps, and there Luigi met the beautiful Caterina Gazzera, from a family higher up the social scale.

They were married at Bene Vagienna and moved down to the coast, to Monaco on the Côte d'Azur, where Luigi first tried his luck in the hotel business, buying the 16-bedroom 'London House'. He registered the birth of Rina at Monaco town hall on 6 April 1896: she was named Catherine Anna Josephine Marie, in later life reduced to Catherine Marie (or Caterina Maria), and then to Rina. But in May 1896, with Rina barely a few weeks old, 'London House' went bust, and the Capelleros moved to London itself, where Rina's sister Anna Marie (known as Annie) was born a year later. By 1901 the Capelleros were in Soho, with Luigi ('Louis') listed as a restaurant waiter. Quite a comedown after the dreams of breaking the bank in Monte Carlo. But Luigi picked himself up: according to family legend he rose to be a head waiter in top London hotels. By 1904 the family had its own restaurant, Capellero's, on Archway Rd, Upper Holloway – then part of Highgate – with a cook, a waiter and two maids. Not quite as glamorous – or sunny – as Monaco, but this was a good time to be offering Londoners the tempting aromas of Italian dishes, coffee and ice cream, in addition to the standard English fare of soup, chops, game pie and pudding.

There had been Italian eating places in London since the

18th century, but in Edwardian times the taste for Italian cuisine was on the rise, fuelled by the 12,000 Italians in the capital alone (Bertorelli's opened in Charlotte Street in 1913). The Capelleros' Archway restaurant (also known as The Toll Gate Cafe) is still there, marooned on a traffic island and overshadowed by the 60-metre-high 1960s era Archway Tower office block. But in Edwardian times it was at the heart of an important road junction, the terminus of Europe's first San Francisco-style cable car (later converted to a tramway).

A studio photograph taken at this period shows a confident Luigi in an immaculate three-piece suit with a fob watch chain and wing collar: a good-looking, straight-backed man, he has sandy hair, a receding hairline, a twisty Edwardian moustache and smiling blue eyes. His wife Catherine, or Caterina, is pretty and dark, with heavy eyebrows and a rather sadder or more preoccupied expression. But she too is in a smart outfit, an embroidered high-necked black dress with long puffed sleeves: her hair is gathered in a bun, with kiss curls on her forehead, and a reticule or drawstring handbag dangles elegantly from the belt of her tightly nipped-in waist. The two girls, in button boots, carry studio props – a badminton racket for Annie and a model ship for Rina. Both girls were regarded as 'highly intelligent – and very determined'.

And so Rina and Anna Marie were brought up in late Victorian and early Edwardian Britain, attending a convent school on Haverstock Hill in Hampstead. When Rina turned 15 and her sister Anna Marie 14 they were sent back to Piedmont to a convent school in Cuneo, the provincial capital, noted for its neo-classical buildings, elegant squares, Turin-style cafes and rum-filled chocolates. Perhaps Luigi and Caterina felt the girls could do with immersion back in Italy to remind them of their origins. Rina's miniature silver diary details their departure for Italy in August 1910 via Calais, Paris and Turin – a journey Rina was to make many times during her adult life.

What interested her most at school was art: she learnt to draw and paint, and to mix pigments such as burnt umber and copper powder. 'In the studio drawing a plant', she wrote on 26 January 1912, even noting the time, 10.55 a.m. 'Went yesterday to the art gallery'. In other entries she described drawing an eye, or painting a portrait of Alexander the Great. But she was 16, and her thoughts were turning from the mountains of Piedmont to the bright lights of London – and dreams of romance. She jotted down a passage in Italian from Dante's famous verses on the forbidden love affair between Francesca da Rimini and Paolo Malatesta: 'Love, that releases no beloved from loving, took hold of me so strongly through his beauty that, as you see, it has not left me yet.'

Within a few years Luigi Capellero bought a share in a more upmarket establishment, The Crichton at Clapham Junction in South London, and the family moved to Wandsworth. Adrian claimed his mother attended the Slade School of Art; she certainly loved to paint, draw and sculpt (DH Lawrence would later borrow her paint box). She was 18 when the First World War broke out in 1914: her mother Caterina took her two daughters back to Bene Vagienna, and they spent the war in Turin, where Anna Marie served with the American Red Cross as a bilingual secretary (Italy had joined the Allies against Germany and Austro-Hungary). Rina's role is less clear: she may have helped the American YMCA in Turin, and Adrian later recalled that his mother had washed for the Red Cross in Europe 'and eventually in Italy'.

A decade or so later she read Ernest Hemingway's celebrated semi-autobiographical 1929 novel *A Farewell to Arms*, the story of a doomed love affair between Frederic Henry, an American lieutenant in the Italian Army ambulance corps, and Catherine Barkley, a British Voluntary Aid Detachment (VAD) nurse, and pronounced it 'rather gruesome and not too true to things as they were'.

When the war ended and Europe began to recover from the slaughter of the trenches, Rina's parents could have stayed in London; instead, they went back to Italy. Luigi, it seems, wanted to pack up in London after a quarter of a century and start again – this time in the sunshine. For a while he lived and worked at Pegli, near Genoa, described by Baedeker as 'a small seaside town with shipbuilding yards and an old castle which occupies a pleasant site protected from the wind and is visited by nervous and dyspeptic patients in winter and by bathers from Genoa in summer (beach mostly sand)'.

He then bought the Hotel Miramare along the coast at Spotorno. Possibly he was influenced by British government advice to those suffering from the effects of the Spanish flu epidemic as well as TB and other diseases to 'seek the sun on the Italian Riviera'. It was at any rate a good investment – and one which had unintended consequences for literature. For by the time Luigi was setting himself up as a hotelier at Spotorno, Rina back in London was getting to know – and falling in love with – Percy Klingender, better known to history as Martin Secker, DH Lawrence's publisher.

Martin was nearly 15 years older than Rina, and already an influential figure at the heart of literary London. He was 'not a tall man', Frank Swinnerton, one of his authors, later recalled: he was 'very dark and very quiet and gentle, and his large, noticeable eyes are set unusually wide apart in a thin, olive-skinned face'. Martin had a mix of pessimism and dry wit, with a 'kind heart and a reluctance to give pain which have landed him in many difficulties'. He was born into a long-established German immigrant family in Kensington and brought up in Carshalton and Beckenham as Percy Martin Secker Klingender: the 'Klingender' was dropped by deed poll in 1910, possibly because it was too Germanic-sounding in the run up to the First World War, and 'Percy' was dropped in favour of 'Martin'.

The re-named Martin Secker first worked as a clerk at the Bank of England, and then as a reader for an established publishing firm before – with a bravado which must have surprised those who thought him rather unassuming – he set himself up as a publisher at the age of just 28, thanks to a legacy from his Irish-born mother, Julia Clark, who died when he was 24. 'When I was in my early twenties I came into a legacy of £1000, a sum which at that time, I need hardly say, was considerably more substantial and impressive than it is today,' he wrote later. He decided to turn the legacy into 'a golden key which would open the door into the world of publishing'.

By the time Rina met Martin, however, there was another formidable woman in his life – his benefactress, Lucy Margaret Lamont, née Smart, known as 'Lammy', widow of the prominent Scottish Victorian artist Thomas Reynolds Lamont. Quite what hold Lammy had over Martin, a man half her age, we may never know. It later caused serious problems in Martin's marriage to Rina, who resented the older woman's influence – one of the causes no doubt of the *nervosa* discontent which struck DH Lawrence.

Lucy Lamont's hold on Martin may even have influenced Lawrence in his creation of Ivy Bolton, the nurse and housekeeper who acquires such a dominance over Sir Clifford Chatterley. 'My dear, you cannot ask a woman to share her home and her husband with another woman, however platonic the situation may be for all three,' Rina wrote to Martin from Alassio in a burst of fury in 1932, seven years after the Spotorno episode. 'There have been two of you against me for all these years ... In this extraordinary *menage à trois* of ours, I have definitely been the one *de trop*.'

While his mother was alive Martin had lived with her and his sister Kathleen near St Peter's Church at Iver in Buckinghamshire; but by 1911 Mrs Lamont, 52, 'widow of private means', was recorded as head of the household at Churchgate, with Martin Secker, by now 28, as her boarder, plus two live-in servants. They moved in 1912 down the hill to Bridgefoot, an elegant early 18th-century Queen Anne mansion owned by the local landed gentry, the Tower family, with a coach house and stables and a Georgian stone bridge over a stream, the Colne. When the First World War broke out Martin Secker somehow managed to avoid military service: Frank Swinnerton recalled that since 'neither of us had been swept into the Army, we lunched together at least once a week', sometimes with other Secker authors such as Gilbert Cannan, Francis Brett Young and 'charming Viola Meynell', who was Secker's fiancée until she broke off the engagement in 1919.

The first novel Secker published, *The Passionate Elopement* by Compton Mackenzie (then only 28), was a runaway success, partly because Mackenzie had the bright – and at the time unheard of – idea of advertising the book in the lifts at London Tube stations. Secker never looked back. He started out with titles by Norman Douglas, Arthur Ransome, Frank Swinnerton, Hugh Walpole, Frances Brett Young, James Elroy Flecker, Ford Madox Ford, Henry James – and DH Lawrence.

When the war that Secker – and Lawrence – hated so much came to an end, travel was again possible, and it was now that Martin and Rina first met – on a train. Adrian Secker claimed his mother had met his father 'on one of her Italian trips – it was on the Rome Express – when he was going out to Capri to stay with Compton Mackenzie, one of his authors and later my godfather'. Mackenzie confirms this in his memoirs, *My Life and Times*, recording that early in the summer of 1921 Martin Secker 'came to spend a week on Herm with Rina Capellero, a charming and extremely able Italian girl who had come to his rescue when his lack of Italian was involving him in difficulties on the way to Capri.'

What Mackenzie did not say was that Martin, still recovering from his split with Viola Meynell, was clearly a fast worker. His letters to Rina in 1920 and 1921 move within the space of three months from 'Dear Miss Capellero' and 'Yours sincerely Martin Secker' to 'Dearest Girl' and 'Darling Rina' from 'Your loving Martin'. Moreover, his Italian was in reality not that bad: when he started to get to know her better he attempted a letter in passable Italian while staying with Mackenzie on Herm in the Channel Islands, signing off 'Martino' and beginning 'Carissima'. He probably spent some time over it, and no doubt used a dictionary, but the letter is good enough to make one wonder if he exaggerated his 'lack of Italian' during the railway journey as an excuse.

He had evidently asked Rina to keep in touch after their encounter on the train – and equally evidently, she was keen to do so, despite the age gap. The relationship was at first professional. 'Dear Miss Capellero,' Martin wrote from his office in John Street, Adelphi, on 2 December 1920 to Rina at her lodgings in a Shepherds Bush boarding house, 'thank you for your note. I was very glad to hear your plans had been satisfactorily arranged.' Her employment at his office had been fixed for the end of the year: 'I am sure you will not find the work onerous.'

He added casually: 'I wonder if you are free for tea, tomorrow Friday, and if so if you would meet me outside Lyons in Shaftesbury Avenue next the Monico at 4.30? Do not trouble to let me know if you cannot manage this, as I shall be there in any case.' A few days later, on 6 December, he wrote to Rina again, this time from Bridgefoot rather than the office, asking her if she would care to have tea with him again at Lyons Corner House at the same time, 4.30, before he took the night boat from Southampton for Guernsey. 'If you were doing nothing afterwards we might go to a cinema,' he added.

Soon the bilingual Rina was working for Secker as a translator: in 1921 he published her English version of *Tre Croci* (Three Crosses) by the modernist Italian writer Federigo Tozzi. By February 1921 they had progressed from teatime meetings to lunches. When he went to Herm on 12 February, Martin wrote to Rina describing his 'marine adventures' at length, including an incident in which his boat's engine had caught fire in a gale. He had thought of their encounters at Lyons 'while tossing about in the waves ... Did you find it dull at the office today, Rina dear? I hope you did miss me a little.'

She did: in a flirtatious letter to Martin the following day, 13 February, Rina told him she was 'very very happy to have such a good friend as you. I am a lucky girl, aren't I?' Martin thanked her for her 'nice long letters'. There had been 'a most wonderful sunset over Guernsey' the night before. 'I am afraid I felt very romantic and sentimental, but it did seem intolerable to be alone on such a night. I think you will love this place, in many ways it is quite as good as Capri and not so sophisticated.'

He returned to England, and by 12 March the die was cast: they had progressed from tea and lunch to dinner dates. Martin was apparently already aware that Rina had a depressive tendency, but overlooked it. 'I hope your little mood of depression was only a transient one for I do so want you to be a happy girl always, as you deserve to be. You have no reason to be sad, darling Rina, or to be dissatisfied with your life so far, and we are going to have some very happy times together in the future.' He added: 'I wish you could realise how much I admire and respect your courage and independence. I want nothing better than to love you and do things for you always.' And he signed off with 'Arrivederci, your loving Martin'.

Within six months Rina and Martin were married: Martin was 39, Rina 25. Secker's friends were much taken with her: 'Dear Martin, I'm so glad you've got a charming wife,' Compton Mackenzie's wife Faith wrote to him from Southampton as she left for Capri for the winter. For the time being, at least, Rina's mood swings and Martin's continuing attachment to Mrs Lamont were put to one side.

The couple's only child, Adrian, was born three years later at Bridgefoot, on 11 March 1924. It was evidently not an easy delivery: Rina's mother Caterina came to England to help, and Martin later recalled how 'the house was crowded with doctors, your mother praying in the nursery'. Many years later Rina wrote to her second husband Carlo Lovioz: 'Tomorrow is Adrian's birthday. It doesn't seem 29 years since he was born. 29 years ago today I started my pains at 8 p.m. and he was born on the morrow at 12.35! What women go through to put a man into the world.'

The following year Rina set off for Spotorno with Adrian, by now just over a year and a half old, and there she waited for Lawrence and Frieda. She could not have foreseen at the time the consequences of her role in persuading Lawrence and Frieda to join her there, but was certainly aware of them later; towards the end of her life, when Martin Secker was preparing Lawrence's letters for publication, Rina wrote on the typescript – in red ink – 'I found them the Villa Bernarda, belonging to Tenente Ravagli, who afterwards became Frieda's 3rd husband.'

7

Down There By The Sea

B<small>Y THE TIME</small> the Lawrences arrived in Spotorno in November 1925, Rina had moved with her baby into the villa adjoining the Hotel Miramare, the two-storey sugar pink green-shuttered Villa Maria – still today the quarters of the hotelier, with the entwined initials VM on the front. She had engaged a local girl 'for two hours every morning and two hours every evening to do our rooms and the young man's washing and generally help.'

She added, almost casually: 'I received a letter from Lawrence – from Baden – an amusing letter. They are arriving here on the 15th or 16th and I have fixed rooms for them at the Albergo Ligure here in Spot. My father has told me of what sounds a very ideal apartment for them in a villa on the hill above Spotorno. We shall probably go to see it this afternoon.' The summery weather which greeted Lawrence and Frieda a week or so later was not yet in evidence – 'I am sitting in my little kitchen, outside my bedroom, over a tiny charcoal fire' – but she was 'very much looking forward to the Lawrences' arrival. The Albergo Ligure is going to charge them 30 lire a day for whatever time they wish to stay there, and it seems very reasonable to me. That of course is an inclusive price. Then when they get here they can look around. Of course, if they decided to stay on all the winter at the Ligure they would have an even better price made at so much a month.'

The Lawrences made their way to Italy via Baden-Baden, where Frieda's mother was now in a retirement home, Lawrence wrote to Martin Secker to say that he had left 'my nice new felt hat' in London by mistake. 'If Rina is bringing a hat box, I wish she'd put it in. It's been worn a few times.' He said he was 'sorry to bother you really – but you're so good natured about these things.' In a P.S. he added 'If Rina's not bringing a hatbox, tell her not to bother at all.'

In a postcard sent to Secker just before leaving for Italy, Lawrence asked if he had received 'a letter from me bothering you about a hat', and added that he had had a letter from 'R', meaning Rina. 'She knows of a house ... The address will be Spotorno now.' On 4 November 1925 he wrote to Brett from Baden-Baden that he had found England 'very damp and dreary', adding: 'Martin Secker's wife lives (her family) in Spotorno, she's just gone there, and we shall probably fix up for a while in that region: don't know yet.'

The 'amusing letter' Lawrence wrote to Rina has survived in the Bridgefoot archives. Writing to her – rather elaborately – c/o (*presso*) her mother Caterina Capellero at Villa Maria, Spotorno, Riviera di Ponente, Provincia di Genova on 3 November 1925, he addressed her as 'Mrs Secker', possibly to impress her parents with his manners. 'Perhaps you will be at home by the time this arrives: your father's home, that is,' Lawrence wrote. He and Frieda were planning to leave Baden-Baden on 12 November and arrive at Spotorno via Lucerne on the 15th, a Sunday, 'or perhaps better Monday, 16th'. He added: 'It would be nice if you knew of a house for us, not very big, three bedrooms or thereabouts.' Meanwhile he was in a place which had once been fashionable and 'grand', and still had 'a sort of *fin de siècle* elegance', but was now 'quite deserted. Nobody comes at all.' His head was 'thick with talking German to old ladies', or rather 'listening to old ladies talk German. My God, what is it that keeps these old ladies trotting and talking for a hundred years? So many people die: but these have the gift of eternal life. And why?

Why, oh why! There should be a law against widows.' His mother-in-law, Lawrence added, was of course 'a dear', 'but she's only seventy five, so far.' He turned his thoughts from his German in-laws to the happier prospect of Spotorno. 'I hope you had a pleasant journey, and the boy fared well, and that you are rejoicing in the bosom of the family. And I hope we shall see you soon, and that we can have some jolly times, all of us, down there by the sea.'

Frieda's account of their arrival in Spotorno in her memoir *Not I, But the Wind* by contrast is rather less than the whole truth. At the end of the summer of 1925, she writes, Lawrence 'became restless again and wanted to go to Europe. To the Mediterranean he wished to go. So on the coast, not far from Genoa, we found Spotorno, that Martin Secker had told us was not overrun with foreigners.'

Under the ruined castle, Frieda says, 'I saw a pink villa that had a friendly look and wondered if we could have it. We found the peasant Giovanni who looked after it. Yes, he thought we could. It belonged to a Tenente dei Bersaglieri in Savona. We were staying at the little inn by the sea, when the bersaglieri asked for us. Lawrence went and returned. "You must come and look at him, he is so smart." So I went and found a figure in uniform with gay plumes and blue sash, as it was the Queen's birthday. We took the Bernarda and the tenente became a friend of ours. Lawrence taught him English on Sundays, but they never got very far.' The 'tenente' was in fact Angelo Ravagli, who would become her lover and – eventually – her third husband. And it was not Frieda herself who found the Villa Bernarda, but Rina.

Rina had first stayed at her father's newly acquired hotel in Spotorno three years earlier, towards the end of April 1922, and had been enchanted. She stopped first at Bene Vagienna, writing to Martin as from 'Augusta Bagiennorum' on 27 April and giving the date in Roman numerals as XXVII-IV-XXII. Bene was 'sleepy and silent', and apart from the fact that she was put in a supposedly haunted room at the family house

– 'I heard several strange noises which I persuaded myself were caused by cats walking on the roofs' – she had 'heard all the gossip there is to hear in Bene, and it's not much.'

However, she had a lot to say about Spotorno. 'You must excuse this missive for daring to present itself to you in mere pencil scribble', she wrote to Martin in a letter postmarked 30 April 1922, 'but I am writing in my little white bed, in a large white room, and everybody else is abed and asleep and I am giving way to an impulse and writing with what material I can find without going beyond my door'. She thought Martin would 'love the place'. 'Dearest, I do wish you were here. It is beautiful. Myriads of roses are in full bloom, and geraniums too, and large large white marguerites. There are also several eucalyptus trees and this afternoon – after a shower – the whole place was scented with them.'

Her room, she wrote, 'faces the sea – in fact I don't think the sea is more than 50 yards away from me, and through my closed shutters I can hear a very gentle swish of waves and if I look out I can see only intense blackness with the faintest edge of paler hue just outlining it and defining the restlessness which continues across and around the world.' She added: 'What a shivery feeling the sea can give one sometimes! It sounds so very gentle just now, but it looks so immense and so restless. Soon the moon will be here, and then the sea will not look so black and fathomless.' The hotel was 'beautifully equipped and spotlessly clean and white. All the rooms are large, airy and scantily but sufficiently furnished. All the walls are painted a nice cream colour and all the floors are of polished mosaic. There is electricity everywhere. There is also a nice garden with enormous palms and a stone balustrade overlooking the sands.' The adjoining villa in the hotel grounds, the Villa Maria, where her parents lived, was 'a charming place, also very sunny, bright and spacious. Altogether, the whole atmosphere is delightful.'

'I do wish you were here to see this sun! – and the sea – it's wonderful,' she wrote from the Hotel Miramare on 6 May

1922. 'It is so clear today that we can just see Corsica on the horizon.' She was missing her husband – 'we really mustn't leave each other again for ages and ages, must we?' – and as promised she returned to England in May via Turin, Paris and Boulogne.

But by the following summer she was back in Italy on errands for the Secker publishing business, visiting the novelist and gossip writer Reginald ('Reggie') Turner in Florence ('a funny old thing') but also finding time to return to Spotorno and the Hotel Miramare ('beach, garage, all modern comforts, prop. L. Capellero'). The Miramare in high summer was 'not so nice now with all these strangers walking about, it has lost its nice privacy and quietness,' she wrote on 4 July. In Florence Reggie Turner, a friend of DH Lawrence, Oscar Wilde and HG Wells, described by Somerset Maugham as 'on the whole the most amusing man I have known', 'was very nice to me and took me out to dinner and to a cinema!' He had been 'most gallant' – but she was longing to be back at Bridgefoot ('how nice it will be to be home'). Despite the fact that both Reggie Turner and Norman Douglas – who would shortly play a key role in the publication in Florence of *Lady Chatterley* – were homosexual, she joked that Reggie Turner was very sorry that Douglas was away in Austria, the country of his birth, visiting an ill sister, 'as he knew positively that Douglas would have fallen in love with me! Imagine!'

What changed her back-and-forth lifestyle, leading to a more or less permanent settling in Spotorno, was her son Adrian, who was deemed to be in need of the climate of the South – the background for Lawrence's story *Sun*. Adrian apart, Rina herself seems to have needed rest on the Riviera after suffering some kind of nervous breakdown or post-natal depression. Her parents found her 'too serious and sad', she told Martin on 19 November 1925 after the Lawrences' arrival, and Frieda 'says the same – what am I to do? I can't laugh and joke to order – and I do feel that life just at present lacks somewhat in lightheartedness and *joie de vivre*.' If it were not for the child 'I should be very restive indeed and would probably come to some drastic decision.' This was probably due to 'some physical weakness left me by the birth of the young man', but she had 'no-one to confide to and my obsessions are my own, kept down under lock and key.'

Mother and baby arrived at Savona on 6 November 1925 via Turin, and were met by Rina's father Luigi. The main drama gripping Italy was an attempt on the life of Benito Mussolini, the Fascist dictator, referred to discreetly by Rina only as 'our friend'. This was not the later attack on the Duce by the Anglo-Irish aristocrat Violet Gibson on 7 April 1926, when she fired at Mussolini and grazed his nose, but an alleged plot by the socialist politician Tito Zaniboni, who was accused of conspiring to kill Mussolini on 4 November 1925 by firing at him with a sharpshooter's rifle from a hotel opposite Palazzo Chigi, the Prime Minister's office, where the Duce had appeared on a balcony.

Some historians suggest the 'plot' by Zaniboni, who was given a 25-year jail sentence commuted to exile on Ponza, was a pretext for Mussolini's crackdown on opposition parties, paving the way for full dictatorship. 'Did you read in the papers what an escape our friend had?' Rina wrote on 10 November. 'It was on the day we were in Turin, but we didn't hear of it until we got here. There have been thanksgiving services in all the churches and demonstrations generally.' Politics, however, was low on her list of priorities, far below the health of Adrian ('his cheeks are very rosy') – and the arrival of Frieda and Lawrence at Spotorno by train on Sunday 15 November.

It was only thanks to Rina's intuition that they were met at all, since their telegram announcing their arrival on the Sunday rather than the Monday had yet to reach the Capelleros. 'Today has been very exciting,' Rina reported to Martin the same day. 'After lunch we set out – my parents, Adrian, the pram and I – for a walk, and when we were some way out of Spot I said to my father, 'What time does the train from

Genova arrive?' He said '2.30'. I looked at my watch and it was 2.25. I said we had better go to the station in case the Lawrences should be arriving today – telegrams have such a way of not finding their way here until long after the senders have themselves arrived – and so we went and reached the station just as the train arrived (ten minutes late), and lo and behold the first person I see is Lawrence himself hanging out of a window! Great excitement!'

Anyone seeking to recreate the scene today should go, not to the present railway station behind the town, but rather to the main road running close to the beach by the former Grand Hotel Palace, where the former railway line ran. Rina 'rushed up the platform to meet them' and 'piloted them out of the station – Frieda, in a brown corduroy velvet coat, looks larger than ever – Lawrence, by contrast, even more fragile.' Their luggage was sent on to the Hotel Ligure, just along the seafront from the Hotel Miramare and the Villa Maria, where the party stopped 'to have Vermouth – my father of course quite incomprehensible and incoherently loquacious, my mother very shy and embarrassed.'

'We got here yesterday,' Lawrence wrote to Curtis Brown on 16 November, 'it is lovely and sunny, with a blue sea, and I'm sitting out on the balcony just above the sands, to write.' Reminiscing toward the end of his life, Ravagli (who called Lawrence 'David') told the Italian author Alberto Bevilacqua that Martin Secker had refused to pay for the Lawrences to have a room at his father in law's imposing hotel, with Rina claiming that all the rooms there were taken, though it appears the Lawrences at some point did lodge in the adjoining Villa Maria – the annex, as it were, albeit a charming one.

Ravagli claimed that Frieda had been furious, seeing the failure to offer them a room at the Miramare itself as a slight and calling Secker 'a usurer, strangler, bloodsucker ...' It was the first time I ever saw Frieda really furious. I never forgot it ... Frieda was screaming, hurling vulgar insults. At a certain point she lifted a pile of papers out of a suitcase and started throwing them in the air, screaming that these were precious papers, David's new masterpiece, which she had brought to give to the publisher, but now she would die rather than hand them over.' He added, 'I still remember that painful scene. Frieda, who wouldn't listen to reason, all the papers floating through the air, and he, David, in humiliation, picking up the papers one after another from the floor and checking the page numbers to put his manuscript back in order again. That was how I knew who these two were – and that David was a famous writer, there on his knees complaining "There's a page missing, stupid German, there's a page missing. It was a very important page, it was really rather good."'

The palm-fringed, pink-painted four-storey Hotel Miramare, though renovated inside, still dominates the seafront. The Hotel Ligure has been rebuilt, but photographs of it in the 1920s and 1930s show a charmingly rustic two-storey building with a pitched roof and peeling shutters facing the beach, festooned with fairy lights and surrounded by newly planted palm trees and outside tables shaded by parasols. 'All modern comforts, splendid position on the sea, modest prices: proprietor Tito Garzoglio', reads the Hotel Ligure business card for 1925.

The Lawrences, Rina wrote, 'seem to like Spot, and certainly they couldn't have chosen a better day. The sun had been shining all day and the air has felt quite summery – it has been a most beautiful day. I escorted them, after the Vermouth, to the Ligure and to their rooms right facing the sea, with a nice terrace on which they had tea and which also belongs to their suite. After tea they joined us again and we went for a walk around Spot considering diverse possible localities. I hope they will stay here and like it.'

What the locals hoped, it seems, was that the arrival of a famous English writer would do for 'Spot' what the English colonies had done for other resorts along the Riviera. 'Wasn't it an inspiration of mine to go to the station? What would they have done otherwise, as they didn't know the name of the Albergo? By now of course all Spot is thrilled at the idea that at last the famous long talked of *stagione inglese* has begun. All Spot is dreaming of itself as a future Alassio.'

8

The Villa Bernarda

'MET LS ON BEACH at 9 a.m.' Rina wrote in her travel diary on Monday 16 November, the day after the Lawrences' arrival. They had walked together to the Pineta, the coastal pine woods: 'Sun, blue seas, gold lights everywhere ... walking in this sunlit air makes one feel so well and happy,' Rina wrote to Martin. After the Pineta walk and lunch, she recorded in her diary, she had gone 'all round Spot with L's and my parents to look for winter quarters for L's.' The Lawrences were 'very comfy at the Ligure, and I think they like Spot', she told Martin. Frieda had even found time to have her hair bobbed and permanently waved 'and looks immensely improved'. Her parents had been 'very charmed' by the Lawrences, especially Frieda. There were morning walks along the front 'halfway to Noli', and a trip to Savona for Lawrence with Rina's father Luigi.

'Here it's sunny,' Lawrence wrote two days after his arrival to Vere Collins at the Oxford University Press, which was issuing an illustrated version of a school textbook on European history he had written to try and make some money. 'We're in a hotel for a bit – probably shall look for a house for the winter here, though the village doesn't amount to much. But if the sun shines on the Mediterranean, that's a lot.'

The following day, Wednesday 18 November, he was already house-hunting with Rina. 'So the Ls have really come,' Martin wrote to Rina from Bridgefoot. 'I expect it is very comfortable at the Ligure, and certainly very cheap, but I do hope that they stop in the neighbourhood, even if they prefer a villa to themselves on higher ground.' He added: 'It was very lucky indeed that you thought of meeting that train, and I am sure their arrival was most impressive.' He was amused at the thought that the 'Spotornesi'– the residents of Spotorno – saw a 'golden future' ahead of them, with the Lawrences heralding a *stagione inglese*.

The villa on higher ground was the Villa Bernarda, which belonged to Ravagli's wife, Serafina Astengo. Ravagli called at the Hotel Miramare and found Rina, who left her son with her mother and walked up the hill to the villa with Ravagli and Lawrence. 'Tenente Ravagli called about Villa Bernarda – left A. with Mamma and went with L and T.R. to see the Villa,' Rina wrote in her diary for Wednesday 18 November. 'Very delightful – Ls very pleased – and decide to take it for the winter.' 'We have at last found an ideal place – a semi rustic little house in the shadow of Spot castle with vineyards and olive groves all around it and the most marvellous view,' Rina reported to Martin the next day, 19 November. 'The Ls are well pleased with it, and they are paying £25 for the whole time they will be here.' Drawing an analogy with the structure of a ship, Lawrence told John Middleton Murry the same day that the Villa Bernarda was 'a three decker – or a four decker, with the contadino in the deeps'.

Ravagli was a highly respected figure in the area. He had humble origins: one of nine children from the small village of Tredozio, 60 kilometres from Bologna in Emilia-Romagna, he had started out making a living by selling aubergines, peppers and tomatoes from a roadside stall. He worked for a time as a builder. Joining the army changed his fortunes: he was decorated for bravery in the First World War, and at the time of the Lawrences' arrival was about to be promoted to captain, becoming referred to – with even greater esteem – as 'Il Capitano'.

He was now stationed at Savona, eight miles along the coast from Spotorno, with Serafina and their two children, Stefano, 5, and Magda, 3, soon to be joined by a third, Federico. Serafina was a good catch for Ravagli: she not only held a prestigious post as a schoolteacher of Italian language and history at Savona, she was a woman of property, having inherited the villa at Spotorno from an uncle. The Villa Bernarda stood below Spotorno's great ruined castle high above the town, with spectacular views over the bay and a caretaker – Giovanni Rossi, the 'contadino'– in the basement. It was, according to Alberto Bevilacqua, who interviewed Angelo Ravagli there in the early 1970s, 'Typically Ligurian in construction – rather monastic, with white, rather roughly plastered walls.'

'We've taken this villa,' Lawrence wrote to Martin Secker, 'move in on Monday. It's just under the castle – the garden goes to the castle itself. It's nice, only hope it won't be cold, I've got a cold, motoring in beastly Switzerland, and feel cross ... Rina's got a little cold too – the boy flourishes. It's been chill and very windy – thank heaven the sun is here again. Hope we'll all have a nice time at Christmas.'

'The village is not much to brag about – but the hills are fine and wild and the villa is above the houses and has a big vineyard garden,' Lawrence informed Dorothy Brett. 'If it won't be cold it will be all right. I wish to heaven they'd just put fireplaces in these houses.' He told his sister Emily the village was not very exciting, but 'they have had some sunny days,' and it was altogether better than the 'damp darkness of England'.

Ravagli – or Angelino, as Frieda came to call him – was five foot nine, and good-looking, with a disarming manner and pomaded black hair. Frieda enjoyed his war stories, his devil-may-care machismo and irreverent sense of humour. It is not clear when they first went to bed: Rina in her letters does not refer to an affair. Some biographers suggest it did not happen until Lawrence stormed off from Spotorno to

Capri in 1926, leaving the coast clear, or even until 1927 or 1928, when the Lawrences were in Florence and Ravagli was posted to Gradisca, on what is now the Italian-Slovenian border.

Others – including Alberto Bevilacqua, who interviewed Ravagli in old age – believe the affair took place almost instantly, given the way Frieda behaved: this after all was the woman who had no hesitation in taking lovers while she and Lawrence were walking across the mountains to Italy in 1912, including the student Harold Hobson. A woman writer who befriended Frieda in 1930–31 claimed Frieda had 'resisted Ravagli's blandishments for a time', which is not only vague but implies that it was Il Capitano rather than Frieda who did the seducing.

At all events the attraction was clearly instantaneous: one of Frieda's confidantes says she was 'infatuated'. Lawrence, ever perceptive, was unlikely to have missed this. It was Lawrence himself, impressed by Ravagli, who urged Frieda to meet their new landlord. Ravagli showed Frieda round the villa: as Lawrence had remarked – and as Rina records in her diary for that day – he and Rina both had colds that day, and to cheer themselves up they had tea together at the Hotel Ligure. And so on a 'wonderful afternoon of sunshine', Frieda was left to her own devices with the dashing Bersaglieri officer. At first Ravagli saw Frieda as 'simply a foreigner, with a difficult character ... I wasn't particularly concerned whether her husband was a famous author,' he told Bevilacqua.

At the villa, however, she walked ahead of him in a clinging skirt which showed her buttocks, Ravagli recalled. When they went into Lawrence's room, Ravagli said, he opened the blinds and felt Frieda behind him, touching him as she felt the soft material of his blue soldier's scarf. 'I was aware of the long, intense rhythm of her breathing ... I accompanied her on a careful tour round the villa. She walked ahead of me, with well-calculated movements of her body: I was trying to work out whether she was just giving herself airs or whether she was trying to provoke me. Then she paid me a compliment, saying "But what a fine way of walking you have, lieutenant". Then she asked a strange question: "Do you have much imagination, lieutenant?"' She sat on the bed, Ravagli said, remarking that it was 'perfect for making love. She was an attractive woman, Frieda, very attractive.' She took off her shoes, complaining that they were hurting her, and started massaging first her feet then her legs while looking at him 'with a lazy smile'. She had 'the eyes of cat, and protruding eyebrows, her hair had a parting down the middle, like two wings round soft ears ... a soft sensuality ran through her whole body.' On this occasion he made his excuses, claiming he had to get back to his wife in Savona.

Biographers have been puzzled by the reference to Ravagli's dress uniform, since the birthday of the reigning queen, Victor Emmanuel III's wife, Queen Elena of Montenegro, was 6 January and not in November. Like the Villa Maria however, this is probably a misunderstanding. Almost certainly the armed forces were marking the birthday not of Queen Elena but of the Queen Mother, the much-loved Queen Margherita of Savoy, widow of the assassinated King Umberto I and mother of Victor Emmanuel III. Queen Margherita's birthday was 20 November: she died a few months later, on 6 January 1926. Ravagli's own birthday was also just a week away: he was born on 27 November 1891 and was about to turn 34. His striking uniform – grey-green trousers and jacket, epaulettes on the shoulders and a blue silk sash across the chest, and above all the black hat adorned with glossy black feathers – must have reminded Frieda of the Bersaglieri soldiers she had admired in Gargnano some 13 years earlier.

Ravagli would therefore have had his fateful encounter with the seductive Frieda at the villa on Friday 20 November, two days after Lawrence had viewed it with Rina. Ravagli later told Alberto Bevilacqua: 'It was the day of the celebration of the Queen's birthday. In the morning I had taken part in a parade and I hadn't had time to change. So I was wearing full dress uniform ... I felt like an actor dressed up in costume to play a part.' The row at the Hotel Miramare over the alleged lack of vacant rooms had made him feel 'strangely uneasy', Ravagli told Bevilacqua. 'Nothing like that had ever happened to me before. I was curious to see whether the meeting would be a disappointment or the beginning of a possible exciting adventure.'

On the Saturday, 21 November, Spotorno was gripped by a spectacular forest fire on the slopes behind the beach, an area known as the Merello, with the flames engulfing a childrens' home. 'Great noise going on outside,' Rina wrote in her diary. 'On going out to enquire cause, Mother discovers that the Merello is on fire.' They had all rushed onto the terrace to watch. 'It is one mass of flames. Dreadful sight. Very windy too, which must make the fight against the flames worse.' The Merello was still blazing late into the evening, 'but we have heard that every child is safe. Thank God for that. Children being carried into Spot wrapped in blankets dazed and very frightened, being billeted all around. All Spot at the Merello.'

If this was a portent of conflagrations to come in the Lawrence ménage, Rina did not see the signs. The rooms at the Villa Bernarda, she reported happily to Martin, were 'small-ish but quite convenient, and I think they will be very comfy.' The villa came with a contadino, a 'nice old man who will supply them with vegetables and wood and so on', and the owners, the Ravaglis, were 'a very nice youngish couple who live in Savona in the winter.' The Ravaglis were 'very generous and are giving the Ls the run of the place, gardens and all ... Altogether I think they have found just what they wanted.' Frieda, on the other hand, instantly admitted she had found Ravagli attractive. 'We have a nice little Bersaglieri officer to whom the villa belongs I am thrilled by his cockfeathers he is almost as nice as the feathers!' she wrote to Brett in early December. Frieda was by now 46.

The Lawrences moved into the Villa Bernarda the following Monday, 23 November, just over a week after arriving in Spotorno. Lawrence wrote enthusiastically to William Hawk, the manager at the Del Monte ranch back in New Mexico, inaccurately claiming Spotorno was close to Monte Carlo. 'It's on the sea, on the Riviera, about three miles from Monte Carlo,' he wrote, though in reality Spotorno is some 60 miles from Monaco. Possibly Rina had told him she was born there, and Lawrence had the impression it was nearer than it was. 'The village is just a quiet Italian village, but we have friends here,' Lawrence added, meaning Rina and her parents. 'The house is nice, just under the Castle, in a big vineyard garden, with a terrace over the roofs of the village, the sea beyond. We do the housework ourselves: Frieda obstinately refused a maid. But there's a gardener lives downstairs, he does all the fetching and carrying, goes shopping every morning at 7.30, pumps the water, and is there when we want him.' Lawrence, Barby wrote later, was 'indulgent' towards Giovanni, the resident gardener and handyman, 'but Frieda and I didn't care for him, because he would get drunk and frighten us.'

The villa was on three floors, Lawrence explained. 'We live mostly on the top floor, high up, where there's a kitchen and bedroom and sitting-room, and a big terrace from the sitting-room; we sleep on the middle floor; the bottom floor we store things in. It's real Italian country style – a pleasant sort of life, easier than America.' The weather, he reported, was 'on the whole sunny and dry, but we've had bitter cold winds.' Lawrence told Hawk they went for walks, with views of the snowy mountains behind, 'and do bits of things. Yesterday we got oranges from the trees, and made marmalade, which I burnt a bit. But it's good.' Barby was in Alassio, 'about 25 miles away. She comes over and stays a day or two with us.' Unlike in New Mexico there were no horses to ride, and no spring from which to fetch water. 'The pine trees are those puffs of umbrella pines all scattered separate on the stony slopes to the sea.'

At the end of November Lawrence wrote to Martin Secker,

this time describing the villa as 'our cottage', adding that they were settled in and it was 'quite comfortable. It has been cold, freezing at night, but we light the stove in the kitchen. And sit there at evening. Today is superbly sunny, and warm – so was yesterday. Rina usually comes with Adrian in the afternoon. She is much better now, was very *nervosa* at first, and a bit trying, no doubt, to her parents.' Adrian, however, was 'very bonny, and growing fast, and perfectly happy and chirpy here. The change is trying for everybody, at first, from England, and especially silent Bridgefoot, to the Mediterranean. When Rina can leave the boy for a few hours with her mother, and get a good walk in the hills with us all, she'll be perfectly happy all right.' Rina Secker, Lawrence wrote to the Brewsters on Capri, was 'a bit out of sorts', but then 'nobody seems very lively nowadays. Time we made a new start.'

Rina's main preoccupation, as her diary for November 1925 shows, was Adrian's health – but also her own. In a phrase which recurs repeatedly in the diary, she was 'sad and anxious' at leaving her husband in England and taking their son to Italy – a state of mind Lawrence was quick to notice. He found Rina overprotective and overindulgent as a mother: Adrian was at times mischievous, Rina recorded in her diary. Lawrence 'strongly advocates a Spartan upbringing to equip him for the world.'

Lawrence must have already begun to take an interest in Rina as a possible source for his fiction, storing away her mood and situation for *Sun*. Certainly Frieda had noticed the change. 'Frieda tells me that I am not the same person I was when she first knew me, and she is right – I am not – and I know it,' Rina wrote to Martin. 'I do try and recapture some of myself as I was then – but it is impossible. All that is gone beyond recall. Only something new, fresh and entirely unexpected might have the effect of lifting me out of my solemnity and dulness (sic) of mind – and that, situated as I am, is of course as highly improbable of taking place as would be the descent of Jupiter.'

No doubt alarmed, Martin broached the idea of coming out to Spotorno to spend Christmas with his wife and the Lawrences, as Lawrence had suggested – but without committing himself. 'I will let you decide by yourself as to whether you should be here by Christmas or not,' Rina told him. 'Of course for me the sooner you come the better, but you must suit your own plans best. I think perhaps you are right about the crowded trains before Christmas.' She regretted worrying him, but hinted at her mood swings. 'I have been through a bad time – not because of the young man's laryngitis, which was slight and from which he has now recovered, but from a variety of other reasons ... However I think the crisis is now passed and we will pull through till your arrival at Christmas.'

She and Adrian, who had 'completely regained his good humour', had spent the afternoon at the Villa Bernarda with the Lawrences to mark St Catherine's Day, the celebration of her name day ('We have been overwhelmed with flowers and cakes'). 'We had tea there and Adrian behaved admirably', she said. Adrian had taken to calling Frieda 'Vida' and Lawrence 'Man', and was learning Italian from her maid, Lina. 'Lawrence and I were alone part of the afternoon and Adrian was pottering around us in the garden, very busy with a wooden spoon purloined from the kitchen and would insist on repeating the final word of every sentence Lawrence uttered. He was a sort of echo and it was very amusing.'

Tea with the Lawrences had become an almost daily fixture, she reported at the end of November. 'Adrian is getting quite attached to Aunty Vida and Man, he is quite *chez soi* at the Villa Bernarda.' DHL was 'busy writing short stories,' she added a few days later. 'Frieda tells me they are good – we go up every afternoon to tea and enjoy it ... The Ls are looking forward to you coming down very much. They are going to Alassio for the day tomorrow as Mrs L's youngest daughter is arriving there tonight.' Spotorno, Lawrence told Brett, was not expensive, 'and we ought to manage on five shillings a day'. As usual Lawrence was busy cleaning, painting, scrubbing floors, making furniture, cooking, making jam. 'Lawrence was always busy,' Ravagli later recalled, 'mostly doing housework.'

But he also – when not making jam or putting up shelves – felt he could write again. He sketched out *Smile*, a brief tale in which a man cannot help smiling incongruously as he looks down at the 'beautiful composure' of his dead wife's body in the care of Italian nuns – a story said to be based on John Middleton Murry's reaction to the death of Katherine Mansfield. He also wrote *Glad Ghosts* for the collection of ghost stories being put together by Lady Cynthia Asquith. She rejected it, partly because it was too long, and too erotic, but partly because its main character, Carlotta Fell, was all too obviously based on Lady Cynthia herself: an aristocrat and graduate of the Thwaite art school – that is, the Slade – who wears pearls and 'affects to be wistful'. The story was replaced in the collection by another ghost story completed by Lawrence at Spotorno a little later, *The Rocking Horse Winner*, in which a boy predicts Derby winners by riding his rocking horse in a trance which eventually kills him.

Winter on the Riviera, Lawrence discovered, was not always sunny but sometimes cold and windy – as it still is, as anyone who has lived there or visited it for any length of time can testify. The Villa Bernarda, Lawrence complained, had no fireplaces, and although the kitchen had a stove around which they could huddle to keep warm, it smoked badly. It was this which brought Ravagli to the house: he visited his tenants to see how they were getting on, was told about the smoking stove and climbed up on the roof to clean the chimney and the flue. Lawrence remarked to Frieda that Ravagli was just the kind of able-bodied man it would be useful to have around at the ranch at Kiowa.

9

Naked in the Sun

*L*ADY CHATTERLEY'S LOVER was preceded by two works of fiction which Lawrence wrote as he sat high above the blue Mediterranean. These were *The Virgin and the Gipsy*, one of his most powerful and enduringly successful novellas, and before that *Sun*, a short story which revolves around the reaction of a nervous and exhausted woman to the sun, elemental nature and the potency of a peasant – based on Rina Secker.

The question of whether and to what extent Lawrence put real people into his fiction is a vexed one. The Cambridge literary critic FR Leavis maintained that 'Lawrence *never* put people into his tales and novels: he was a great creative writer.' For Lawrence's biographer David Ellis, this is 'quite plainly wrong': Lawrence clearly had 'a tendency to base characters in his fiction on people he knew.'

Frank Swinnerton, a fellow Secker author, certainly thought so; he observes in his autobiography that Lawrence 'made up stories about real people with a kind of malicious innocence'. John Middleton Murry wrote to Frieda in 1955 that he recognised himself as Pan in *The Last Laugh*, adding 'Quite a good picture of me'. Lawrence often admitted he had drawn on his parents and Jessie Chambers in *Sons and Lovers*, and told Achsah Brewster he felt he had not 'done justice' to his father in the novel.

On the other hand Lawrence's friends and acquaintances often only provided the starting point for his characters, and he transformed them as he developed the story, sometimes drawing on aspects of his own personality. In John Worthen's words, 'DHL always did far more than take an outward characteristic and reproduce it. He re-created people.' In that sense Maurice, the grey, dull, conventional husband in *Sun* who is shocked when his wife spends months on the Riviera without him and goes 'naked in the sun' is and is not Martin Secker.

Lawrence found that Secker, with his neatly parted hair, waistcoats and bow ties, did not 'sparkle'. But Compton Mackenzie, a shrewd and often waspish judge of men (and women), recorded in his memoirs that 'Martin Secker's company was always a joy to me. I have known few people with such an overwhelming sense of the ridiculous. He would relate some story and be so much overcome by the absurdity of it that he would have to mop the tears in his eyes.'

Swinnerton, who had been a witness at Martin and Rina's wedding, had a similar impression: Secker was kind-hearted, 'dark, quiet and gentle', but with a powerful sense of humour: 'When he laughs he makes hardly any noise, tears fill his eyes and roll down his cheeks, he turns away and is forced by weakness to sit down.' On his occasional visits to the Riviera, moreover, Secker enjoyed the South as much as anyone: 'Your description of your life at Spotorno makes me jealous,' Swinnerton wrote to him at the Villa Maria from Cookham Dean in Berkshire in January 1926. 'My advice to you is not to come back till you are forced to by need or a sense of propriety.'

Similarly 'Juliet' in *Sun* is and is not Rina – but was certainly inspired by her, with little Adrian the model for Johnny, her toddler son, and Maurice based on Martin making visits to Spotorno now and then from London. But whereas in the story Lawrence mocks the husband, in real life he was more sympathetic toward Secker – hence his remark that if Martin was 'a nice gentle soul, without a thrill', Rina was 'a living block of discontent'.

In *Sun*, which Lawrence sent to Brett for typing in mid-December, a young woman from New York who has a young child and is suffering from what Rina would have called 'neurasthenia' is advised by her doctor to head for Italy and sunbathe naked, which she does in the olive groves. Rina certainly sunbathed and went for walks in the olive and lemon groves, though we don't know whether she did so naked or whether Lawrence imagined it.

One Sunday in February 1926 she wrote to Martin: 'I have on the table here four tumblers and two soap dishes filled with the most exquisite, deep coloured, rich scented violets – rich and sturdy – large perfect flowers on long, straight stems – all of which were picked by me on a solitary ramble in the olive groves yesterday afternoon. I wish I could send you a few. They are better than any I have ever seen. They are perfect.' She added, however, that she, her mother and her maid all had colds: 'For a cold catching chill giving clime, recommend me to the Sunny Riviera!'

There were times when she wanted to be back in England because of her health and – more especially – her son's. 'I can't bear really to be away from home,' she wrote to Martin. 'It's all right as long as we are well, but it is too much risk when we are not.' She felt 'lonely and lacking in moral support', and wanted 'to get back as soon as possible – sun or no sun'.

But this mood did not last, and – as in Lawrence's story – the sun proved more powerful. She was 'enjoying gorgeous sunshine', she wrote to Martin in March 1926. 'I wish I could post you some of the warmth and sun we are basking in here.' In January 1927 she was indulging 'the *dolce far niente* which seizes one in this wonderful sunshine'. The weather was 'positively glorious, not a cloud in the bluest of blue skies all day long and every day. The sea is a sheet of blue and silver, and there is only the gentlest of gentile breezes. It is heavenly.'

The following month she went for a walk in the hills

behind Spotorno with a painter friend which 'left the most wonderful pictures in my mind – blue sea, blue sky, the island shimmering in the sun over a perfectly still sea, and behind us fold after fold of hills and mountains (snow-capped) stretching beyond Savona into Piedmont. It made one feel quite drunk!' She was writing about all this, she said, 'sitting on the sands in brilliant sunshine'. The intoxication of sunshine did not leave her; 'The weather here is *glorious*,' she wrote to Martin from Alassio in October 1931, three years after *Sun* was written. The women of the English colony were taking full advantage: 'We are still wearing our summer frocks and basking in brilliant sunshine. Unbelievable climate this is!'

Intriguingly, there are two versions of *Sun*, the second – revised in 1928 – fuller and more explicit than the first version written at the Villa Bernarda three years earlier. Harry Crosby, a wealthy American admirer of Lawrence who founded the Black Sun Press in Paris in 1927 and was an obsessive, indeed increasingly demented sun worshipper (he even had a large sun tattooed on his back), had asked Lawrence for an expanded version of the story.

'A friend in Paris, Harry Crosby, wants to do a little edition of the short story *Sun* – a hundred copies only,' Lawrence wrote to Martin Secker in 1928, choosing to cast a veil over the fact that the story was based on Rina. The revised version was to be 'more or less de luxe. He wants to do it because he bought the ms. from me, and found the printed version so much expurgated, he wants to print it whole.'

In fact, the first version is itself pretty explicit. The story (in both versions) begins '"Take her away, into the sun," the doctor said.' The 'her', Juliet, is apparently going through some kind of crisis, and her marriage is under strain. She is 'sceptical of the sun', but allows herself to be 'carried away, with her child, and a nurse, and her mother, over the sea'. Her husband Maurice boards the ship with her and stays for two hours before it sails, the Hudson 'swaying with heavy blackness, shaken over with spilled dribbles of light'. The husband is apprehensive, 'clinging to the last straw of hope', as he tells Juliet, 'These partings are no good, you know'. But she recalls 'how bitterly they had wanted to get away from one another, he and she'.

When the cry 'all ashore' goes up, Juliet thinks 'For him it is all ashore! For me it is out to sea!' as the quayside recedes and Maurice is left waving his handkerchief, just 'one among a crowd'.

IN OTHER WORDS, Italy offers a new start, a new life. The Atlantic is 'grey as lava', but in Italy Juliet's house is 'above the bluest of seas, with a vast garden, or vineyard all vines and olives dropping steeply, terrace after terrace, to the strip of coast-plain'. She can see lemon groves, smell the scent of mimosa, and hear a goat 'bleating in an empty tomb'. Below the house a spring issues from a cavern, 'where the old Sicules had drunk before the Greeks came'. This draws on Lawrence's memories of Taormina in Sicily, especially the references to the Sicules – the original inhabitants of Sicily – the Greeks and the volcano. But volcano apart, it applies equally well to the view from his terrace at the Villa Bernarda in Spotorno.

At first the Italian landscape has little effect on Juliet: she finds it 'soothing', but inside her the 'anger and frustration' and 'incapacity to feel anything real' are still there, and she finds her child irritating. Her mother reminds her that the doctor told her 'to lie in the sun without your clothes', and is rewarded with an earful of abuse: 'When I am fit to do so, I will ... For God's sake, leave off wanting to do me good.' The 'hurt and incensed' mother departs – understandably – and to make matters worse it is raining and the 'house built for the sun' is cold.

But here comes the sun: the house faces south-west and Juliet, lying in bed, sees the sun 'lifting himself naked and molten, sparkling over the sea's rim'. The image is unmistakably sexual: 'Juliet lay in her bed and watched him rise. It was as if she had never seen the sun rise before. She had never seen the naked sun stand up pure upon the sea-line, shaking the night off himself. So the desire sprang secretly in her, to go naked in the sun. She cherished her desire like a secret.'

Juliet decides to sunbathe naked after all – but away from people – 'not easy, in a country where every olive tree has eyes and every slope is seen from afar'. She finds a rocky bluff overgrown with cacti, out of which rises a phallus-like single cypress tree 'with a pallid, thick trunk, and tip that leaned over, flexible, up in the blue'. Juliet takes off some of her clothes, using the 'forest' of cactus leaves as a cover – presumably avoiding the spines – and offers her bosom to the sun.

She is still hesitant – rather like Lady Chatterley hesitating over her affair with the gamekeeper – and sighs against 'the cruelty of having to give herself'. But she surrenders as she feels the sun and the soft sea air on her breasts, which had once seemed 'as if they would never ripen' but are now 'warmer than ever love had been, warmer than milk or the hands of her baby'. They were now 'like long white grapes in the hot sun'.

She slides off all her remaining clothing and lies naked, looking up through her fingers at the sun, which envelops her breasts, face, throat, 'tired belly', knees, thighs and feet with fire while she lies with her eyes shut and feels 'the colour of rosy flame through her lids', the sun penetrating into her bones, emotions and thoughts. She turns over to let the sun warm 'her loins, the backs of her thighs, even her heels', and lies 'half stunned with wonder at the thing that was happening to her. Her weary, chilled heart was melting, and in melting, evaporating.'

Juliet goes home, 'only half-seeing, sunblinded and sundazed', to be met by her small son, whom she resents – 'he should not be such a lump' – and who she fears will grow up 'like his father – like a worm that the sun has never seen'. She takes the boy's clothes off so that he too can sunbathe naked, but he is frightened and starts to cry: he is bothered by the prickly thorns ('ickly thorns') and at one point rouses a sleeping snake – an echo of Lawrence's celebrated Taormina poem.

All she can think of however is 'the sun in his splendour, and mating with him', watching at dawn from her bed to see if the sun will rise 'all molten in his nakedness'. The sun is described as male: 'Sometimes he came ruddy, like a big, shy creature. And sometimes slow and crimson red, with a look of anger, slowly pushing and shouldering'. Although it is winter there is sunshine most days, so she goes every day to the cactus grove at the foot of the 'powerful cypress tree', wearing a 'dove grey wrapper and sandals', but ready to be 'naked to the sun' at any moment.

Her devotion to the sun, which she feels 'knows' her, 'in the cosmic, carnal sense of the word', gives her a contempt for people, including the peasants she sees every day passing up the rocky paths with their donkeys, who are 'sun-blackened, but still have a core of fear' in them. So too does her son, who is turning 'bonny and healthy' (Lawrence's phrase for the real-life Adrian) from toddling naked, but still keeps his spirit inside himself 'like a snail in a shell', incapable of any 'gesture of recklessness'.

Juliet, by contrast, turns golden, washing in the clear green basins of water beneath the lemon trees and rubbing olive oil into her skin, knowing that if a peasant spots her 'he would be more afraid of her than she of him'. Sunbathing makes her 'a different person ... It was not just taking sunbaths. It was much more than that. Something deep inside unfolded and relaxed ... she was put into connection with the sun, and the stream flowed of itself from her womb.' She is escaping 'the vast cold apparatus of civilisation', and her rosy golden breasts are 'alert, full of sap'.

When Maurice turns up from New York in March – by now the sun is growing 'very powerful' – he looks 'pathetically out of place' in his grey felt hat and dark grey suit. He is dull: he manages his business efficiently, Lawrence tells us, but 'without startling success'. Picking his way through 'the tangle of Mediterranean herbage' he looks up to see his wife 'standing erect and nude by the jutting rock, glistening with the sun and with warm, life. Her breasts seemed to be lifting up, alert, to listen, her thighs looked brown and fleet.'

Maurice averts his gaze, embarrassed. Watching the 'lifting and sinking of her quick hips' as she goes to pick up the child, he is 'dazed with admiration' at her beauty, muttering 'splendid, splendid', but also 'at a deadly loss'. Juliet tells him that she cannot possibly go back to New York, and Maurice – 'powerless against her rosy, wind-hardened nakedness' – quickly agrees that she can stay as long as she likes in Italy, perhaps 'even for ever', and he will visit her in the holidays.

In a conventional story, this would open the way for Juliet to have an affair – and in fact she is tempted by their neighbour, 'a rather fat, very broad fellow of about thirty five' with powerful shoulders, a sunburnt face, big blue eyes, a cropped brown moustache and thick brown eyebrows whom Juliet sees having his midday meal with his watchful, jealous, 'stiff and dark faced' wife under an almond tree in the adjoining property, with bread and wine laid out on a white cloth on the ground.

Although 'stout and broad', the unnamed peasant has vitality, with a 'peculiar quick energy which gave a charm to his movements', and is at least clean, with well-laundered white trousers, a coloured shirt and an old straw hat. Watching him from a distance, Juliet concludes that although shy he is like a 'quick animal', and they become aware of one another, even 'intimate, across the distance' in the sense that she knows when he will arrive with his donkey and he looks up when she appears on the balcony. When he sees her naked one hot day, 'his eyes and her body' are aflame, and she thinks: 'Why shouldn't I meet this man for an hour, and bear his child?'

Lawrence is not here suggesting that Juliet should submit to one man rather than another: on the contrary, her sunbathing and the desire it awakens are symptoms of her independence and – in the jargon of today – empowerment. She had always been mistress of herself, he writes, but now she felt within her 'quite another sort of power'. 'Why should I have to identify my life with a man's life?' she asks herself. She sees the 'flushed blood' in the peasant's sunburned face and the 'flame in the southern blue eyes' and the answer in her is a 'gush of fire'. Her idea is to meet him for an hour to make love to him on her terms for 'as long as the desire lasts, and no more'.

But she doesn't: instead she resigns herself to bearing her dull husband a child again. This is partly because Maurice gamely agrees to sunbathe naked as well, taking off his grey suit to show her he is 'not entirely quenched in his male courage'. But if Juliet holds back from an affair it is because she lacks the courage to take the final step and do what Connie Chatterley will later do. Consequently 'her next child would be Maurice's. The fatal chain of continuity would cause it.'

The second, expanded version of *Sun* is even more explicitly erotic than the first version, with Juliet only prevented from sex with the peasant by the unwitting intervention of her little son. Lawrence emphasises Juliet's womb 'coming open wide with rosy ecstasy, like a lotus flower' as the sun penetrates her. Lawrence allows himself to refer several times to the peasant's aroused penis, which Juliet is thrilled to think is erect 'for her' beneath his thin cotton trousers. In the privacy of the little ravine she is suddenly overcome by weakness as the peasant moves toward her.

They are interrupted by her son, who runs up shouting 'Mummy, a man!' – an echo no doubt of little Adrian, who at the Villa Bernarda had taken to calling Lawrence 'Man' and Frieda 'Vida'. The peasant watches her 'naked, retreating buttocks rise and fall' as she and the boy retreat. In this revised version, when Maurice arrives she feels 'a little flame' inside her and 'thrills helplessly', because 'at least he was a man' – whereas the peasant is the kind of man who will always wait for the woman to make the first move.

The first, shorter version of *Sun* appeared in the Autumn

1926 issue of the London literary magazine *New Coterie*, and then in a collection of Lawrence's stories published by Martin Secker in 1928; the second, so-called unexpurgated version was published on its own the same year, in a special edition by Crosby's Black Sun Press in Paris. Lawrence wrote to Crosby, 'I wish the story had been printed as it stands there, really complete. One day, when the public is more educated, I shall have the story printed whole.'

In fact Lawrence had not really 'expurgated' the earlier version of *Sun* when sending it for publication; he had merely expanded it when Crosby asked him to. At any rate the reworking was financially rewarding: Crosby paid him with five gold twenty-dollar pieces, followed later by three more gold pieces and (to Lawrence's embarrassment) a snuff box which had reputedly belonged to the Queen of Naples. Crosby, a playboy who used his wealth to indulge in a decadent lifestyle – his aunt, Jane Norton Grew, was the wife of JP Morgan – later shot himself and one of his many mistresses in New York. Lawrence commented that Crosby had been 'too rich and spoilt', leaving him with nothing to do but commit suicide in a 'last sort of cocktail excitement'.

Rina, oddly, never refers to either version in her letters; she mentions stories such as *The Captain's Doll* and *The Man Who Died*, and novels such as *The Lost Girl*, but not *Sun*. Either she was unaware of it – which is unlikely, given that she and Martin discussed Lawrence and his fiction in their letters throughout their lives – or she preferred to put it on one side as too personal.

Lawrence continued to believe in the power of the sun – 'the great gold sun' as he called it – to renew, regenerate, revive and heal. 'Come to Sicily with me,' Connie Chatterley's lover Michaelis says to her. 'It's lovely there just now. You want sun! You want life!' Lawrence also continued to think of Rina. A few months after telling Secker he intended to publish the 'unexpurgated' version of *Sun*, Lawrence wrote to him from Bandol in the South of France that it was 'dull

– a bit like Spotorno … Frieda gets rather bored without a house, but I don't know where I want to settle … How is Bridgefoot? Is it wintry? I can hardly believe it, it is so sunny here. How is the boy? – getting a real big lad now. It is three years since Spotorno! Remember me to Rina.'

He was also aware that all was not well in the Secker marriage: from 1925 until his death in 1930 he repeatedly mentions Rina in his letters to Martin, and asks for his best wishes to be conveyed to her. But in November 1929 he wrote to Secker that he was 'sorry Bridgefoot is a bit of trial', and advised his publisher to spend more time at work: 'There's no home like the office, as a man said to me.' The following month Secker informed him that Rina had gone with Adrian to Alassio for the winter. 'I'm glad Rina is in Alassio, she will probably enjoy it, and you will have a bit of peace,' Lawrence wrote, in one of his last letters. He added: '*Dio mio*! How awful is a dissatisfied woman.'

10

The Virgin and the Gipsy

CHRISTMAS 1925 seems to have passed off peacefully enough: Martin Secker duly arrived from England on 12 December, and stayed with Rina at the Hotel Miramare. 'Secker is here – with wife and child, down on the road, with her parents – for a month,' Lawrence wrote to Murry. 'He's gentle and nice, seems to me'.

He was savouring life at the villa. 'Now it is evening,' Lawrence wrote to his German mother-in-law on 16 December. 'We are sitting in the kitchen high under the roof. The evening star is white over the hill opposite, underneath the lights of the village lie like oranges and tangerines, little and shining. Frieda has devoured her whipped cream from Savona at one gulp, and now she moans that she hasn't kept any to eat with coffee and cake after supper. Now she sits by the stove and reads. The soup is boiling. In a moment we call down into the depths: *"Vieni, Giovanni, è pronto il mangiare"*. Then the old man runs up the stairs like an unhappy frog, with his nose in the air, sniffing and smelling. It is nice for him to know that there is always something good for him to eat.'

'Soon Christmas comes again: here the children have written "Natale" on every door,' Lawrence added. 'But it isn't a great fact in Italy' (he wrote in German: the translation is Frieda's). He told Frieda's mother he had been to Savona with Martin Secker, 'but you can't buy much there, not much of interest.' He had bought figs, dates and raisins and was sending them to her in a parcel. To Brett he complained there was 'absolutely nothing to buy here': he recommended Strega, 'a yellow liqueur made of citrons', with San Pellegrino mineral water to settle the stomach. Frieda had painted a watercolour of the campanile and roofs below the villa.

It was colder: 'In the daytime we live in the sitting-room with a terrace over the village and the sea, but at night we dwell in the kitchen,' he told the Brewsters. The kitchen at the Villa Bernarda had a kind of stove known in Italian as a *stufa economica* which was 'anything but economical', but still a blessing. 'The Seckers come up in the afternoon, to get thawed out. Oh icy Italy, where is thy fireplace, thou heartless and bitter cold!' He felt a bit like 'a chipmunk hibernating'. He would have liked to spend Christmas on Capri, but 'Frieda had her daughter over from Alassio for a few days; she is coming again; and the elder daughter in January'. Barby had been 13 when Frieda walked out on her husband and children in 1912 to set off with Lawrence: she was now 21, and apparently willing to at least try and reach out to both her mother and her famous step-father.

At Lawrence's insistence the Christmas lunch was turkey, English-style, with Frieda and Lawrence, Barby, Martin, Rina and Rina's parents eating it not, oddly enough, at the Capellero's own hotel, the Miramare, but at the Ligure, where the Lawrences had stayed when they first arrived in Spotorno before moving into the Villa Bernarda. It sounds like a rather sticky occasion, with not much jollity, at least according to Lawrence himself. Sending the MS of *Glad Ghosts* to Brett afterwards, he allowed himself some ungenerous remarks about Martin, Rina and her parents: 'We had a very mild Christmas Day – went down to the inn and had a turkey (my dinner) with Seckers and Capelleros,' he wrote, adding 'But they *are* dull people.'

Lawrence was at first wary of Barby, telling Brett in November 1925 'I can't stand Frieda's children ... When they appear I shall disappear.' Barby had arrived on the Riviera in December 1925, staying not at Spotorno but in a pensione at Alassio because her father disapproved of her staying any closer to her mother and Lawrence – or as she put it in her memoir of Lawrence, 'for reasons of family decorum'.

Italy seemed 'a kind of paradise' to Barby. Alassio, once a fishing village, had become 'a sort of retreat for English gentlefolk living there to benefit from the favourable exchange rate'. Many of the expats there, Barby found, were army officers or civil servants who had served in colonial India – the Raj – and 'who looked on the Italians as a slightly improved kind of "native"'. Lawrence had thoroughly disapproved when an 'English admiral' who had admired Barby's painting took her out to tea in Alassio. 'You want to be very careful of that kind of man,' Lawrence warned her.

Despite 'family decorum' Barby did make visits to Spotorno, enjoying a supper of chicken and red wine on her first night at the villa, a 'haphazard sort of house' beneath the castle ruins. 'I remember so well walking in darkness up the narrow streets of the village, enthralled by its romantic ancient feeling and the wonderful foreign smell,' she recalled. 'From the villa, a little way up the hill, I saw the light of an upstairs balcony window shine out towards the sea.'

Lawrence seems to have changed his mind about her as he got to know her better. 'Barby Weekley is here since Christmas Day,' he reported to Brett after Christmas, 'nicer this time'. She had attended the Slade School of Art (as Rina is said to have done), and was busy painting, with 'faint hopes of one day selling something'. The Slade, however, had taken 'all the life out of her work. That Slade is a criminal institution, and gets worse.'

They went for walks together, and Lawrence offered Barby advice on her painting. In part this was to get away from Frieda, who was also trying to paint: Barby recalls an incident in which she sprang to her mother's defence after Lawrence had flung half a glass of red wine in Frieda's face, shouting at him, 'She's too good for you; it's casting pearls before swine!' He retorted, 'Look what I've done for your mother! Haven't I just helped her with her rotten painting?' Frieda, he complained, always wanted to be 'important' and seemed incapable of talking to him naturally, 'as you do, like a woman'.

In her memoir Barby says that 'in 1926 I spent a very happy spring with Lawrence and Frieda on the Italian Riviera,' evidently preferring to forget the rather less happy time before Christmas, when Lawrence was still being unkind about her. She resented, however, any suggestion that she and Lawrence had been romantically involved, and thought Lawrence 'mean' for telling others that 'Frieda's daughter tried to flirt with me.'

'Went for a long walk today with L and Barby.' Rina told Martin on a postcard in January. Lawrence thought she should translate *The Lost Girl* into Italian – 'What do you think?' The weather had been lovely, but 'turned rather heavy this evening'. It was not only the weather however – tempers were fraying at the Villa Bernarda. Lawrence was getting restless, considering a trip to Calabria, Sicily or the Balearic Isles, or Tunisia, or Montenegro, or Russia. Or anywhere. 'The sea is most tempting, and I am really pining for the lugger,' he told Brett. He added that Martin Secker was leaving for London 'next Monday', 18 January.

'My sister arrives on Feb 9th – for two weeks, Frieda's daughter Elsa on Feb 12th,' Lawrence informed Brett on 25 January. 'Barby is here since last Wed., and we're settling down better – do paintings.' Rina wrote to Martin on the same day: 'I spent yesterday afternoon with the Ls. Barby is there and we sat out in the garden – Frieda, Barby and I – and talked while B was making herself a cotton frock in the most haphazard way imaginable (I became very worried to see her cutting a sleeve shorter than the other and doing other absent-minded things).' Lawrence was upstairs trying to make jam with some over-ripe persimmons, 'which wouldn't and couldn't do anything but remain in a state of perfect and unchangeable liquidity. He gave it up at last and was very annoyed.'

Beneath all the tensions, Rina shrewdly observed, lay the love-hate relationship between Frieda and Lawrence. 'While Frieda was upstairs preparing the tea I had a few details of domestic life at the Bernarda given to me by Barby. It appears that DH alternates between great love and great hate for Frieda – mostly hate. It also seems that they really do throw things at each other!' Lawrence had had a bag packed and ready for some days, 'and threatens vehemently and noisily that he will start the next moment for Capri as he is fed up. He then disappears and noises and bangs are heard as though he were flinging things into his trunk. Then he re-appears and makes jam or cooks the soup, and goes on until the next spasm seizes him.' 'The Lawrence menage sounds rather a strain to live in – a lack of repose,' Martin replied from Bridgefoot. 'Poor Frieda, and poor DH too, for he cannot be very happy. It is sad that with his great gifts he does not have more balance, and one cannot help admiring Frieda's dog-like fidelity. Do you think he would be too temperamental to drive a car? I think it would do his nerves good to have a small Fiat and get rid of the cooped-up feeling he no doubt has at the Bernarda.'

It is difficult to know which is more peculiar – the idea of Lawrence behind the wheel of a Fiat or the notion that Frieda was faithful. Secker, however, always tended to sympathise with Frieda, seeing her actions in terms of what she had to put up with in dealing with a temperamental genius. Although he later told Rina he had never thought of Frieda as 'perfectly sane', he seems to have taken the view that it was Frieda rather than Lawrence who was sorely tried. Barby seems to have agreed: she was, Rina reported, 'surprised that Frieda takes all his tempers so quietly – because as a girl Frieda was the sort who would throw an ink pot at her professor's head when he found any reproach to make to her! An amusing ménage altogether, isn't it?' Also 'rather amusing' was the fact that she had taken a 'long walk over the castle' with Adrian, ending at the Villa Bernarda for tea as usual, to find Ravagli – 'the Tenente' – 'having an English lesson from DH.'

After *Sun*, Lawrence embarked on *The Virgin and the Gipsy*, drawing – sympathetically – on the character of Barby for the heroine Yvette and – less sympathetically – on Professor Weekley, who is clearly caricatured as Yvette's father, the Reverend Saywell, a literary vicar whose wife has left him and their children. The gipsy – memorably played by Franco Nero in Christopher Miles's 1970 film version, with Joanna Shimkus as Yvette – enters Yvette's life when she is motoring with friends in Derbyshire and the girls in the party decide to have their fortunes told by the gipsy's wife. Yvette feels the gipsy staring at her with a frank sexual desire she has never come across before.

The 'virgin and the gipsy' finally come together when the rectory in which Yvette lives is flooded and the gipsy rescues her by carrying her to an upper room where he takes off his clothes and holds her naked body against his – to warm her up, protect her from hypothermia and protect her from shock. Lawrence does not spell out whether they also make love. The story offers a barbed account of the staid Weekley family – not only the vicar himself but also the spinster aunt, modelled on Weekley's sister Maude, who is shown as harbouring a deep and bitter resentment and envy of the young and her own wasted opportunities.

Above all the story is shot through with sexual symbolism – not least the dramatic flood – with the gipsy acting as the catalyst for Yvette's awakening to a new life. Just like the sexual encounters with departed spirits in *Glad Ghosts* and the response of Juliet to the elemental and reviving power of the sun's rays in *Sun*, so in *The Virgin and the Gipsy* the physical contact with the gipsy makes Yvette aware of 'some hidden part of herself which she denied; that part which mysteriously and unconfessedly responded to him'. Like Parkin (later renamed Mellors) in *Lady Chatterley's Lover*, the gipsy is described as having survived the First World War despite nearly dying of pneumonia.

Oddly, although *The Virgin and the Gipsy* is one of his best tales and clearly had commercial possibilities, Lawrence did not send it off to his agent or publishers, and it was only published after his death in 1930. This may have been because Lawrence had reservations about his portrayal of friends, enemies and acquaintances in his fiction, and also because he had grown rather fond of Barby, who was commuting back and forth from Alassio.

'BARBARA HAS BEEN HERE A WEEK, goes back tonight,' Lawrence wrote to Martin Secker on 20 January 1926. 'My sister arrives this day fortnight, for two weeks. Rina and Barby and I walked to the top of the ridge this afternoon, and made plans for outings when you come again.' Shortly afterwards he reported 'It's been a lovely day, Rina here to tea, after a small walk behind the castle ... I had a good whack at my gipsy story tonight and nearly finished it, over the climax and on the short down slope to the end.' Rina 'thinks she would really like to start translating *The Fox* or *The Captain's Doll*. You might send her that vol. And let her try. *Tanti saluti*!'

Lawrence had finished writing *The Virgin and the Gipsy* by 21 January 1926. 'Here is the rest of the gipsy story,' he wrote to Secker that day. The previous day had been lovely, 'but today is cold and rainy. Barbara came last night. We wanted to go to Savona and buy colours, but the day's not good enough, leave it till tomorrow.' He adds, to reassure Martin that Rina is keeping warm, 'All well at the Villa Maria – the paraffin stove a great success. It will be useful today.'

He was, at last, productively happy. There was no point in killing oneself like Keats 'for what you've got to say' he wrote to Murry. This would be 'to mix the eggshell in with the omelette'. He hoped to have enough money to live on, but that was about it. He was now 40, 'and I want in a good sense, to enjoy my life'. On 1 February Lawrence thanked Secker for sending him the ms of *The Virgin and the Gipsy* ('Frieda doesn't like the title'), adding – using an Italian or Germanic word order – 'On the 9th arrives my sister, with a friend which will make an interlude, while Barby and Elsa Weekley are apparently going into the Ligure with a friend, a Mrs Seaman. *Vive les femmes e la stagione inglese*!'

Ellen Seaman was Elsa's future mother-in-law; Ada's Nottingham friend was called Lizzie Booth. Women were descending on the little Spotorno colony, creating tensions which would shortly boil over, and which apparently had an affect on Rina and her parents as they awaited the new arrivals. 'A bit of friction down at the Villa Maria,' Lawrence reported to Martin in a postscript, 'but probably it's only the weather. Rain again today.' The following day he wrote to Brett, who was in Capri, to thank her for typing *Glad Ghosts*, adding that he had sent it off 'but they'll never find a magazine to print it'. It was 'beastly weather' in Spotorno, 'cold and rainy and all the almond blossom coming out in the chill'.

He felt a 'revulsion from America ... We might keep this house on till April. But I simply don't know what I shall do. I wish I wanted to go to the ranch again; but I don't, not now. I just don't. The only thing is to wait a bit. I've left off writing now: I am really awfully sick of writing.' He added: 'I send a couple of snapshots – Rina Secker takes them; they're good, for such a tiny camera, don't you think?' He then went down with flu, which a week later he told Brett had given him a bronchial haemorrhage 'like at the ranch, only worse'. He noted that his sister Ada had arrived the previous day with her friend Lizzie Booth, and that Elsa, Barby's sister, was also due at Ventimiglia: Barby had gone to meet her and they would stay at 'the little hotel Ligure till my sister has gone

– she leaves on the 25th – then they two move up here.' He added 'But I like Barby.'

He also indicated that Frieda's hostility to Brett had re-emerged, and that he and Frieda were going through a difficult patch: he doubted that they would ever visit Brett in Capri together because 'Frieda declares an implacable intention of never seeing you again, and never speaking to you if she does see you – and I say nothing.' 'I've been in bed six days with flu,' Lawrence reported to Martin Secker. 'Hope to be up tomorrow however – not feeling very happy – and vile weather here, cold and wet. My sister came, with friend, last evening – entered Italy in snow and gloom then streaming rain, but still thrilled. Elsa Weekley arrives Ventimiglia tomorrow.'

The English colony at Spotorno was about to 'spread', Rina now reported to Martin from the Villa Maria. 'Life at the Villa B sounds hectic,' he wrote back. 'I can almost see its walls palpitating from the pent up storms of emotion. I suppose the truth is that Frieda's patience and forbearance has for a long time been at breaking-point, and now the strain has been too much, probably from some quite trivial and accidental occurrence. Spot will be much intrigued at these changes of ménages, trying to puzzle out the relationships. *Pazzi inglesi, davvero*! [Mad English indeed!] I cannot imagine how the situation is going to resolve itself. At least it adds an excitement to life.'

Lawrence himself was feeling far from excited however. 'I've been in bed six days, and feel rather downcast,' Lawrence told Earl Brewster on 11 February. 'My sister is here with a friend, in this fireless house – and it pours with rain, is cold, and dismal as Hades: self in bed and Frieda cross.' Rina agreed the weather was 'dismal' on the Riviera – 'grey skies and rain for four or five days now', with very heavy seas and waves which 'shake the house when they break.'

Instead of moping, however, she was turning her attention to translating Lawrence's works into Italian. Since *The*

Lost Girl was 'rather terrifyingly long' she was making a start on *The Captain's Doll*, Lawrence's story of an affair between a German aristocratic woman and a widowed British army officer left 'dehumanised' by the trauma of the Great War. 'Don't expect any quick work, will you?' she wrote to Martin. 'I am rather nervous of it, as DH will keep an eye on the translation and I doubt whether I shall ever be able to interpret what he calls his "feelings" about his work. However, I'll try.'

Frieda meanwhile was 'becoming very agitated about the arrival of her many guests', Rina reported. 'She is going to have a grand scrub-up and a polish at the Villa B, and I have offered to help her in the afternoons. We are to begin this afternoon. I am longing to show her how to really clean up that place and make it tidy. I was in her bedroom the other day with her, and there were dried orange and tangerine peels everywhere – but *old* ones, you know, quite black with age – and cigarette ends all over the furniture – not on trays but just anyhow – and the chaos!'

There were also 'heaps of all sorts of heterogeneous substances and things on the beds, on the chairs, on the window-sills, on the night-table – everywhere! I am longing to have a go at it all.' Lawrence and Frieda had furious rows during this period, according to Barby. At one point she heard 'loud bumping noises' overhead and rushed upstairs to find that Lawrence had scratched Frieda's neck. There was worse to come: a row which would see Lawrence fleeing what Rina called the 'frightful scenes' at the Villa Bernarda for the safety of Capri and the arms of Dorothy Brett.

11

'Such Combustible People!'

BARBY'S SISTER ELSA arrived to join the growing Lawrence ménage at Spotorno in early February 1926, after first flying to Paris – 'quite an enterprising thing to do' in 1926, as Barby noted. Elsa found the atmosphere at the villa 'spiteful', and Lawrence agreed, blaming Barby, who he said always had a vendetta against someone or other. 'I wouldn't marry you, Barby, if you had a million pounds,' he told her, by her own account. 'If the Archangel Gabriel came down from Heaven and asked you to marry him, you'd find fault.'

Rina was briefly distracted from the Lawrences at the beginning of February by the death of her maternal grandmother, Anna Dompé, from a stroke at Bene Vagienna. 'I left poor Grandmother unconscious, and knew that it would be but a matter of hours before she expired,' she wrote to Martin after her return to the Riviera coast from Piedmont. Back in rainswept Sportono, she found that 'at Capo Noli the waves are up to the level of the road, and you know the road is pretty high up there'.

She also found that her father had succumbed to a mild attack of phlebitis while 'poor DH is laid up with a touch of influenza'. She herself was now in bed with 'a bad cold caught in the snows' of Bene, she told Martin in a postcard from Spotorno, though her paraffin stove was 'a great comfort'. Her mother had returned from Bene after a 'very impressive funeral', Rina reported, adding: 'Bad weather here – DHL laid up with 'flu – Frieda depressed.'

By 14 February Spot was in the throes of the Italian Carnival, involving 'masked balls which are bringing dissipation and late hours and intrigues and heartaches into the hitherto peaceful houses of the populace,' Rina wrote, though Lawrence was unable to enjoy the festivities since his flu had turned to 'bronchitis and haemorrhages, which depress him'. His illness, however, was the least of it. 'There are terrific happenings at the Villa Bernarda. His sister and her friend arrived last Wednesday. They were escorted here to tea on Thursday by Frieda – apparently the best of friends.' However Rina had later heard 'the most amazing tales' from Lawrence's sister's friend, Mrs Booth, who asked Rina to show her where the chemist and post office were in Spotorno, and relayed the gossip from the villa.

It appeared that 'Frieda, the evening before, had had the most frightful scene with Mrs Clarke [DHL's sister] and had accused her of wishing to alienate DH from her – and had in fact thoroughly frightened everyone by the violence of her language, and had then gone off and declared she would go to the [Hotel] Ligure with her daughters and stay there as long as DH's sister and friend stayed at the Villa B.' Frieda, Barby and Elsa had duly decamped to the Ligure, with the result that 'poor Mrs Clarke is now doing all the cooking and the cleaning and the nursing of DH! – assisted of course by her friend Mrs Booth (I must say the Villa B looks a different place already). She [Ada] says DH wants looking after and feeding carefully, and she swears she won't leave him alone with Frieda again. I think she is a very nice, capable, straight forward, sensible woman who very much knows what she is about. Her friend, Mrs Booth, also I think very nice but of rather a more shy disposition than Mrs Clarke. And so there they are, in possession of the Villa B!'

Barby's account of the upheaval is rather understated by contrast: 'In February Lawrence's sister Ada came with a friend to stay at the Bernarda, so Elsa and I moved to the tiny Hotel Ligure. As we breakfasted on the balcony over the sea, Frieda appeared looking angry and upset. Ada and the friend had been "bossy", she said. They had tried to oust her from her kitchen, where she managed so well.' In the war between Lawrence's wife and his sister, Rina clearly sympathised with Ada, with whom she shared a sense of order and tidiness. 'I am quite sure that DH will stand a much better chance of recovery with his sister's gentle, systematic housekeeping than with Frieda's slapdashery,' she wrote. She could also, however, see that Frieda and Lawrence had a stormy but dynamic relationship, which was out of the ordinary. 'Frieda's chief complaint apparently is that Ada dotes on him too much and is too sentimental and is spoiling him.'

'My sister's coming was occasion for another rumpus,' Lawrence told Brett on 16 February, Shrove Tuesday – the start of Lent. 'F. abandoned the ship and stays down in the little hotel with her two daughters, pro tem. On Saturday or at latest next Monday I hope to be able to go with my sister to Monte Carlo – or some little place near – for a week. She has booked her ticket home that way, returning on the 25th. After that I don't know what I shall do. I might stay alone in S. France for a while; I hardly feel up to F. and two daughters.' It was a spectacular female falling out. Ada clearly felt the shambolic Frieda was deficient as a nurse and not looking after her brother properly, whereas Frieda resented Ada acting as if she and not Frieda were the mistress of the house.

'I feel absolutely swamped out,' Lawrence wrote to William Hawk, 'must go away by myself for a bit, or I shall give up the ghost. I expect Frieda will stay here till end of March; then I don't know where. The almond blossom is out in clouds here, and it's warm. That's one blessing. But somehow everything feels in a great muddle, with daughters who are by no means mine, and a sister who doesn't see eye to eye with F. What a trial families are!'

There was a real risk of Frieda and Lawrence parting

company, Rina thought. 'DH says that as soon as he is really well again he is going away with his sister and leaving Frieda here with her daughters. I am placed in a very awkward situation, for when I go to the Villa B I get long outpourings from the three of them as to their woes and difficulties – and when I come down into Spot I meet Frieda and then I get her version of the talk – and of course it is a direct contradiction of the other.' Her diplomacy and tact and 'resources of all similar species' had been 'quite exhausted long ago. I now just stand and listen to them and try to look sympathetic – but my head swims and my mind is a blank. They are all such combustible people! They go off like so many rockets all around me and one rocket has no sooner gone off than they are already setting a match to another and another and another. Good heavens, but the Villa B really will go off one of these days with the noise of a hundred bombs.'

The outcome, Rina told Martin, was that Lawrence, his sister Ada and her friend Mrs Booth were 'removing themselves from Spot' the following Saturday, 20 February, and going to the South of France. Lawrence 'will go on to Spain by himself – not coming back here at all. So that is the end of DH here – isn't it a pity? The Villa B will be left to the sole possession of Frieda and her daughters. All this time Frieda has been taking her meals at the Ligure with Elsa and Barbara, and only going up to the Villa B to sleep. Isn't it silly? I shall be sorry to lose DH, and I imagine that my long walks will now come to an end as Frieda sleeps most of the afternoon. However he has returned me my paint box and I shall paint instead and on dull afternoons I shall translate *The Captains Doll*.'

By 24 February the weather was 'hot and lovely, with flawless dazzling skies of perfect blue', but Lawrence was not there to enjoy it, Rina reported. 'The Villa Bernarda is in possession of a feminine colony now. DH left, with his sister and her friend, last Monday, for Monte Carlo. I heard from him this morning. He will then go on to Spain when the other two leave for England. He says he may come back to Spot when 'those girls' have left. In the meanwhile a very subdued Frieda rules over the Villa B with Elsa, Barbara and a Miss Hermes, an art student friend of Barbara's. They have their lunch at the Ligure. I think Frieda is very sorry that DH has gone away without her.'

Frieda's own account in her memoir *Not I, But the Wind* puts the blame on Ada – and on Lawrence. With Ada's arrival at Spotorno, she says, 'there were two hostile camps. Ada arrived and above me, in Lawrence's room with the balcony, I could hear him, complaining to her about me. I could not hear the words but by the tone of their voices I knew.' Ada, Frieda claims, 'felt he belonged to her and the past, the past with all its sad memories. Of course it had been necessary for him to get out of his past and I had, of equal necessity, to fight that past, though I liked Ada for herself. Lawrence was ill with all this hostility. I was grieved for him. So one evening I went up to his room and he was so glad I came. I thought all was well between us.'

The next morning she and Ada had had 'bitter words'. '"I hate you from the bottom of my heart," she told me. So another night I went up to Lawrence's room and found it locked and Ada had the key. It was the only time he had really hurt me; so I was quite still. "Now I don't care," I said to myself.' Lawrence then 'went away with Ada and her friend, hoping at the last I would say some kind word, but I could not. Lawrence went to Capri to stay with the Brewsters.' Frieda was right in saying that Lawrence stayed with his friends the Brewsters on Capri; what she does not say is that he also went to see Brett. He may not have decided to head for Capri until the last minute; his remark to Rina that he intended to spend some time on his own in Spain may even have been sincere. He certainly gave no advance hint of his plans to Brett herself, writing to her on 16 February only that he was 'up and creeping about', and although still 'shaky with flu' was leaving Spotorno to accompany Ada Clarke and

Lizzie Booth to Monte Carlo and see them on to their train for England at Nice.

He duly did so at the end of February, arriving in Monaco on 24 February. 'You were right about the Riviera,' he wrote to Martin Secker in a postcard from Monte Carlo, meaning on this occasion the French Riviera, 'it's deadly boring, but very sunny and rather romantic to look at.' He and his sister were planning to motor along the Grande Corniche to Nice the next day, 'and in the afternoon she leaves for England. I don't know where I shall go – but Italy is certainly much nicer than here.' This was the first indication that he was thinking of Capri – and Brett – rather than Spain. He now sent a telegram to Brett from Ventimiglia on the French–Italian border to announce that he was coming, and he arrived in Capri on 27 February. He told Frieda only two days later – and she was furious.

'DH is at Capri – enjoying himself,' Rina told Martin at the beginning of March – though whether she knew about Brett is unclear. Martin was about to make another of his – comparatively rare – visits to Spotorno to see her and their son. 'I still go up to the Villa B and Barbara, Elsa and I have walks and then have tea with Frieda.' Rina told her husband. Her mind was on domestic matters: she asked Martin to bring with him two packets of 'Canary Creeper' seeds for her mother's frost-damaged garden, because Lawrence – a keen botanist and gardener – had recommended them as quick-growing.

On Capri Brett thought Lawrence appeared frail and delicate despite sporting a new grey suit, a new brown overcoat, a brown Homburg hat and brown shoes. They toured the island together, and played charades at the Brewsters' villa (Lawrence was noted for his comic impressions). 'I am in Capri with the Brewsters for a few days,' he wrote to Martin Secker disingenuously. 'Capri is about the same, only more built over, and rows of bathing houses on the Piccola Marina.' He wrote to Ada to say how sorry he was that the 'bust-up' with Frieda had spoiled her holiday at Spotorno, adding 'I had so wanted you to have a nice time.' According to Brett, Lawrence told her he was worn out by his constant battles with Frieda, remarking 'you have no idea how humiliating it is to beat a woman'. Brett in turn showed him a painting she had done of the pagan god Pan holding up a bunch of grapes to Christ on the cross, both with Lawrence's own face (he didn't like it, so she destroyed it, only to recreate it later).

It had been a 'muddled unsatisfactory sort of winter,' Lawrence wrote to Catherine Carswell, explaining that he was on Capri and Frieda was at Spotorno with her daughters, without going into details – or mentioning Dorothy Brett. When the Brewsters left Capri for India on 10 March, Lawrence and Brett went to Ravello on the Amalfi coast. They went on painting trips together in and around Ravello – until Brett left abruptly, for reasons which have been the subject of dispute ever since but which appear to have to do with a bungled attempt by Lawrence to have sex with her.

In her memoir, Brett said she left because she had been summoned to the American consulate at Naples to deal with her application for immigration to the United States. In a later account, however, she said this was only an excuse, and gave a quite different version, saying that one evening Lawrence had walked into her room – they had adjoining rooms in an annexe of the Hotel Palumbo – in his dressing gown and got into bed with her, saying there was no such thing as a 'close relationship' if it was not physical.

According to Brett, she was 'passionately eager to be successful' and felt 'an overwhelming desire to be adequate', but had 'no idea what to do' to help Lawrence make love to her. He tried again the next night, and again Brett tried to be 'loving and warm and female', but again the encounter was 'a hopeless horrible failure'. 'I was frightened as well as excited', Brett wrote. 'He got into bed, turned, and kissed me. I can still feel the softness of his beard, still feel the tension, still feel the overwhelming desire to be adequate.' When 'nothing happened', Lawrence got up, said 'It's no good' and 'stalked out of the room. I was devastated, helpless, bewildered.'

Given how seriously Brett took all this, there is unintentional hilarity in the disagreement over the remark Lawrence is said to have flung at her as he left her room in humiliation: one version of Brett's memoir has him saying 'Your pubes are all wrong', while another renders this parting shot as 'Your boobs are all wrong'. It is difficult to imagine Lawrence saying either; on the whole the former is more likely, since the word 'boobs' was only used for breasts much later, after the Second World War, and is not a term which Lawrence ever otherwise used – or indeed is likely to have used.

Whatever the truth, Brett left in such haste that Lawrence had to deal with the laundry she left behind in her room, writing to her on 17 March, 'Am sending your washing.' The next day he wrote again to reflect on the fiasco of his attempt to make love to her, saying 'One has just to forget, and to accept what is good. We can't help being more or less damaged. What we have to do is stick to the good part of ourselves, and of each other, and continue an understanding on that. I don't see why we shouldn't be *better* friends, instead of worse. But one must not try to force anything.'

He added 'I'll let you know my plans, as soon as I make any. Just be quiet, and leave things to the Lord.' Aware that she blamed herself rather than him for what had happened, he told Brett she should have learned from her affair with John Middleton Murry not to 'mope and lie around' in 'sloppy self-indulgent melancholics', as Murry himself tended to do. 'The greatest virtue in life is real courage, that knows how to face facts and live beyond them. Don't be Murryish, pitying yourself and caving in. It's despicable ... Rouse up and make a decent thing of your days, no matter what's happened.' Brett, he told the Brewsters a few weeks later, was too possessive: 'I can't stand it when she clings too tight.' Some biographers have doubted whether the 'fiasco' took place, suggesting Brett invented it. On the other hand, Lawrence's own subsequent remarks appear to confirm that something of the sort happened. Brett herself said she felt devastated by 'the whole misery, the torment of the failure in Ravello.'

Lawrence gave no outward indication of these dramas. Martin Secker had arrived in Spotorno, staying with Rina at the Villa Maria, and Lawrence now sent him a jaunty postcard from Ravello with a black and white photograph of the 13th-century cathedral altar on the front. He was sorry to hear that Martin had flu (which he spelled 'flue'), and hoped it was a mild attack. 'The weather isn't worthy the name,' Lawrence wrote. 'I leave for Rome on Monday and wend my way slowly north so shall no doubt see you if you don't leave till about March 30.' Together with two painter friends who were also staying at Ravello, Mabel Harrison and Millicent Beveridge, Lawrence duly went to Rome – where he arrived on 22 March 1926 – and then to Assisi ('too museumish'), Perugia (where he conceived the idea of his book on the Etruscans) and Florence before going across to Ravenna near the Adriatic coast and then back up to Spotorno on 3 April 1926, Easter Saturday, after an absence of a month and a half.

'I have been moving around a bit,' he wrote to Mabel Luhan; Frieda was in Spotorno but was talking of leaving it for good and going to Germany. This apparently alarmed him – 'I do think we are all changing pretty drastically' – but if so he needn't have worried: Frieda had been persuaded by Barby and Elsa to make it up with him. In her memoir Frieda claims she was happy with Barby and Elsa in Lawrence's absence, with Barby 'rushing up the hills with her paint box, her long legs carrying her like a deer' as they enjoyed the spring sunshine under the almond blossoms and fig trees. 'But I was still angry. Finally Lawrence came from Capri, wanting to be back. The children tried like wise elders to talk me round. "Now Mrs L (so they called me) be reasonable, you have married him, now you must stick to him". So Lawrence came back. "Make yourself nice to meet him," the children said. We met him at the station all dressed up. Then we all four had peace. He was charming with Elsa and Barby, trying to help them live their difficult young lives ... But for his sister Ada he never felt the same again.'

Lawrence's version is rather different: 'Got back here yesterday afternoon, everybody very nice and pleased to see me,' he wrote to Martin Secker. They were leaving Spotorno, but Frieda 'is no longer so keen on Germany. We might go to Perugia, and I might do a book on Umbria and the Etruscan remains. What do you think?' He asked Secker to send him 'any good book, modern, on Etruscan things,' since he had only read Dennis' classic *Cities and Cemeteries of Etruria*. Elsa's and Barby's attitude had made him 'die laughing', Lawrence told Brett, with quiet glee. Frieda had 'caught more than she bargained for in her own offspring. Makes her really appreciative of me.'

Lawrence felt better for his break, he told Frieda's mother in a letter on Easter Sunday. He was well, apart from a touch of bronchitis – 'but they say an Englishman at forty is almost always bronchial'. 'I am back,' he told her. 'The three women were down at the station when I arrived yesterday, all dressed up festively – the women, not I. For the moment I am the Easter-lamb. When I went away I was very cross, but one must be able to forget a lot and go on.' Frieda's daughters were 'nice girls really', he wrote to Frieda's sister Else. 'It is Frieda who, in a sense, has made a bad use of them, as far as I am concerned.' Frieda 'undoubtedly loved Lawrence, even if he drained her emotional reserves or failed to fulfil her needs', is the judgment of Frieda's biographer, Janet Byrne. But equally, Lawrence believed in marriage, and his union with Frieda was in a sense 'his life's work'.

In letters to her mother, Frieda expressed her frustration at the constant self-sacrifice of living with an invalid. 'Just as I want to travel, L gets ill,' Frieda wrote. 'I can't bear always just living this illness and always *just* sacrificing myself. That's not what I understand by life.' She was bound to Lawrence, yet wanted to live her own life. Richard Aldington claimed that Frieda had told close friends (presumably including himself) that Lawrence had been impotent since 1926 – that is, their time at Spotorno and later in Florence. Aldington was often spiteful, and had fallen out with Lawrence, as had John Middleton Murry, who apparently made similar allegations which were rebutted by Frieda.

'Fancy,' she wrote, 'Murry says he [DHL] was impotent, the lie, the lie, I ought to know, far from it.' There seems little doubt, however, that Lawrence's sexual desire was on the wane. In one of his *Pansies* poems, written later at Bandol in the South of France, Lawrence wrote, 'I cannot help but be alone for desire has died in me.' When Lawrence started writing *Lady Chatterley's Lover* at Scandicci outside Florence, John Worthen writes, it was striking that he 'should have embarked on such a project when Frieda had taken a lover (Ravagli) and when his own illness probably ensured that he was less sexually involved with her than in their entire life together ... it is not too much to say that the second and third versions of *Lady Chatterley's Lover* were verbal acts of love to Frieda.'

12

The Villa Mirenda

'ITALY IS STILL VERY NICE, and I feel more at home here than in America,' Lawrence wrote to a friend as he prepared to pack up at the Villa Bernarda in April 1926. But it was time to leave Spotorno. 'We shall leave this house on the 20th,' he informed Brett. 'I feel I don't much care where I go, so long as it's no effort.' Barby and Elsa were 'beginning to regret they haven't seen more of Italy. But it's all very expensive.'

Lawrence, Frieda, Elsa and Barby arrived in Florence toward the end of April 1926, staying first in the Pensione Lucchesi on the Lungarno della Zecca Vecchia. Elsa and Barby went back to England after a little over a week, having been shown round the Uffizi Gallery by Lawrence, who commented on Botticelli's *Venus Rising from the Sea*, remarking that it was 'full of air'. This was true, Barby later observed: the figure of Venus did indeed seem 'to float in sea air'. 'We came here ten days ago, and the girls only left yesterday, for London,' Lawrence wrote to Martin Secker from the Pensione Lucchesi. 'It poured with rain all the time they were here – till the day they left, then it was gloriously sunny, as it is also today. Nevertheless they hated leaving. Ask Rina to send them a line sometime – 49, Harvard Road, Chiswick, W.'

Lawrence knew Florence – 'the flowery town', the 'perfect centre of the human world' – from earlier visits: in *Aaron's*

Rod Rawdon Lilly is almost certainly speaking for Lawrence when he says he loves the pale pink Duomo (Cathedral) and its adjoining Giotto belltower, finding them not 'gimcrack and tawdry' as some 'gothic souls' do, but rather 'delicate and rosy', with dark stripes 'like the tiger marks on a pink lily'. This time, however, he preferred the countryside outside Florence: he found the city itself 'very full and noisy, but I still like Tuscany. Today we went out into the country – half an hour by tram, half an hour walk – to look at a villa.'

This was the 16th-century Villa Mirenda, properly called the Villa L'Arcipresso (Cypress Tree) but known then (and now) by the surname of its owner, Raul Mirenda. It still stands on a hill in the hamlet of San Polo, overlooking Scandicci and the Val d'Arno. Here Lawrence and Frieda rented six bare rooms on the top floor for 3,000 lire a year – i.e. £25, the sum he had paid for half that time at the Villa Bernarda. 'It was April, the young beans were green and the wheat and the peas up, and we drove into the old Tuscan landscape, that perfect harmony of what nature did and man made,' Frieda recalled later. 'On the top of one of those Tuscan little hills stood a villa. My heart went out to it. I wanted that villa.'

The villa – as Lawrence informed his friends – was reached by taking a tram from the Duomo to the terminus at Vingone, then taking a pony and trap and walking up a lane lined with cypresses. In his memoir *Adventures of a Bookseller* Pino Orioli (who had first met the Lawrences in England and would later publish *Lady Chatterley* in Florence) recalls that the journey consisted of an 'endless tram ride and then the walk up', and describes the villa as 'a distant and dilapidated place among the hills with no water supply and only one small fireplace'.

Raul Mirenda lived in Florence and used the San Polo villa, a former hunting lodge for a noble Tuscan family, as a summer retreat. It has passed to Alessandro Mirenda, Raul's nephew, and the tram – nowadays a smart 'supertram' which leaves from the Santa Maria Novella station rather than the

Duomo – has made a comeback after a long period in which Scandicci was reachable only by bus. On a recent visit we were met in a Fiat Panda rather than a pony and trap, and Scandicci has grown from a settlement of 2,000 souls into a suburb of Florence with a population of over 50,000. But the isolated villa high in the hills above is still much as it was in the 1920s, with a well in the garden from which water was winched to the upper floor where the Lawrences lived.

They were happy there, with Lawrence – as usual – 'managing his own washing and scrubbing and mending and needlework and cooking and marketing', as Orioli noted. Their neighbours were English, a middle-class Bohemian family called the Wilkinsons. Arthur Wilkinson 'seems nice', Lawrence told Secker: 'red beard, rucksack, violin-case – you can see him'. He was tempted to get the Wilkinsons to stage puppet plays from a caravan, 'and I'll go with them and bang the drum, in the Italian villages'. He added: 'But I forget, you don't know Florence.' The villa 'crowns a hill, as usual in old Tuscany'. Tuscany was 'much lovelier' than the area around Genoa, 'but of course, doesn't get the winter sun as Spotorno does'.

They moved in on 6 May 1926. The villa had (and still has) breathtaking panoramic views over the Tuscan city, and the Lawrences had rooms with a view. 'I love this place in easy reach of Florence,' Frieda wrote from the Villa Mirenda to Rina at Bridgefoot a week later. They were busy making 'this empty place more liveable'. It had 'a bit of the old splendour about it. I am just reading the *Decameron* and it seems a bit like that, but alas sadly so much of the gay spirit gone – you must come and see it.'

She liked Florence itself, though there were too many foreign visitors ('*forestieri*'). Lawrence was 'happy as the sun shines', though 'we also have vile weather. There are a few nice people in Florence – our nearest neighbours a high brow family who insist their unfortunate children shall be geniuses!' Frieda recalled 'the good times at Spot', when 'sometimes we were alive anyhow!' and casually mentioned the 'Tenente's' plans to transfer to Imperia at the end of the month – but without admitting to Rina that if she had 'come alive' at Spotorno, it was because of her attraction to Ravagli.

Barby, who stayed at the Villa Mirenda in the spring of 1927 and again a year later, found it 'a house of magic'; two large horse chestnut trees stood in front of the villa (as they still do), and inside there were oil lamps, a stove with pine logs, a piano hired from Florence, fine woven rush matting on the floor and paintings by Lawrence on the wall, including a 'Holy Family'. In the evenings they sang Hebridean songs with Frieda on the piano and Lawrence singing in his high-pitched voice. This gave the songs a 'suitably other world sound', Barby noted, 'although orthodox musicians would no doubt have shuddered'. They also went to a party at the Wilkinsons' and had to do party turns: Lawrence played an imaginary harp and in a falsetto voice recited WB Yeats's 'I will arise and go now, and go to Innisfree' in the manner of the actress Florence Farr, a friend of Yeats and mistress of George Bernard Shaw. Lawrence had seen her perform in London. He later regretted this comic turn, Barby recalled, and 'on the way home raved at Frieda for having allowed him to do it'.

Apart from the first few weeks, when the weather was rainy, Lawrence spent much of his time writing outside, leaning with his back against an olive tree. He wrote *Two Blue Birds*, a short story in which a wife who lives abroad – apart from her author husband – and has numerous lovers, visits him and berates him for his dependent, though apparently platonic, relationship with his secretary, Miss Wrexall, accusing her of writing his books for him. This has been interpreted as an acid portrait of Faith and Compton Mackenzie, but also no doubt reflects Frieda's complaints about Lawrence's relationship with Brett.

Lawrence was anxious about the miners' strike in England, and the General Strike to which it led. This was partly because of the impact of strike action on his family in the Midlands, and above all on his sisters, whose husbands were shopkeepers dependent on the mining communities for their income. But it was also because he feared it would lead to 'class warfare', which would be 'the beginning of the end of all things'. He was unsure what to write next: apart from *Two Blue Birds* he wrote *The Man Who Loved Islands* – another lampoon of Compton Mackenzie, or so both Mackenzie and Secker believed – but his public wanted something more like *Sons and Lovers*. He had high hopes of *The Plumed Serpent*, which he had finished with supreme effort after his collapse at Oaxaca in Mexico, but was disheartened by the relative lack of enthusiasm with which it was greeted when published. In July he wrote to Brett 'I am not doing any work ... Pity one has to write at all.'

At about this time, in June 1926, he and Frieda were invited to meet Sir George and Lady Ida Sitwell, parents of what Lawrence called 'the writing trio' – Edith, Osbert and Sacheverell. The Sitwells lived at an imposing castle, the Castello di Montegufoni, 14 miles from Florence, which they had bought derelict in 1909 and restored. Lawrence was impressed by Sir George's vast collection of beds, 'four poster golden Venetian monsters that look like Mexican high altars', but taken aback when told they were not for sleeping in but were 'museum pieces'. Lawrence gave a similar account to Martin Secker: 'We've been out very little – only to the Sitwell parents, Sir George and Lady Ida. They have a castle about fourteen miles out – queer old place – a bit disheartening. He collects, of all things, beds – room after room, bed after bed, as if he were providing for all the dead.' When he sat down in a carved gilt chair his host barked out, 'Those chairs are not for sitting in.' Lawrence was not impressed. But then Lady Ida was not impressed with him – or Frieda either, writing to Osbert that they had had a visit from a Mr DH Lawrence, a funny little man with a beard who 'says he is a writer and seems to know all of you. His wife is a large

German. She went round the house with your father, and when he showed her anything would look at him, lean against one of the gilded beds and breathe heavily.' As usual, Frieda gave as good as she got. 'We have met the Sitwell parents Sir George and Lady Ida,' she reported to Rina. 'They have a *big* castello 126 rooms and terrific golden beds, and cannon balls and a tower. He *very* polite, she nice but drinks.' The young Sitwells called their father 'Ginger', she revealed.

Edith Sitwell later remembered that after the Lawrences' visit to the castle she and her brother Osbert had gone to Montegufoni to stay with their parents, to be greeted by her father with the news that 'a most extraordinary man came over here – a man with red hair. I *think* he is a writer; he *said* his name was Lawrence. He had heard of you: he brought his wife'. Frieda, in his version, had not merely leaned on the beds breathing heavily but had 'jumped on all the beds after luncheon – to see if the mattresses were soft'. Lawrence and Frieda then asked Edith Sitwell and her brother to tea at the Villa Mirenda. 'We drove through the Tuscan countryside to their tall, pink house, that looked as if it were perched upon a hen's legs,' Edith recalled. 'It was full of Lawrence's pictures.' Lawrence had 'a rather matted, dank appearance. He looked as if he had just returned from spending an uncomfortable night in a very dark cave.' He was courteous and amiable, with 'a kind of eager quickness, as if he were afraid of something being left unfinished'. But his once very red hair was 'dimmed by illness, as though dust, or ash, had quenched that flame', and he seemed obsessed with the differences between his humble origins as a 'son of toil' and the Sitwells' privileged upbringing, even though 'this was not our fault and our childhood was hell, anyhow'.

Osbert Sitwell also wrote about the visit, in a 1935 collection of essays and recollections called *Penny Foolish*: Lawrence was extremely courteous and made the tea himself, 'which grieved one, for he looked so ill'. Osbert saw Lawrence as 'a fragile and goatish little saint': he had the face of a genius, with 'hollow, wan cheeks and a rather red beard', a 'curious but happy mingling of satyr and ascetic'. The rooms were charming and simple, with 'none of that broken, gold junk one so frequently encounters in the homes of the English in Italy'. He was appalled, however, by Lawrence's paintings, which some had praised but which he found 'crudely hideous and without any merit save that he painted them and in so doing may have rid himself of various complexes which might otherwise have become yet more firmly rooted in his books.' The feud with the Sitwells continued after the appearance of *Lady Chatterley's Lover*, which they were convinced Lawrence had based on them; they believed Wragby Hall was modelled on Renishaw, the Sitwell estate in Derbyshire, and Sir Clifford on Osbert, who as an army officer had served in the trenches in the First World War. Lawrence's response was that the Sitwells 'want to be important at any price, poor souls'.

Thanks to Reggie Turner, the Lawrences also met the eccentric painter, composer and playwright Lord Berners, misspelt by Frieda in her letters to Rina as Lord Bernis. He came to tea at the Villa Mirenda in 'a *huge* Rolls Royce', Frieda told Rina, but was 'a nice man'. She added, evidently not altogether accurately, 'Florence is getting empty now, we haven't seen many people', also telling Mabel Luhan 'We hardly see anybody'. Rina had sent them a family photo, which Frieda declared was 'jolly'. Rina had changed her hairstyle again: 'Lawrence at once noticed your hair, he hadn't seen the "bang", he liked it.' Their plans, Frieda said, were 'a bit uncertain still'. They planned to come back to England, but the weather in Italy was 'not so *very* bad' and it was fun 'to rattle in an old tram full of healthy contadini and workmen into Florence and here at the end of the tram one of the peasants meets us with a little cart'.

In July 1926 Frieda and Lawrence left the sweltering Tuscan heat for Baden-Baden, and then went to England, for what would turn out to be his last visit. 'In the hot weather, the days slip by, and one does nothing, and loses count of time,' Lawrence wrote to Martin Secker from Florence before setting off. 'In the real summer, I always lose interest in literature and publications. The cicadas rattle away all day in the trees, the girls sing, cutting the corn with the sickles, the sheaves of wheat lie all the afternoon like people dead asleep in the heat. *E piu non si frega* [One can't be bothered any more].' He added 'I don't feel much like doing a book, of any sort. Why do any more books? There are so many, and such a small demand for what there are. So why add to the burden, and waste ones vitality over it. Because it costs one a lot of blood.' In England, he told Secker, a friend was offering a flat in Chelsea, 'so we shall see you and Rina, and I hope we'll have a pleasant time'. Despite claiming that he saw no need to add another book to the pile, Lawrence was sketching out *Lady Chatterley's Lover* – and Ravagli was on his mind. 'The Tenente still writes occasionally from Porto Maurizio, where he is transferred, rather lachrymose and forlorn,' he told Secker, adding 'Remember us both to Rina.'

Lawrence and Frieda arrived back at the Villa Mirenda at the start of October 1926. Lawrence devoted himself to repainting the shutters and chairs, writing to Monty Weekley: 'I have painted window frames by the mile, doors by the acre, painted a chest of drawers till it turned into a bureau, and am not through by a long chalk.' 'We got back here just a week ago – very warm, almost hot,' he wrote to Martin Secker. The annual grape harvest, the *vendemmia*, had just ended 'and we are hung all around with grapes. It is very nice, after so much moving, to be still, in these big, empty, silent rooms.' He had promised to come to England in November to help with the proposed staging of his play *David*, and this turned his thoughts to Buckinghamshire. 'How is Bridgefoot – and Rina and the boy? I guess it is lovely autumn there as here.' 'It will be fun to see you and Rina here in January,' he wrote a fortnight later. 'The time flies by.'

Frieda too urged Rina and Martin to come and stay

with them. She rather regretted having made fun of the Wilkinsons – 'the Wilkies' – she wrote to Rina at the end of November, because they had generously offered the use of their house to friends while they were away. 'So there you are, it would be *very* nice if you both came, it would be cheap and you need not give the Wilkies *really* anything. It would be *such* fun having you there and I could give you one meal anyhow and there are 2 girls that help and lots of peasants and a *stove* called the pig!' Lawrence had not been well, but was now painting a 'somewhat doubtful picture' of a scene by Boccaccio. 'I shall have to run and hide it if ever a proper English visitor comes! Wouldn't do for your mother.'

She was writing on her knee, Frieda told Rina, because Lawrence was also painting furniture and had 'painted the table legs yellow and I have already a yellow stripe on my green dress'. She loved the Villa Mirenda, and although it was not Florence as such it was 'so lovely when the sun shines'. Oh yes, and the Tenente – or rather 'Capitano' – had been to visit and was 'so glad to see us and interested in everybody – it must have been dull for him in Spot without us all'.

13

Florence and *Lady Chatterley*

LAWRENCE NOW BEGAN the first version of *Lady Chatterley*, sitting with his back against an umbrella pine tree in a wood of thyme, anemones, violets and gladioli. Lawrence, Frieda reported to Rina, had recovered from a cold and had no wish to go to England. 'Your letter as usual made me laugh: you made it so damp and chilly our desire to come to England melted like butter in the sun.'

Lawrence 'seems very fit', Frieda added. 'He goes in the umbrella pine-wood to write, only comes home in a rage when some louts discover him and stare!' He thought at first it would be a novella, like *The Virgin and the Gipsy*, she recalled later. 'There he would sit, almost motionless except for his wrist writing. He would be so still that the lizards would run over him and the birds hop close around him.' His favourite spot was close to a spring and a cave dedicated to St Eusebius, a 4th-century Roman martyr.

As for what he was writing, if there is one word which he used repeatedly to describe it, it is 'improper'. 'I have begun a novel in the Derbyshire coal mining districts – already rather improper,' he wrote to Martin Secker from the Villa Mirenda in mid-November 1926. As if the two facts were unconnected, he added. 'Our Tenente – now Capitano – came for the day from Gradisca, in the Udine district – he is so miserable there, and descended on me with a dense fog of that peculiar inert Italian misery, dreariness, that I am only just recovering. The Italians are certainly more dreary than the English just now.'

'The novel goes pretty well – is already very improper – and will apparently be quite short,' Lawrence wrote to Secker just over a week later, adding that his neighbours, the Wilkinsons, had left their villa for two months and were willing to rent it out for a pound a week. 'If you and Rina would like it from Christmas till about the 20th – say 18th Jan – write at *once*.' There was a cleaning woman for 20 lire a week 'and everything provided. If it strikes Rina's fancy, write at once.' He wrote his novel in the morning and read the results to Frieda over lunch. She told her son Monty it was 'breaking new ground', with the class struggle and the mind's struggle with the body as its themes. It was in fact a development of *Sun* and *The Virgin and the Gipsy*, taking the story further to ask whether a woman such as Yvette or Juliet – or Connie – could have a permanent rather than passing relationship with a man not of her class.

Lawrence wrote three versions of *Lady Chatterley*, which he at first wanted to entitle *Tenderness*. In the first version, which he wrote in just six weeks, the gamekeeper is called Parkin. Connie becomes pregnant by him and wants to use her private income to buy them a farm so that they can live together: he, however, takes a job at a Sheffield steel works and becomes a Communist. Undeterred, Connie renounces Wragby Hall and decides to live with Parkin, though how they can reconcile their class differences is not made clear. Lawrence evidently realised the novel did not work. He faced not only objections to sexual descriptions and use of Anglo-Saxon words but also reservations over his use of the device of a husband deprived of his virility – 'only half a man' – by the First World War, still very much a sensitive issue in 1926.

In his essay *A Propos of Lady Chatterley's Lover*, which he published in 1929 to explain and justify his 'defiance of convention' and use of 'taboo words', Lawrence admits these drawbacks, but insists that 'the story came as it did, by itself, so I left it alone'. The problem was as much class as sex: his theme was adultery, but it was adultery with a social inferior. Was the relationship between the militantly left-wing Parkin and Connie plausible? The impotence of Clifford Chatterley was not negotiable, however delicate an issue it might be after the war: according to Frieda, Lawrence identified with both Clifford and the gamekeeper. He began rewriting the novel almost immediately, this time over a period of two and a half months – still remarkably fast, especially since he also took time off now and then to paint. In the second version (known as *John Thomas and Lady Jane*) the gamekeeper – still named Parkin – remains uneducated and working class but is no longer a political radical: he has no faith in Communism or any other political system, only in the individual.

Far from toning down the sex, however, Lawrence makes the sexual language even more explicit than in the first version. 'I'm getting on with the novel,' Lawrence wrote to Secker at the beginning of January 1927. It was not a likely bestseller, he told his publisher. 'It's already what the world would call very improper, and not inclined towards popularity'. 'It won't take me very long, I think, to finish the novel, so it won't be too lengthy – 80 to 90 thousand, I suppose,' he wrote to Secker a month later. 'But you'll probably hate it. I want to call it *Lady Chatterley's Lover*, nice and old fashioned sounding. Do look up in Debrett or Who's Who and see if there are any Chatterleys about, who might take offence. It's what they'll call *very* improper – in fact, impossible to print. But they'll have to take it or leave it, I don't care. It's really, of course, very "pure in heart"'.

Rina was still on his mind: 'Is Rina in Italy? She has given no sign,' he wrote to Secker on 12 January. Now in February he reported 'We heard from Rina – she said she was going to Milan, so we asked her to come round this way and stay a day or two with us. She hasn't answered yet.' He asked to be remembered to Mrs Lamont. 'Oh by the way, if you re-print

The Lost Girl, do spell Ciccio with three c's.' He was going to
Ravello to stay with the Brewsters, Lawrence wrote to Secker
in March 1927, despite a bout of flu 'nagging at me these last
three weeks, seeming to get better, then coming back worse.'
It was a 'lovely spring', he reported, 'the wheat full of big blue
anemones and primroses and many violets and grape hya-
cinths by the stream, and purple anemones and scarlet, and
the wild tulips all in bud. Tuscany is very flowery. I'm sorry
Rina didn't pop over. Then she stayed much longer in Spotorno than she said.'

'Had a letter from DHL the other day *insisting* that I
should go to Scandicci to stay with them,' Rina told Martin
from Spotorno in February 1927. 'But of course I couldn't, as
I didn't have enough cash, for one thing, and then no more
time. Pity, really. But *pazienza*.' Lawrence was evidently
keenly disappointed: he had some marionettes for Adrian,
he wrote to Secker, 'but they'll keep, and so will he!' (He later
asked Barby to take them to England). 'Frieda says did Rina
get the scarf sent to Bridgefoot?' He added, almost casually:
'I've finished my novel *Lady Chatterley's Lover* – not long –
but about 80,000 I suppose, or ninety. It's verbally terribly
improper, but I don't think I shall alter it. I'll send it you
one of these days, am not keen somehow on letting it go out.
What's the good of publishing things!'

He completed the second version in February 1927, but
did not immediately send it off for publication. He told Brett
on 9 February he would 'let it lie and settle down a bit before
I think of having it typed'. Instead in March, in a change of
pace – and subject – he put *Lady Chatterley* on one side and
set off with his American friend Earl Brewster in search of the
Etruscans, the ancient and mysterious vanished inhabitants
of central Italy who had long fascinated him. He and Brewster visited Cerveteri, Volterra and Tarquinia as well as the
Etruscan museum in Rome, the Villa Giulia. Lawrence saw
in the vanished Etruscans evidence (from their tomb deco-
rations) of a people who had tried to live in harmony with

nature and the world rather than seeking to exploit or domi-
nate it, as the Romans did – and as their Fascist self-styled
successors were doing under Mussolini. The Fascist 'will to
power', he thought, was alien to Italians, who instead were
more like the Etruscans as he imagined them: sensitive, dif-
fident, given to symbols and mysteries, 'able to be delighted
with true delight over small things', violent only in spasms,
and altogether without any 'natural will to power'. Lawrence
also noted the use by Etruscans of the phallus as a decoration,
and concluded they had had a 'phallic consciousness'. He was
pondering his third (and final) version of *Lady Chatterley*,
and no doubt his visions in the painted Etruscan tombs of
'vivid feeling throbbing over death' and man moving 'naked
and glowing through the universe' informed his fiction.

By April he seemed a bit more optimistic about his
'improper' novel, writing to Secker that it was for him to
judge how 'possible or impossible' *Lady Chatterley's Lover*
was, adding, 'But there is much more latitude these days, and
a man dare possibly possess a penis.' In real life he was getting
rather fed up with Ravagli's continuing attentions to Frieda.
Frieda went to Baden-Baden, almost certainly travelling via
Trieste so that she could see her lover, who was now stationed
at Gradisca, a former Habsburg town on the border with Slo-
venia. Ravagli had made the reverse journey from Gradisca to
Florence to visit Frieda at least twice, to Lawrence's irritation.
In November 1926 Frieda told Rina Secker that 'the Tenente
– Capitano – wrote he will come and see us, has a "pro-
cesso militare" (military trial) in Florence,' and Ravagli duly
turned up in the first months of 1927. Ravagli later admitted
that Lawrence thought he was using the trial as a cover to
visit Frieda, and became cordial only after insisting on seeing
Ravagli's military travel documents.

Frieda rejoined Lawrence at the Villa Mirenda on 11 April,
and Barby arrived the next day. He was ill again, deciding
this time it was bronchial trouble aggravated by malaria. In
May the weather quickly turned hot, and he felt 'drowsy like

an insect'. Barby, Frieda told Rina at Bridgefoot in May, had loved coming, but 'could only stay 3 weeks'. The situation was always 'a little difficult', but 'the children feel they have a right to me and L. feels the same'. She added that 'women will have it that I am a peculiarly unattractive female' and that Lawrence '*must* always be dashing after somebody else! For all that, I flourish.' She did not admit that she was flourishing because it was she rather than Lawrence who was 'dashing after somebody else'.

Rina had been to Spotorno again to see her parents, but was now back at Bridgefoot with Gemma, their Italian maid. Frieda was intrigued. 'I wish I could hear Adrian and Gemma together – and how does she like England?' Iver 'will begin to look splendid now – but I do wish you could see the woods here now, such absolute masses of flowers, the earth seems quite inexhaustible'. She mentioned the visit from Edith and Osbert Sitwell – 'really *liked* them, not a *bit* bouncy or conceited, but simple and "simpatico"' – and was amused to note that when any guests in a 'rich American motor' arrived at the villa their normally barefoot peasant girl, Giulia, 'flings on her high heeled shoes when she hears them and flies up from her house and is there to receive them: every inch a parlourmaid!' Frieda added: 'I get such fun out of the peasants, their lives are so *real* and they are so shrewd! I do love the life here anyhow, I can't tell you how closed up Germany seemed, not open and gay like here.' Once again Lawrence had not been very well, 'but is better and loves the woods and is much chirpier than he used to be, has just finished painting a queer resurrection.'

In June he felt well enough to go swimming with the Huxleys at Forte dei Marmi on the Tuscan coast, but had a serious haemorrhage in July. As Frieda recalled later: 'One hot afternoon Lawrence had gathered peaches in the garden and came in with a basketful of wonderful fruit – he showed them to me – a very little while after he called from his room in a strange, gurgling voice. I ran and found him lying on his bed: he looked at me with shocked eyes while a slow stream of blood came from his mouth.' He and Frieda once again escaped from the Italian heat, this time to Villach in Austria, where he translated stories by Verga, the author of *Cavalleria Rusticana*, and then to the summer house of Else, Frieda's sister, in the Bavarian countryside. 'It's a relief to be here after the friction and bossiness of Italy,' he wrote to Secker in August 1927. 'Remember us nicely to Rina and the boy and to Mrs Lamont.'

They returned to Villa Mirenda in October. At a meeting in Florence with Reggie Turner and Pino Orioli Lawrence decided to resolve the *Lady Chatterley* problem by having his 'improper' novel published privately. He finished the third and final version by 8 January 1928, and made substantial changes to produce the novel we now know. Clifford was now more like Lawrence himself, a literary intellectual and author of short stories, while Connie has an affair before she meets the gamekeeper (now called Mellors), sleeping with Michaelis, an Irish playwright known as Mick. Mick is not an effective lover – he suffers from premature ejaculation – and so leaves Connie unsatisfied and ready for a more virile contender such as Mellors.

Mellors himself has also evolved: unlike the working class Parkin, he is described as having won a scholarship to Sheffield Grammar School, and having risen through the ranks during the war to gain a commission, serving in India and Egypt. He is more articulate and educated than Parkin, and speaks middle-class English as well as dialect, just as Ravagli would have spoken correct official Italian and the local vernacular. But in a sense, Mellors is also Lawrence himself, as is Clifford – indeed all the characters. The final version ends with Mellors writing to Connie from a colliery-owned farm where he is working while waiting for his divorce from Bertha. He can see 'a bad time coming, death and destruction for these industrial masses', but is content: Connie is pregnant, and he is chaste ('How can men want wearisomely to philander?').

A man, Mellors concludes, 'has to fend and fettle for the best, and then trust in something beyond himself'.

Looking back in old age, Ravagli told Bevilacqua that Frieda had stimulated Lawrence's imagination – and hence his fiction – at Spotorno by telling him what she and her lover got up to both at the villa and in the nearby bushes, olive groves and vineyards. There was certainly complicity between Lawrence and Frieda at Scandicci, where he read *Lady Chatterley* to her as he wrote it: at times, according to a visitor from Nottingham, Enid Hopkin, they laughed over it, and at other times Frieda sounded shocked 'and in her deep, throaty voice said "Lorenzo, you cannot say that".' 'It is frankly a novel about sex, direct sex,' Lawrence wrote to Martin Secker while at Les Diablerets above Lake Geneva where Aldous Huxley, his brother Julian, the biologist, and their wives were skiing. 'I think it's good, but you may not like it. I expurgated it all I can – it's a pity one has to do it. You'll have to see what you think of the result ... It's a bit of a revolution in itself – a bit of a bomb.'

It was still too much of a bomb. In the end, back in Florence, he had 1,000 copies printed privately by the Tipografia Giuntina, supervised by Pino Orioli, complete with numerous misprints, since none of the typesetters knew any English. *Lady Chatterley*, Lawrence insisted, was 'phallic, but tender and delicate'. Instead of a future in which people accepted the superiority and authority of others, he hoped for a new relationship between men and men and men and women based on tenderness and sensitivity, 'not the one up one down, lead on I follow, ich dien sort of business'.

Frieda and Lawrence were still urging Rina to come to Florence, but time was running out. There was an inn at the tram terminus, Frieda told her in March, 'about 20 minutes from us', and although the owner had had a heart problem 'he will have recovered by that time'. There was the prospect of nice walks, 'especially when all the flowers have come'. They were happy at the Villa Mirenda, but would give it up on 1

May: 'It's sad, but as high up in Switzerland did Lawrence such a lot of good I'll find something there again for a few months.' Lawrence was 'busy printing the novel and is enjoying it'.

An exhibition of his erotic paintings – many of them done at the Villa Mirenda – opened at the Warren Gallery in London in June 1928: it had been suggested by Barby, who as a graduate of the Slade knew Dorothy Warren, the gallery owner (and niece of Lady Ottoline Morrell), and put it to her that Lawrence's artistic efforts were worthy of a London show. The daring subject matter did indeed draw the crowds, but police raided the gallery in early July and confiscated 13 paintings on the grounds that they were obscene.

Frieda visited Barby at Alassio, together with her sister Else Jaffe, but then 'went off alone' to Spotorno, according to Barby – ostensibly to spend time with Rina's parents, Luigi and Caterina Capellero, but also to see Ravagli again. 'Frieda was away a week with Barby in Alassio,' Lawrence wrote to Secker in April, 'went to Spotorno, saw the Tenente and the Capelleros and all. She came back the other day, and we are spasmodically packing up.'

Rina had missed her chance, Frieda told her: the climate in Italy was not helping Lawrence ('this has been an absolute muff of a spring') and 'I think we must go away sooner than I said – we shall go to Capri I think: so I am awfully sorry to have to put you off. I shall only just come back for a few days and disperse the Villa Mirenda, it will make me sad. I am sorry you never saw it, it can be so very attractive!' Frieda asked Rina to tell Martin that for a year she had been 'scared' of *Lady Chatterley*, and had 'run past the book shelf where the manuscript was', but now 'I think it's art and stick by her'. The Huxleys had been 'thrilled by it. Lawrence is deep in his printing, it's interesting to see the printer and everything all rather on a small scale and old fashioned.'

Three years after Lawrence's death, while Rina was on holiday in Scotland, she received a letter from the Swiss film producer in Paris, JE Siebenhaar, to whom Frieda had sold the film rights of *Lady Chatterley's Lover*. Siebenhaar, it seems, had met Rina in Paris and was aware of her role in helping to inspire the novel. 'It is not because you have had no news from me that you must think I have forgotten all about our meeting in Paris,' he wrote. 'But things go on slowly and with all sorts of ups and downs as is usual in all cinema affairs.' He and his team were coming to England to discuss the idea of a film version of *Lady Chatterley*, and he wanted to meet Rina again so she could 'supply personal reminiscences that would be of great interest'. He also hoped she could give him a list of 'the most interesting newspaper cuttings containing criticisms of *Lady Chatterley's Lover*'. She chose, however, to stay firmly in the background, and asked her husband to send Siebenhaar the cuttings he wanted on her behalf.

14

Death in Vence

LAWRENCE SPENT HIS LAST YEARS – as he had spent
much of his life – wandering from place to place. A sick
man in need of rest, he rattled around Europe by train and
ship for all the world as if he were in rude health and looking
for new experiences.

He accepted an invitation to join Richard Aldington
for five weeks at a converted island fortress Aldington had
rented called La Vigie (The Lookout) on the Ile de Port
Cros, in the Gulf of Hyères near Toulon. Frieda went back to
Italy to pack up at the Villa Mirenda, and joined him later,
making a detour via Trieste – not far from Ravagli's posting
at Gradisca. Lawrence and Frieda then moved on to Bandol,
between Toulon and Marseilles, where they stayed for four
months at the Beau Rivage, the hotel where Katherine Mansfield had stayed in 1916 in a vain attempt to regain her health.
In April 1929, with Frieda in Baden-Baden, he set off by train
for Paris ('terribly noisy and full of traffic, no elan,' he wrote
to Secker) to oversee the publication of a cheap edition of
Lady Chatterley's Lover, accompanied by Rhys Davies, a
young Welsh writer who had become his acolyte in Bandol,
who was shocked by the sight of Lawrence's El Greco-ish
'frail, wasted body'.

Lawrence and Frieda then took a ferry to Majorca (Mallorca), but he did not much take to it: the wine was foul,

and 'made cat's piss seem like champagne', Lawrence wrote
to Davies. Frieda was happier: 'We are enjoying it here, right
on the sea, the days just dream themselves away, the Mediterranean at its best!' she wrote to Rina from the Hotel Principe
Alfonso at Palma de Mallorca. 'I hope it's coming to Bridgefoot too, the spring!' The Ravaglis, who had had another
baby, their third, 'asked us to be godparents, they seem to
take it rather stoically,' Frieda reported to Rina. Majorca was
full of 'amusing people, nobody very rich, a few really jolly
ones, but also decrepit generals and colonels! I will come
to England this summer and hope to see you – end of this
month we make a tour: Granada, Madrid, then Germany!'

They returned to France, and despite Lawrence's worsen-
ing health Frieda left for London to deal with the aftermath
of the confiscation by police of pictures from the Warren
Gallery exhibition while Lawrence joined the Huxleys again,
this time at Cannes. His feverish attacks were getting worse,
and he was short of breath. An alarmed Pino Orioli, visiting
Lawrence in Cannes, got him back to Florence by train and
alerted Frieda, who came at once. Bizarrely, instead of sum-
moning another doctor, she whisked him off to Baden-Baden
in August to celebrate her 50th birthday and her mother's
78th birthday. Not surprisingly Lawrence found this celebration distasteful: the sight of his mother-in-law – a 'terrible
old woman' – and her 'depressing and fat guests' made him
feel ill, he wrote to Orioli.

They went to Bavaria, where Lawrence wrote his celebrated
Last Poems, about death: the poem on gentians, inspired by
the flowers in a vase by his bed: 'Bavarian gentians, big and
dark, only dark/darkening the daytime, torch-like with the
smoking/blueness of Pluto's gloom'; and *The Ship of Death*:
'I am ill because of wounds to the soul.' 'I don't like Germany
this year, I want to go away,' he wrote to Harry Crosby and
his wife Caresse, who had published the expanded version
of *Sun*. He was dreaming of Italy again, he said. Instead he
and Frieda returned to Bandol in the South of France, this

time renting the Villa Beau Soleil, an imitation Roman villa where he wrote his defence of his 'lewd and obscene' novel, *A Propos of Lady Chatterley's Lover*, and *Apocalypse*, his reflection on the Book of Revelations and ancient pre-Christian writings on the cosmos.

'WE'VE GOT A COMMONPLACE little house on the sea,' he wrote to Secker at the beginning of November, 'but it is pretty comfortable, a good bathroom, and a central-heating system that warms up very quickly. But mostly we don't need it, because the sun shines in warm off the sea, very lovely.' He added: 'It seems a long time since we were at Spotorno, yet being on the same coast, I often think of it. I wish I were as strong as I was then.'

'Have you had any communication from the Lawrences at Bandol?' Martin wrote to Rina in Alassio in January 1930. 'I had a letter from him the other day saying that his health was worrying him, and wishing he was as well as he was at Spotorno. And that was nothing great, was it? I expect one would see a change in him after four years. He does not seem able to do any sustained work now, like a novel.' In reality, as Aldous Huxley observed, 'For the last two years he was like a flame burning on in miraculous disregard of the fact there was no more fuel to justify its existence.' Examined at Bandol by a doctor sent by his concerned friends, Lawrence was warned that if he did not enter a sanatorium he would be dead within three months. He reluctantly moved to the Ad Astra sanatorium above Vence in the Maritime Alps, not far from Cannes.

He was miserable at the Ad Astra, and lost more weight as he wasted away. 'Yes, it was better for Lawrence to come here but I do hope it may do him good,' Frieda wrote to Martin Secker from the Ad Astra. 'Anyhow I was at my wits ends. It's that he is so *thin*, his lungs if they tell me the truth don't seem much worse than they were in Mexico 6 years ago, when they took an X ray photograph. It's most mysterious and we fed him so well!' She added: 'If Rina would like to spend a night or two with us *soon* at Cagnes (I believe it isn't so very far from Alassio) we would be so glad. *We* is Barby and I.' They were renting a villa at Cagnes sur Mer, 'the next little place to this', but were staying nearer the Ad Astra for a few weeks because the villa at Cagnes was too cold. 'It is lovely to have Barby; it's horrid weather and Lawrence is miserable today.'

Barby, who had spent a fortnight during the winter of 1928 with Lawrence and Frieda at the Hotel Beau Rivage at Bandol, returned at Frieda's request to help care for Lawrence, cooking porridge for breakfast and putting her arm round him to comfort him. At the Ad Astra sanatorium the manager told Barby: 'Monsieur Lawrence is a lamp that is slowly failing.' 'This winter makes me know I shall just die if I linger on like this in Europe any more, and what's the good of my dying!' Lawrence wrote to Brett. He dreamed of a return to New Mexico from Marseilles via New York or San Francisco: 'I wouldn't mind a long sea trip. But I do want to do something about my health, for I feel my life leaving me.'

At the beginning of March he moved to the Villa Robermond in Vence, which Frieda had rented to be near the sanatorium where he was being treated, and which – like the Villa Bernarda – has since been replaced by a block of flats. He had a stream of final visitors, including HG Wells, who according to Barby unhelpfully told Lawrence his illness was mostly hysteria. Lawrence asked Frieda to sleep beside him to warm him, but began to have hallucinations, seeing his own dead body 'over there on the table'. He called for more morphine and asked Frieda to hold him, saying 'I don't know where I am, I don't know where my hands are.' A short time later his last words were 'I am better now.'

His first love, Jessie Chambers, said that the day Lawrence died – 2 March 1930, a Sunday – she heard his voice 'as distinctly as if he had been in the room with me,' saying to her 'Can you remember only the pain and none of the joy?'

His voice was 'so full of reproach that I made haste to assure him that I *did* remember the joy'. He then said 'in a strange confused way', 'What has it all been about?' Jessie said his death had reinforced her conviction that he had been 'a living manifestation of God'. Frieda recorded that an hour after his death, when she pulled back the sheet covering his face, she felt that 'all suffering had been wiped from it, as if he was someone she had never seen before' – just as Elizabeth Bates in his story *Odour of Chrysanthemums* feels she has never known her dead husband before as she surveys his body.

LAWRENCE, IT SEEMS, also appeared to Rina. The letter in which she described to Martin seeing Lawrence in a dream has not survived, but Martin's reply has. 'How strange that he should have been so much in your mind and that you should have dreamt of him the night of his death,' Martin wrote to Rina from Bridgefoot.

Frieda, it has to be said, does not come out of the death scene particularly well: for one thing, when John Middleton Murry came to Vence after Lawrence's death to pay his respects, she had no scruples about immediately going to bed with him. She wore a red dress to the funeral at Vence, which Achsah Brewster found inappropriate. Some 30 years later, on New Year's Eve 1963, Martin Secker wrote from Bridgefoot to Rina in Cannes: 'I saw Frieda on her last visit to England, not long before her death. She had become very eccentric looking ... As we walked up Lower Regent Street together people turned to look back at her.' He found it ironic that the Lawrence estate had generated 'all this money' when 'at the time of his death DHL could not afford the luxury of a bottle of brandy'. Yet it was Frieda above all who saw Lawrence through his last months, as Secker acknowledged in 1970, 40 years after Lawrence's death. Despite everything, he wrote, he would 'like to pay a tribute to Frieda, to her devotion and to her loyalty'. Lawrence had only had a short life to live, Secker said, but if it had not been for Frieda, 'it would have been shorter still'.

Frieda Lawrence and Angelo Ravagli left for America in May 1931 on the SS *Conte Grande* from Genoa: she described herself on the ship's manifest as 51 and a widow, he as a 40-year-old married officer. He gave his wife Serafina in Spotorno as his nearest relative. At Taos Ravagli, who had worked as a builder before he joined the Italian army, made the chapel for Lawrence's ashes above the ranch at Kiowa in 1935, and acquired a modest reputation as a ceramicist and painter. Accounts vary as to how Lawrence's ashes were brought there, if in fact they ever were: Ravagli told Bevilacqua that he had 'built the shrine myself, with these bricklayer's hands of mine: I mixed his ashes into the cement, beside his typewriter and a sculpture of the phoenix, his personal symbol'.

Ravagli had taken the urn from Marseilles to America: he was met at Lamy railway station in New Mexico, 17 miles south east of Santa Fe, by Frieda and Mabel and Tony Luhan, but they left the ashes by mistake on the platform. 'If I hadn't gone back to get them, they would have remained there on the ground'. According to other accounts, however, Ravagli admitted he was apprehensive about trying to take them through US customs, and had substituted other ashes for the real ones when he got to America. The real ashes were disposed of – or so Ravagli told some visitors to Taos after a certain amount of bourbon had been drunk – somewhere at sea between Marseilles and Villefranche, where he embarked for America. In a way it is rather fitting to think that Lawrence's ashes may not have been interred in New Mexico after all but rather scattered in the Mediterranean, the sea which he loved and which inspired him.

As far as we know, Rina never saw Frieda and Lawrence again after Spotorno, despite their close relationship. She continued to spend time there, although the resort's hopes of a 'golden age' of English tourism to rival Alassio had mixed results. In February 1926 Rina wrote to Martin that Spotorno was 'in a great state of preparation as there are 30 English people coming from Bordighera in charabancs to lunch at the Ligure and look at Spot! A pity the sun isn't shining. The owners of the Palace Hotel have also got an hotel at Bordighera and they are responsible for this invasion.' In January 1927, when she visited Spotorno again, she was reporting, 'There are over a hundred Inglesi here. But Oh! Such specimens!' They wandered over the hills all day, and played tennis, but were alas 'all very plain, very old, and very prim!' The Hotel Miramare was sold to the owners of the Grand Hotel Palace after Luigi Capellero's death in 1931; Rina's mother Caterina invested the proceeds in apartments in Alassio.

Quite why Rina detached herself so completely from Lawrence and Frieda after the Spotorno drama we can only guess. She never went to Florence to see them, despite repeated invitations, even though she had only to take the train down the Ligurian coast past La Spezia to Pisa, and then the short distance across to Florence and Scandicci. Neither did she go to see Lawrence as he lay dying in Vence, even though Alassio and Spotorno were not too far along the coast, and even though Frieda implored her to come. 'No, I haven't had any news from the Lawrences,' Rina wrote to Martin from her flat in Palazzo Genova in Alassio in January 1930. She had heard of Lawrence's rapid decline: 'I feel sorry for poor DH'. Later the same month she wrote that she was 'sorry to hear about poor DH, although I suppose it was to be expected sooner or later. Poor DH. He has put up a very valiant fight, but I suppose he must now definitely recognise his debilities. I wonder what Frieda thinks about it? I don't think she can possibly be blind to the real state of things. Lord knows what she'll do without DH!'

Visiting Spotorno from Alassio in April 1931 to see her father shortly before his death, Rina wrote to Martin 'I always think of poor DHL when I am in Spot. I wonder where Frieda is?' Years later, in 1950, when she was in a clinic in Zurich – she had a series of treatments for unspecified 'female ailments' in the post-war years – Rina came across an article by Frieda in an American magazine and sent it to Martin with the comment 'Amusing, *nicht wahr*? Wonderful old thing, Frieda!'

Possibly Rina felt she had become too intimately involved with Lawrence and Frieda: she must have been aware of the publication of *Sun*, and she was certainly aware that had unwittingly provided Frieda with a lover by introducing her to Ravagli. Perhaps she had had enough drama.

There was, after all, growing drama in her own life: she was increasingly preoccupied with the breakdown of her marriage, and the consequences for herself and her young son. By 1930, the year Lawrence died, Rina was still spending much of the year apart from Martin, wintering at Alassio, where five-year-old Adrian attended the English PNEU (Parents National Education Union) school on the seafront. The little Alassio school had premises in a rented seaside villa, the Villa delle Palme, where the ghosts of the British expat children who had their lessons there – within sight and sound of the beach below, which must have been an added torment – can still be sensed. The building still has its original decorated ceilings, parquet floors and chandeliers. In the grounds, with its palm trees, a venerable Mediterranean pine of immense age leans against the round summer house overlooking the sea, carved out of the remains of a 15th-century stone lookout tower built to guard against Saracen invasion.

Throughout the 1930s Rina divided her time between Iver, Bene Vagienna and Alassio, where she lived first in a family-owned flat, then at the Villa Scozia above the town on the road to Solva, and from 1932 at the Villino Mio on Viale Hanbury. Although her letters to Martin in the mid 1920s are full of loving affection, by the 1930s the tone was more distant and business-like. The strain of leading a double life in England and Italy was beginning to tell. 'I suppose I had better pack all the household things like curtains, sheets, blankets, rugs, cushions etc up and leave them here in storage in case we decide to come again next winter,' she wrote in March 1931. 'Lord – what a business.'

Her mood had changed. 'I have got past the age when one wakes up in the morning and thinks that something miraculous will be sure to turn up during the day which will make everything different. To lose that feeling is, I imagine, the first real sign of age. I have definitely lost it since last summer so I am definitely getting old.' The black moods which had gripped her at Spotorno, only to be dispelled by the excitement of the Lawrences' arrival, now returned, worsened by the bizarre machinations of Mrs Lamont in conveying supposed spirit world 'messages' from a medium called Alice Coltman, warning Rina and Adrian not to return to England.

Rina spent ever longer periods apart from her husband: the summer of 1933 found her on holiday with Adrian at Pitlochry in Scotland, and then at Blair Atholl in the Grampian Mountains, which reminded her of Garessio. She pleaded with him to join them – in vain, as usual. 'When I think of all my disillusions of the last ten years I shiver,' she wrote to Martin. 'One has only one life to lead, and to have that one life just made up of one broken ideal after another is hard luck!'

She was also feeling the tug of Italy more and more strongly. Already in March 1930 she had warned Martin from Alassio, where she and the young Adrian were spending the winters, that although the summers were too hot for the boy she was 'loath to leave this place ... I hope that Bridgefoot will be looking its best to welcome us and make us forget our hills and sea and sun! Of course I am looking forward to your seeing Adrian, but otherwise I am really rather sad!'

The Riviera coast and the flower-filled valleys behind it were 'bewitching'. Her mother Caterina's funeral at Bene Vagienna seven years later in February 1937 only reinforced her sense of '*Italianita*'. At Alassio afterwards she stayed at a seaside hotel, the Minerva, with 'one window looking south to the sea and the other south-west towards the hills which are covered with blossom. There is an orange tree loaded with fruit just opposite my window.' 'We are having simply glorious weather here,' she wrote again later in the month. 'Brilliant sunshine and warmth – why does one live in England? I have just been for a solitary and lovely walk to Solva and beyond, and found many violets. It is heavenly up in the hills. Everything looks very well kept and clean and prosperous.' She would continue coming to Italy every year, 'if I don't decide to stay out here altogether – and I must say the temptation is strong.'

'Really, England is an impossible place to live in!' she wrote from Spotorno in May 1931, comparing the delights of Italy to dull and 'pseudo genteel' English boarding houses. The more time she spent in Italy, she told Martin in a letter written on Spotorno beach on 14 February – St Valentine's Day – 1927, the more she realised that despite her upbringing in London she found it increasingly difficult to leave 'this wonderful sunshine, the sea and the hills, and all that makes Italy. The older I get the more I realise that I belong here and am a bit like a fish out of water in England, even in a Queen Anne House!' In the same letter she even refers to 'us poor foreigners'.

Adrian was eventually sent back to prep school in England at Swanbourne House at Bletchley, not far from Iver, and then to Ampleforth School in Yorkshire. Rina was aware of the gathering clouds on the international scene as Nazism and Fascism took hold: 'I wish somebody would be brave enough to shoot Mussolini and let the world have some peace,' she wrote from the Cowdray Club at Cavendish Square to Adrian at his prep school in October 1935. 'But I suppose that is too much to hope.'

Tensions were no doubt further exacerbated by Secker's business difficulties: in 1935 his firm went into receivership, and it was bought the following year by Fredric Warburg and Roger Senhouse, taking the new name Secker and Warburg. Rina had invested £2,000 pounds in the family business, which she lost. There followed tiresome tussles over her allowance and the sale of land at Bridgefoot to make up for business losses. 'It is very lovely out here,' Rina wrote to Martin from the family-owned Hotel Lido in Alassio in February 1937, where she was dealing with the aftermath of her mother Caterina's death. 'But for seeing Adrian I wouldn't want to come back at all.' She was willing to help out with 'reasonable' debts, but 'if you mismanaged your business affairs I don't see why I should have to pay for it'.

In 1938 Martin and Rina were divorced. Within a year she had re-married: her husband this time was Carlo Lovioz, an Italian banker who had lived in London for 20 years. Lovioz was director of the London branch of the Banca Commerciale Italiana (BCI), and Rina became his private secretary in 1937: before long she was overseeing the decoration of his London flat and he was taking her out 'to all the nice and right places to lunch and dinner ... I hope to make myself quite, quite indispensable!' Lovioz, who was 'as bald as a billiard ball' but 'kindness itself', subsequently became head of the BCI in Como.

The Second World War dashed Rina's hopes of resolving her Anglo-Italian identity problem by identifying wholly with Italy, however. She was in Rome with Adrian when the war broke out: Italy was not at first involved, but when Mussolini entered the war on Hitler's side in 1940 Adrian was first interned and then sent to a prison camp at Kreuzburg in German Upper Silesia. Rina waited out the war anxiously with Lovioz in Nazi-occupied Merano in the Italian South Tyrol. In 1952 she told Carlo she was reluctant to live in Italy ever again. 'There are too many indelible memories,' she wrote. 'In any case I can hardly look upon Italy as my own country when I have been brought up and educated in another country. My whole outlook is too different ... you are a little apt to overlook what my position was in those days with an Italian husband and an English son, and the scars it has left behind.'

After the war Rina became for a while assistant in Rome to Cyril Ray, Rome correspondent of the *Daily Express*, working at the Stampa Estera (Foreign Press Club). After Lovioz' death in 1954 she lived at Vevey in Switzerland, but eventually moved back to England permanently, living at Richings Park in Iver, close to Bridgefoot, even though Martin had by then re-married.

She rarely referred back to her days at Spotorno or her association with Lawrence and other writers – although writing from Locarno in January 1950, she told Adrian she had been looking again at Compton Mackenzie's *Sinister Street*, and 'I find it doesn't bear re-reading. It is too much *all'acqua di rose*, and terribly terribly snobbish. Also, I don't think the characters ring true. I can't think how I was ever impressed by it.' In November 1950 she told Adrian she was sorry to have heard on the BBC that George Bernard Shaw – 'brave old GBS' – had died: 'He made a truly noble effort, but at 94 I suppose it was hopeless – my great grandfather in Bene died at the age of 96 because of a broken ankle, and he was furious!'

Rina died at 12 Somerset Way, Iver, on 3 December 1968, taking with her her memories of Spotorno, Alassio and the 'combustible' days with DH Lawrence and Frieda. They live on, however, in her letters.

15

DHL the Italian

'IT IS EXTRAORDINARY the change, when one crosses the Alps,' Lawrence wrote from Spotorno on returning to Italy after America and Mexico. 'I think on the whole I like the Mediterranean countries best to live in.'

WHAT, IN THE END, did Italy mean for DH Lawrence? When I asked the late Italian author Alberto Bevilacqua he replied 'Above all, the sun. For him Italy was full of sunny places. But in addition it was full of people he found interesting.' Lawrence, Lina Waterfield records in her memoir *Castle in Italy*, 'had a real understanding and liking for the Italian people, especially the peasants and workers. They often irritated him, but their friendliness and lust for life overshadowed their faults in his eyes.'

He found Italy refreshingly free of the class distinctions which blighted England. The reason for Lawrence's obsession with sex and 'mystical phallicism', Compton Mackenzie believed, was his discovery that sex was a 'social equaliser'. 'Nobody had less reason to bother about class, but it forever tormented him and this was why Lady Chatterley had to be the wife of a baronet'. *Lady Chatterley's Lover* is in effect a lament for the England he could see disappearing under urban and industrial sprawl. When in 1915 he visited Lady

Ottoline Morrell at Garsington Manor, her estate in Oxford-shire, he wrote: 'When I drive across this country, with the autumn falling and rustling to pieces, I am so sad, for my country, for this great wave of civilisation, 2,000 years, which is now collapsing, that it is hard to live.' He later wrote a lyrical recollection of Garsington, with its stone windows and pillars, its Tudor arch, the wet lawn, ilex trees and elms, 'a gleaming segment of all England'.

But this was an elegy written by a wanderer. As Jeffrey Meyers has observed, travel was for Lawrence not just 'a pilgrimage from country to country in search of warm climate and good health'. Travel intensified his sense of being English at the same time as it removed him from England and allowed him to see his own country more clearly. Like Joyce, he was a 'regional novelist who became a good European'. Lawrence's discovery of Italy 'was also a discovery of himself'. *The Virgin and the Gipsy* and *Lady Chatterley's Lover* were written not in the Midlands but in Italy, the country to which Lawrence felt bound all his adult life, and which he first explored shortly after he met Frieda. Italy is the country to which Connie Chatterley offers to take Parkin (later Mellors) to at the end of *John Thomas and Lady Jane*, the second version of the novel ('We can go to Italy if you like').

Italy meant different things to him at different times: a source of sunshine and inexpensive food and wine, but also the land of simple and enduring peasant values, the landscape of his search for an ideal community. As Simonetta de Filippis notes, Lawrence was often sharply critical of Italy, but it none the less represented to him 'everything England was not: freedom, the pagan landscape, the source of primitive passions, the authenticity of life, the way towards re-birth'. He at first found the Sicilian writer Giovanni Verga 'not at all good', describing *Cavalleria Rusticana* – best known to us as Pietro Mascagni's searing opera of love and betrayal – as 'a veritable blood-pudding of passion'. But the more he immersed himself in Italy the more he understood Verga's depictions of peasant life, telling Edward Garnett that in fact Verga was 'extraordinarily good', even 'Homeric', and he took on the challenge of translating him, remarking 'If I don't, I doubt if anyone else will – adequately, at least.'

For Leo Hamalian, Lawrence felt that Italy offered 'a kind of natural magic' not yet at that stage 'diminished by modern industry and tourism'. The Italian attitude toward the 'dictates of passion' was 'tolerant and subtle, and Lawrence, weary of English inhibition, felt that he could happily adjust to this less frigid psychological (as well as geographical) climate.' There was also religion: Alan Sillitoe, a later Midlands-born writer, has suggested that although he was brought up as an evangelical Christian, Lawrence deliberately travelled to Roman Catholic parts of the world – Italy, Mexico – 'where the female spirit of the Virgin Mary was in the ascendant, where mother-worship of the Latins was the norm', combined in the case of Mexico with Aztec sun worship and in the case of Italy with the legacy of the Etruscans. As Jill Franks notes, Lawrence fused the Resurrection and the Apocalyptic themes of Christianity with the pagan myths of rebirth to create 'a religion of his own'.

Three travel books about Italy by the ever-restless Lawrence are still published – and widely read – because of their vitality and descriptive power, even though they depict the Italy of a hundred years ago: *Twilight in Italy*, a collection of essays about his experiences on and near Lake Garda in 1912–13, published in 1916: *Sea and Sardinia*, the account of his visit to Sardinia in January 1921 while he was living in Sicily between 1919 and 1922; and *Sketches of Etruscan Places*, written in 1927 and published posthumously in 1932 simply as *Etruscan Places*. Lawrence, who on arrival at Lake Garda in 1912 with Frieda admitted he had hardly any knowledge of the language, by the end spoke 'clear and excellent Italian', according to Raul Mirenda, their landlord in Florence.

What he loved about Italians was their spontaneity and vitality. In his account of a performance of *Hamlet* at the village theatre by a travelling troupe, Lawrence notes the self-absorption in the audience of the Bersaglieri who 'sit close together in groups, so that there is a strange, corporal connexion between them. They have close cropped, dark, slightly bestial heads, and thick shoulders, and thick brown hands on each others' shoulders. When an act is over they pick up their cherished hats and fling on their cloaks and go into the hall.'

Long before his wife met Angelo Ravagli, Lawrence was fascinated by the Bersaglieri. They were 'like young, half-wild oxen, such strong, sturdy dark lads, thickly built and with strange hard heads, like young male caryatids'. There was 'a strange, hypnotic unanimity among them as they put on their plumed hats and go out together, always very close, as if their bodies must touch ... They are in love with one another.' Their leader, he observed at the theatre on Lake Garda, was 'very straight and solid, solid like a wall, with a dark, unblemished will. His cockfeathers slither in a profuse, heavy stream from his black oil-cloth hat, almost to his shoulder'. 'He is reminded of Agamemnon's soldiers on the seashore at Troy, except that they all look 'as if their real brain was stunned, as if there were another centre of physical consciousness from which they lived.'

This is in much the same vein as an observation a century earlier by the French novelist Stendhal when he was staying with his friend Fabio Pallavicini at Recco near Genoa in 1814 and recorded his envy of the local Italians on the Riviera, joyously unconscious of anything much beyond their daily existence in villages nestling among the vineyards and terraced fields: 'History, for them, is no more than the dates of accession and death of Popes and Kings,' Stendhal wrote amid the merrymaking of a local festa by the seashore. 'They have never had the misfortune to fall in love with mankind. They firmly believe that in a hundred years everything will be as it was a hundred years previously, and this fortunate mistake kills any spiritual concern over such matters.'

Lawrence evidently found this fatalism and connection with earthy realities stimulating. Within seven months of arriving at Lake Garda with Frieda, Lawrence had written the final version of *Sons and Lovers*, two plays, most of the poetry collection *Look! We Have Come Through* about his stormy relationship with Frieda, and had begun both the revised version of *The Lost Girl* and *The Sisters*, which would become *The Rainbow* and *Women in Love*. It is remarkable that he found the time to write *Twilight in Italy* at all, let alone the passionate passages in it which have stood the test of time.

He was stimulated not only by the people but by the Italian landscape itself. 'Conscience is sun awareness, and our deep instinct not to go against the sun,' he wrote in the poem *Conscience*. When he went back to Lerici on the Gulf of the Poets in November 1919 he wrote to Cecily Lambert: 'Yesterday Italy was at her best, such brilliant sun and sky … I shall go further south – feel I want to go further and further south – don't know why.' In the Mediterranean, he wrote to Cynthia Asquith from Capri the following year: one 'sheds ones avatars and recovers a lost self'.

The spell of Italy had been cast 13 years earlier, on Lake Garda. In *Twilight in Italy*, looking down on the lake he sees 'a blood-red sail like a butterfly breathing down on the blue water, whilst the earth on the near side gave off a green-silver smoke of olive trees, coming up and around the earth-coloured roofs'. But he knew that there were limits: just as in the poem *Snake* he understands that he and the serpent inhabit different worlds, so in *Twilight in Italy* he encounters an old woman with a dark red kerchief spinning and knows that she is beyond his grasp, as much part of the landscape as the stones on the hillside.

Lawrence had a sharp eye, as Anthony Burgess observed. Lawrence found the Sicilians 'terribly physically all over one another. They pour themselves one over the other like so much melted butter over parsnips. They catch each other under the chin, with a tender caress of the hand, and they

smile with sunny melting tenderness into each others faces.'
So they do, Burgess comments, 'but who but Lawrence
would have thought in terms of buttered parsnips?'

He was of course aware of, and alarmed by, the development of a different Italy, one in which – as in the West
as a whole – there was a movement towards 'the modern
money-driven neurotic life', with young Italians emigrat-
ing to America and either staying there or bringing back its
ethos and way of life, the dominance of machines and money.
Meeting Italians who worked in a textile factory in Switzerland, he wrote that 'it is the hideous rawness of the world of
men, the horrible, desolating harshness of the advance of the
industrial world upon the world of nature that is so painful.'

In *Women In Love* Hermione, who has spent her girlhood
in Italy and even speaks Italian to her cat, remarks to Rupert
Birkin that she is interested in Italy's 'coming to national consciousness' – to which, however, Birkin (Lawrence's *alter ego*)
retorts that this 'only means a sort of commercial-industrial
consciousness', adding 'I hate Italy and her national rant.'

Writing just before the First World War, Lawrence was
alarmed at the phenomenon of mass Italian emigration to
America: Italy was 'a country on the change, and suffering
acutely. Fifty years ago, almost every man was a peasant. In
one generation it has all changed.' There were also bouts of
irritation: in *Sea and Sardinia* Lawrence and Frieda find that
the ideal Italy of Anglo-Saxon dreams is in reality a land of
rude and obstructive officials, cheating shopkeepers, taxi
drivers and hoteliers, and often squalid towns which look
attractive enough from the sea but rather less attractive on
closer inspection.

Sea and Sardinia is often very funny, enlivened by his
constant disagreements with Frieda – 'an interfering female',
referred to as the queen bee, or q-b. But above all it reflects the
dichotomy between the real and the ideal Italy, all too familiar to anyone who has lived in the country for any length of
time. At Sorgono in the Sardinian interior Lawrence allows

himself almost incoherent rage at 'the degenerate aborigines, the dirty breasted host who *dared* to keep such an inn, the sordid villagers who had the baseness to squat their beastly human nastiness in this upland valley.' No picturesque villas, terracotta-lined swimming pools and Renaissance architecture here, then.

If tourism was under-developed in Sardinia the opposite was true of Venice, at least if *Lady Chatterley's Lover* is any guide: Connie goes to Venice in a trial separation from her husband, but finds 'sun-pinked bodies' heaped up like seals and altogether 'too many gondolas, too many motor-launches, too many steamers, too many pigeons, too many ices, too many cocktails, too many men-servants wanting tips, too many languages rattling, too much, too much sun, too much smell of Venice.' What Lawrence would have made of today's Venice, with residents all but outnumbered by day trippers, we can only imagine.

There was sometimes 'too much sun' in Tuscany too: 'It is still lovely to see the meadows lush green, instead of that parched Tuscany,' Lawrence wrote to Martin Secker from Austria in 1927, during his years at the Villa Mirenda. 'The Austrians are really very nice, so happy-go- lucky and easy, and on the whole, healthy and handsome. It is a relief to be here, after the friction and bossiness of Italy.' 'I'm not eager to go back to Italy,' he confirmed to Secker a month later. 'I like it here. Did Rina just go to Spotorno? Didn't you go away?'

In October, back in Florence, he was still in one of his anti-Italian moods: he found Tuscany 'warm and cloudy with bits of sun, very still', adding 'I'm really not very keen on being here – but Frieda loves it. The space indoors, and the quiet, I like – but suddenly I don't care for Italy any more – have a sort of revulsion from it – it seems so stupid, somehow.' He put this disenchantment down to his illness ('my health is far from satisfactory'), but the impression is that – like many expats – he found Italy seductive and irritating in equal measure. 'I was at Forte dei Marmi two weeks, not bad, but a place I should never love,' he wrote to Secker in 1929. 'Italy seems a bit *flat* to me, deflated – like a flat tyre. I don't like it much'. The muggy weather had given him 'one of my Italian colds, all hot and feverish inside. I seem only to get them in Italy.'

He found the ideal Italy not so much in modern times as among the tombs of the Etruscans, that mysterious race which at one time dominated central Italy but was exterminated by the Romans in an act of genocide – or as he memorably put it, a people 'whom the Romans, in their usual neighbourly fashion, wiped out entirely in order to make room for Rome with a very big R'. Precisely because so little is left of the Etruscans, apart from their painted tombs, Lawrence was free to imagine how they might have lived and behaved.

In his exploration of Etruscan territory north of Rome in March 1927 – Cerveteri, Tarquinia, Volterra – with his American friend Earl Brewster he found a lost ideal, a life-enhancing people – their symbols were the phallus and the womb (the ark) – which had been overcome by mechanistic, militaristic Rome but which Lawrence set out to resurrect, interpreting their tombs as copies of their 'homely and happy' houses when alive. He believed, rightly, that there were Etruscan traces in the local Tuscan population, with the local women displaying much the same traits he had seen in the tomb paintings.

He also found comfort in the Etruscan heritage as he approached his own death. Steeped in Christian imagery from his Nottingham boyhood, Lawrence rejected monotheism but was not an atheist. Instead he looked for hope and inspiration to the pagan, pre-Christian cultures, finding in the Etruscans a view of death as a 'pleasant continuance of life, with jewels and wine and flutes playing for the dance' and with the ship of death – the title of one of his last poems – loaded with cakes and wine for 'the dark flight down oblivion'. Lawrence believed he had found in the Etruscans a life affirming culture in which instinct was more important than reason, and the loins, not the brain, were the centre of life. By contrast, in the crucifixes of the Alps on his first Italian journey he had seen a 'worship of death' which was 'crude and sinister', even depraved, a 'form of reverting, turning back along the course of blood by which we have come'.

For Aldous Huxley – who knew him well – to be with Lawrence was 'a kind of adventure, a voyage of discovery into newness and otherness.' He 'looked at things with the eyes, so it seemed, of a man who had been at the brink of death and to whom, as he emerges from the darkness, the world reveals itself as unfathomably beautiful and mysterious.' He seemed to know 'what it was like to be a tree or a daisy or a breaking wave or even the mysterious moon itself. He could get inside the skin of an animal and tell you in the most convincing detail how it felt and how, dimly, inhumanly, it thought.' There was in Lawrence 'a continuously springing fountain of vitality' which went on welling up 'long after the time when, by all the rules of medicine, he should have been dead'.

This, in the end, was the secret of Italy and the Mediterranean for Lawrence – the 'continuously springing fountain of vitality'. Take this passage written during his stay in Sicily after his excursion to Syracuse 'We came back, and the world was lovely: our own house above the almond trees, and the sea in the cove below: Calabria glimmering like a changing opal away to the left, across the blue, bright straits and all the great blueness of the lovely dawn-sea in front, where the sun rose with a splendour like trumpets every morning, and me rejoicing like madness in this dawn, day-dawn, life-dawn, the dawn which is Greece, which is me.' In England, he wrote in *Etruscan Places*, 'winters and summers shadowily give place to one another. But in the sunny countries, change is the reality, and permanence is artificial and a condition of imprisonment.'

In the north, Lawrence said, 'man tends instinctively to imagine, to conceive that the sun is lighted like a candle, in an everlasting darkness, and that one day the candle will go out, the sun will be exhausted, and the everlasting dark will resume uninterrupted sway. But to the southerner, the sun is so dominant that if every phenomenal body disappeared out of the universe, nothing would remain but bright luminousness, sunniness.' The South, the Mediterranean, the ancient Greek landscape of southern Italy, all hold out the promise of re-birth. When the sun shines, Lawrence wrote, even death 'does not have many terrors. In the sunshine, even death is sunny.' And in his poem *The Sun in Me* he wrote: 'A sun will rise in me, I shall slowly resurrect'.

Postscript

'Far be it from me to suggest that all women should go running after gamekeepers for lovers. Far be it from me to suggest that they should be running after anybody.'

DHL, *A Propos of Lady Chatterley's Lover*

'THE THING TO REMEMBER about Lawrence's exile is that it enabled him to serve England, or at least England's literature, far better than if he had stayed at home.' So wrote Anthony Burgess in the preface to *Flame Into Being: The Life and Work of DH Lawrence*. Aldous Huxley makes much the same point in the introduction to his 1932 edition of Lawrence's letters, adding, however, that Lawrence 'never found a society to which he could belong'.

The nearest he came, I would suggest, is Italy. We have a tendency to airbrush out of our consciousness the fact that some of the greatest English, Scottish and Irish writers lived abroad; many of them, such as the Romantic poets, in Italy. James Joyce, who we associate with Dublin, in fact spent much of his life in Zurich and Paris, and lived for ten years in Trieste; Muriel Spark lived for nearly 40 years in Rome and Tuscany. Graham Greene lived at Antibes on the Côte d'Azur and then at Vevey on Lake Geneva, and in 1948 bought a house on Capri, Il Rosaio, which he kept and visited for over 40 years. Lawrence, too, spent most of his life outside England, but paradoxically this only reinforced his Englishness.

Some suggest that DH Lawrence is now unfashionable. To quote Birkin's final remark to Ursula Brangwen at the end of *Women in Love*, 'I don't believe that.' To modern ears his prose may sometimes seem overblown, with its talk of blood, phalluses and cosmic rhythms. But can we be sure the issues he so fearlessly confronted have been truly resolved? As he wrote in *A Propos of Lady Chatterley's Lover*, 'Man has little needs and deeper needs. We have fallen into the mistake of living from our little needs till we have almost lost our deeper needs in a sort of madness.'

It is true that even in his native Nottingham, as the University of Nottingham website frankly admits, he was for a long time regarded with 'disdain', partly because of the lingering scandal caused by his affair and elopement with Frieda Weekley. As a young man Lawrence attended the Day Training College of what was then University College, Nottingham (in Shakespeare Street, not the present campus) from 1906 to 1908 to study for a teaching diploma. From the college's point of view his affair with the wife of Professor Ernest Weekley – whom Lawrence himself admired at first – was not a wise move. As the university website puts it, 'Their marriage, and Weekley's great popularity with staff and students at University College, were certainly factors in the lack of interest shown in Lawrence's writings at Nottingham.' I remember arriving as a student at Nottingham some 35 years after Lawrence's death – and just six years after the *Lady Chatterley* trial – to find that although there was a bust of Lawrence in the university library, it was not exactly prominent.

But this has changed: there is now a Lawrence Collection of manuscripts, correspondence and books at Nottingham, described as 'one of the University's great resources'. There is even a bronze statue of Lawrence on campus, unveiled in 1994. His poetry and travel writings are more highly valued than ever, and his novels remain classics. *Women in Love* was dramatised for television in 2011, with Rosamund Pike as Gudrun and Rachael Stirling as Ursula. His lyrical, pulsating descriptions of the English countryside – in *The Rainbow*, for example, as well as *Lady Chatterley* and the poems and short stories – have never been surpassed. At the last count, there were six different film versions of *Lady Chatterley's Lover*, a novel which although it is not his best and now appears in some ways more outdated than outrageous, retains its power as a timeless story of love across the class divide and a call for honesty in relations between men and women.

Even the tired old cliché that Lawrence was a misogynist is finally under attack: in April 2013 Andrew Harrison of Nottingham University published a hitherto undiscovered letter which Lawrence wrote to John Middleton Murry's journal *Adelphi* in 1924, lambasting a male contributor for suggesting that beautiful women bore within themselves 'the seed of terrible, unmentionable evil'. This was an attitude which stemmed from 'meat-lust' for women, Lawrence wrote, adding that 'even the most beautiful woman is still a human creature'.

This will come as no surprise to those familiar with the musings of Rupert Birkin, Lawrence's alter ego in *Women in Love*. Men and women, he argues, should be 'two pure beings, each constituting the freedom of the other, balancing each other like two poles of one force'. For that matter, Lawrence's fiction is full of strong and independent-minded women, including Gudrun and Ursula Brangwen, Connie Chatterley – and Juliet/Rina in *Sun*.

'Why should I have to identify my life with a man's life?' Juliet asks herself as she considers the choice between her husband and the Italian peasant to whom she feels drawn. She is tempted to meet the peasant for an hour to make love to him – but on her terms, and for 'as long as the desire lasts, and no more'.

Perhaps it is time to re-assess DH Lawrence – as a feminist.

Dramatis Personae

Rosalind Baynes, briefly DH Lawrence's lover in 1920, died in 1973 at the age of 81.

Dorothy Brett remained for the rest of her life at Taos in New Mexico, and died there in 1973, at the age of 93.

Anna Marie Capellero, Rina's sister, known as Annie, married Edward Burrall Frysinger, a farmer from Texas whom she met while working for the Red Cross in Turin during the First World War. Frysinger divorced his first wife to marry Anna Marie and moved back to his native Illinois, working as a real estate agent in Chicago. The couple later moved to the West Coast. Anthea Secker remembers Anna Marie as 'rather fun. She was a completely different character to Rina, always very bubbly, and thin'. Anna Marie became a naturalised US citizen in March 1925, and she and Frysinger had two children. Frysinger died in Pasadena in 1963; Anna Marie moved to Manhattan Beach, a suburb of Los Angeles, where in old age she was interviewed in a local paper as an enthusiastic and energetic Republican Party campaigner who still had a trace of an English accent. She died in 1991, at the age of 93.

Luigi and Caterina Capellero are buried in the cemetery at Bene Vagienna. Luigi Capellero died at Savona on 13 June 1931, and his wife Caterina, née Gazzera, at Alassio on 27

January 1937, but Rina had her parents re-buried together at Bene Vagienna, next to the Gazzera family mausoleum. The Latin dedication on their tombstone, from the Roman Catholic Mass for the Dead, reads 'Requiem Aeternam Dona Eis, Domine et Lux Perpetua Luceat Eis': 'Grant Them Eternal Rest Lord, and Let Perpetual Light Shine on Them'.

Lucy Lamont died in 1953, at the age of 96.

Frieda Lawrence married Angelo Ravagli in the US in 1950, and died six years later, on 11 August 1956, the morning of her 77th birthday. She was buried beside Lawrence's shrine, to the sound of a recording of her voice reading Lawrence's poems and Psalm 121: 'I will lift up mine eyes unto the hills, from whence cometh my help'. Her tomb, made of Colorado granite, is adorned with her coat of arms and photograph.

Carlo Lovioz died at Locarno on 29 May 1954, at the age of 67.

Viola Meynell, Martin's first fiancee, became a well-known novelist and poet: she died in 1956, at the age of 71.

Angelo Ravagli returned to Spotorno after Frieda's death in 1956 and was taken back by the long-suffering Serafina. In his 1994 memoir *Hermit in Paris* (*Eremita a Parigi*) the Italian writer Italo Calvino recalled visiting 'Angelino' at Taos after Frieda's death and speaking to him in Ligurian dialect, since although Ravagli was born in the Romagna 'he is really from Spotorno'. Calvino found that Ravagli 'does not really know what to do with himself in Taos on his own'. Ravagli's American divorce and his marriage in 1950 to Frieda – there was no divorce in Italy until 20 years later – were not recognised in Italy. He died in 1975, at the age of 84, and is buried in the cemetery at Spotorno. Serafina had died six years earlier, in 1969, also at Spotorno.

Adrian Secker went to Ampleforth and claimed to be the only English public schoolboy who spent the Second World War in a prison camp. When war broke out in September 1939, Rina was not at first concerned since Italy was not involved: she and Adrian were on holiday in Italy and headed for Rome, with the idea that he could enrol in the University there. Rome in 1939, Adrian later recalled in an unpublished memoir of his wartime imprisonment, 'encouraged the illusion' that nothing much had happened: he and Rina stayed at the Hotel Eden, above the Spanish Steps, with trips back to Alassio for sea air. Rina rented a studio in Via Margutta, the artists' quarter near Babington's Tea Rooms and the Spanish Steps, and sculpted. Even when Mussolini finally sided with Hitler and declared war on the Allies from his balcony on Piazza Venezia in 1940 – an event which the young Adrian witnessed – Rina did not react: 'My mother continued sculpting, but was plainly worried for me ... With hindsight, we were lax to drift on.' Rina had dual nationality, but he was 16, British and 'approaching military age', and so was taken to Merano in the South Tyrol and placed under police surveillance there as an enemy alien. Rina and his stepfather Carlo joined him there, first at an hotel, later in a rented house. But in 1943, after the Italian armistice with the Allies and the subsequent occupation of Italy by Nazi Germany, Adrian was arrested, driven with others 'in an open truck through the jeering population of Merano', and transferred first to a Nazi work camp at Innsbruck in Austria. Rina, not surprisingly, was 'shattered' by his 'summary removal' from Merano, Adrian recorded later. Some of Martin Secker's friends suspected Rina had calculated that Adrian would be interned in Italy and thus would sit out the war. She had not however foreseen the Nazi occupation. 'So Adrian is caught!' Faith Mackenzie wrote to Martin on 7 October 1940. 'I suppose it's just what she wanted. But possibly not what he wanted.' Adrian was transferred to a German internment camp at Kreuzburg in German Upper Silesia (now the Polish town of Kluczbork),

Ilag VIII-B. With Russian troops poised to capture Kreuz-burg toward the end of the war, Adrian and other POWs were evacuated by train to a camp at Spittal in Austria. After the war he was taken on as a trainee reporter with Reuters in Rome before returning to England to read modern languages and then international law and medieval history at Cambridge. After graduation he was given a full-time job with Reuters reporting from Bonn, moved to Paris as a correspondent for the *Daily Telegraph*, and in 1966 joined the *Financial Times* as Foreign Manager, increasing overseas revenues for the paper by putting out a monthly foreign supplement backed by advertising. In 1958 Adrian married Anthea Fairfax-Ross. He died in 1998, at Bridgefoot, at the age of 74. He was, *The Times* obituary said, 'a distinguished foreign correspondent of a kind now almost extinct', courteous, a generous host and a 'firm all weather friend', an affectionate husband and father, and a man of charm and wit. Lord Drogheda, the *FT* chair-man, said Adrian had had an 'agreeably vague manner which concealed a very shrewd judgement'.

Martin Secker's publishing firm went into receivership in 1935 and was bought by Fredric Warburg and Roger Sen-house, taking the new name Secker and Warburg. The firm later became part of Random House, and in 2005 was merged with the Harvill Press to form Harvill Secker. Secker at first stayed on with Secker and Warburg in charge of production, but left after two years to join The Richards Press, until he retired in 1960. Martin re-married on 17 February 1955: his new wife was Sylvia Hope Broadbent, née Gibsone. 'I am delighted to hear of your marriage to that delightful girl,' Faith Mackenzie wrote to Martin. 'The best news I've heard for a long time.' He was increasingly blind in old age: on New Year's Eve 1963 he wrote to Rina at the Canberra Hotel in Cannes to thank her for her Christmas wishes, adding 'My eyes are getting very dim and Sylvia has to read the paper to me'. He died in 1978, and Sylvia Secker in 1999.

Barbara Weekley had a nervous breakdown at Vence in 1930 after Lawrence's death; Frieda is said to have connived with a local doctor in prescribing sexual relations with a male servant at the Villa Robermond as part of the cure. Her family were horrified; her brother Monty and sister Elsa took her back to England, where she fully recovered. In May 1934, four years after Lawrence's death, Barby married John Stuart Barr, a Scottish journalist and left-wing politician: he died in 1986. She later lived near Florence, and died in 1998. When the jury found in favour of publication of *Lady Chatterley* at the 1960 trial, Barby observed 'I feel as if a window has been opened and fresh air has blown right through England.'

A Note on Sources

The letters and papers of Rina and Martin Secker are preserved in the Secker family archive at Bridgefoot, Iver, Buckinghamshire, together with letters to Rina Secker from DH Lawrence and Frieda.

Like all who write about DH Lawrence I acknowledge a debt to *The Letters of DH Lawrence*, published in eight volumes by the Cambridge University Press; and the 1932 edition of the letters edited by Aldous Huxley. Also, the monumental three volume Cambridge biography, *DH Lawrence: The Early Years 1885–1912* by John Worthen (1991), *DH Lawrence: Triumph to Exile 1912–1922* by Mark Kinkead-Weekes (1996) and *DH Lawrence: Dying Game 1922–1930* by David Ellis (1998); John Worthen's one volume biography, *DH Lawrence: The Life of An Outsider* (2005); and biographies and studies listed in the bibliography, notably those by Keith Sagar, Brenda Maddox, Harry T. Moore, Janet Byrne and Geoff Dyer.

I have also drawn on Adrian Secker's notes in the Bridgefoot archives, including carbon copies he made of his replies to the editors of Lawrence's letters; Lawrence's letters to Martin Secker, 1911–30, published privately in a limited edition of 500 copies and made available to me at Bridgefoot; Secker's letters to Lawrence, also privately published, in 1970; the 2007 Penguin edition of Lawrence's writings on Italy, with introductions by Tim Parks and Anthony Burgess; Keith Sagar's invaluable *DH Lawrence: A Calendar Of His*

Works; and Italian studies of the British relationship with the Riviera, including *Vacanze a Spotorno* by Giulano Cerutti, *The British Colonies in the Italian Riviera in '800 and '900* by Alessandro Bartoli, and *Daniel Hanbury and the British colony of Alassio* by Maura Muratorio.

The recollections of Lawrence, Alassio and Spotorno by Frieda's daughter Barbara Weekley Barr (Barby) provided insights, as did Lina Waterfield's memories of Lawrence in *Castle in Italy*, Compton Mackenzie's memoirs, *My Life and Times*, especially the fifth volume, or 'Octave Five', covering the years 1915–23, and a conversation at Spotorno with Angelo Ravagli in the early 1970s conducted by the Italian author Alberto Bevilacqua and published in Italy in 2002 as *Attraverso Il Tuo Corpo* ('Through My Body'), of which I have made selective use.

Bevilacqua's title is taken from a prose poem he claims Lawrence wrote for Ravagli and Frieda, which reads: 'Through your body, my friend, I have re-found the last breath of life in my body, through your body, Frieda, I have re-found the last splendour of the senses which you have lived through the body of Angelo, and through my body you two have given your bodies the sense of a God who, if we ask him to, takes on the substance of the whole which is the desire of love'. ('*Attraverso il tuo corpo, amico mio, ho ritrovato l'ultima vita del mio corpo, attraverso il tuo corpo, Frieda, ho ritrovato l'ultimo splendore dei sensi che tu hai vissuto attraverso il corpo di Angelo, e attraverso il mio corpo voi avete dato ai vostri corpi il senso di un Dio che, se glielo chiediamo, prende sostanza nel tutto che è desiderio d'amore*').

Bevilacqua had planned to write a play about Lawrence and Spotorno for Giorgio Strehler's Piccolo Teatro in Milan; instead he turned his conversations with Ravagli into a novel. He claimed that his recollections were '*esattissime*' (extremely exact) when I interviewed him in Rome in September 2010, adding that he had told 'the absolute truth' in his account of life at the Villa Bernarda. 'I devoted a lot of time to my book to avoid any ambiguity or mystery ... Ravagli was old by then and had just been knocked down by a motor scooter (*motoretto*) which had left him with a slight limp. However his face was very young, with a look which was full of extreme curiosity and rather disturbing.'

Bevilacqua, who died on 9 September 2013, never produced the original of the prose poem, and Ravagli's memories as recorded in a novel written so long after the events it describes should obviously be treated with caution. I have left open, for example, whether Frieda went to bed with Ravagli immediately (as Bevilacqua has it) or later. On the other hand this does not mean that all of Ravagli's memories as recorded by Bevilacqua are invalid: on the contrary, I find some passages thoroughly convincing, including Ravagli's description of Frieda's behaviour in showing him round the villa and her fury over the Hotel Miramare episode.

Endnotes

Introduction

1. Lawrence wanted to write *Lady Chatterley* all his life: Frieda Lawrence, foreword to *The First Lady Chatterley*, published in the US in 1944, by Heinemann in 1972 and Penguin in 1973.

2. Ravagli showed Frieda round the villa: Alberto Bevilacqua, *Attraverso il tuo corpo*, 2002, p. 28ff. On Bevilacqua's reliability as an observer see Note on Sources.

3. 'My search for Rina and Lawrence began': 'Doors Open on Writers' Inspiration', in The Register, *The Times*, 20 March 2004. Another English legacy is the museum at Bordighera founded by the botanist and archaeologist Clarence Bicknell: see the website www.clarencebicknell.com, run by his great great nephew, Marcus Bicknell.

4. 'We got here yesterday': DHL to Curtis Brown, from Spotorno, 16 November 1925.

5. Rina ought to write her literary reminiscences: Adrian Secker to Rina Lovioz, from Bridgefoot, 14 March 1962 and Rina to Adrian Secker in the prison camp at Kreuzburg, from Merano, 9 January 1944, Bridgefoot Archive. Bewley (1888–1969) was Irish Minister Plenipotentiary in Berlin in the 1930s.

1: Nottingham to Lake Garda

1. The Lawrence's arrival at Spotorno by train on a 'quite summery' day: Rina Secker to Martin Secker, from Spotorno, 16 November 1925, Bridgefoot Archive. The former railway line was removed – together with the old wooden station buildings – and re-routed in 1977.

2. 'It's a nice old house': DHL to Blanche Knopf, the wife of his American publisher, 23 November 1925.

3. *The Origins of Prohibition*: by JA Krout, published by Knopf, Lawrence's own publisher in the United States.

4. 'There is something forever cheerful': DHL to Edward McDonald, from Spotorno, 11 January 1926.

5. 'It is a relief to be by the Mediterranean': DH Lawrence, in the essay *Europe versus America*, November 1925.

6. 'Italy feels very familiar': DHL to Earl and Achsah Brewster, from Spotorno, 25 November 1925.

7. Frieda Weekley's meeting with DHL in 1912: *Not I But the Wind, the Autobiography of Frieda Lawrence*, pp. 4ff.; *The Married Man, A Life of DH Lawrence*, Brenda Maddox, 1994, p. 113ff.; and John Worthen, *DH Lawrence, the Early Years 1885 to 1912*, 1991, p. 371ff. Some accounts suggest Frieda had Lawrence in bed within 20 minutes of his arrival: others find this unlikely given that the Mapperley house was full of children and servants.

8. Frieda an aristocrat: her father was Baron Friedrich Ernst Emil Ludwig von Richthofen, her mother was Anna Elise Lydia Marquier, from an aristocratic family of French origin.

9. 'Frieda was pretty and voluptuous': Janet Byrne, *A Genius for Living, A Biography of Frieda Lawrence*, 1995, p. 31. In 1950 Martin Secker wrote to Rina that he was sending her Richard Aldington's book on Lawrence which had 'a splendid photograph, new to me, of Frieda as a young girl, most good-looking and attractive'. He said Frieda had clearly been an '*echt deutsche Backfisch*, if ever there was one', using the German word for a pretty

adolescent girl (literally 'fish to fry'). Martin Secker to
Rina Lovioz, from Bridgefoot, 5 May 1950. Bridgefoot
Archive.

10. Lawrence's parents: 'I was born hating my father',
    Lawrence wrote to the Aberdeen poet and critic Rachel
    Annand Taylor, adding that by contrast there was 'a kind
    of bond between me and my mother'. He later revised
    this view, accepting that his mother had taunted his
    father, who had had a hard life in an area scarred by the
    industrial revolution. DHL to Rachel Annand Taylor,
    from Eastwood, 3 December 1910.

11. 'What was then University College, Nottingham': it
    opened in 1881. The building is now part of Nottingham
    Trent University. Lawrence disliked the later university
    campus and wrote a sardonic poem beginning 'In
    Nottingham, that dismal town/Where I went to school
    and college/they've built a new university/for a new
    dispensation of knowledge'.

12. Other women in his life: Alice Dax said she 'gave Bert
    sex' to release his creative energies and praised his sexual
    stamina; he was also close to Agnes Holt and Helen
    Corke, fellow teachers in Croydon, though as far as is
    known neither went to bed with him (neither did Louie
    for that matter). The agonies of youthful sexual longing
    are the theme of his first two novels, *The White Peacock*
    and *The Trespasser*.

13. Lawrence seeks Weekley's advice on Germany: an
    additional reason was that his aunt Ada Beardsley had
    married the Cambridge orientalist Fritz Krenkow, and
    they were living near Trier in Germany.

14. 'Travelled to Metz': their adventure came to light
    following a farcical episode in which Lawrence, busy
    making notes for an article on *Fortified Germany* – Metz
    was a garrison town – was arrested for trespassing in
    a military zone. He gave as a reference Frieda's father,
    who extricated Lawrence from the police but packed

him off to Trier, where Frieda joined him. According to David Garnett Lawrence's real offence was not spying but making love to Frieda in the Metz fortress. David Garnett, *Frieda and Lawrence* in Stephen Spender, op. cit., p. 38.

15. 'Offering herself to a no doubt startled woodcutter': David Garnett recorded the incident, saying Lawrence 'must have told me'. Garnett in Stephen Spender op. cit., p. 39. The Harold Hobson incident: Lawrence and Frieda took a room in a farmhouse at Mayrhofen where they were joined after a week by David Garnett and his friend Hobson, an engineer and son of the left-wing economist and journalist JA (John Atkinson) Hobson, author of *Imperialism*.

16. Riva on Lake Garda 'quite beautiful and perfectly Italian': DHL to Edward Garnett, 7 September 1912.

17. 'Out here seems so much freer than England': DHL to Louie Burrows, 15 September 1912.

2: Gargano to Lerici

1. 'I am here on the border of Italy', DHL to Alice Dax, from Riva, 17 September 1912.

2. 'A funny place, rather decayed': DHL to Louie Burrows, from Riva, 15 September 1912.

3. GM Trevelyan on the Bersaglieri from *Scenes from Italy's War*, 1919, pp. 83–6. Trevelyan was a generous donor to Sir Walter Becker's ambulance unit near Turin: see Chapter 3.

4. 'They are beautiful creatures': Frieda Lawrence to David Garnett, from Gargnano, 19 November 1912.

5. Lawrence on the Bersaglieri and the Villa Igea: letter to Edward Garnett, from Gargnano, 3 October 1912. Lawrence wrote 'ceccia' in Italian for persimmons: the normal word is 'cachi', an Italian transliteration of Kaki, the botanical term for Japanese persimmons.

6. 'I live in sunshine and happiness': DHL to Ernest Collings, from Villa Igea, 7 November 1912.

7. Hobson turned up without warning: 'Harold Hobson is here and it's very jolly' DHL to Arthur McLeod, from Gargnano, 17 December 1912.

8. 'In the morning I often lie in bed': from *The Spinner and the Monks*; 'rows of naked pillars' from *The Lemon Gardens*, both in *Twilight in Italy*.

9. 'Italy is a country to keep you in a temper': DHL to Violet Monk, from Taormina, 12 October 1921.

10. 'My great religion is a belief in the blood': DHL to Ernest Collings, from Gargnano, 17 January 1913. 'One must love Italy if one has lived there' DHL to Arthur McLeod, from Irschenhausen, near Munich, 26 April 1913. See also *Memories I* by Julian Huxley, Penguin 1972, p. 153.

11. 'I don't know any Italian, but it doesn't matter': DHL to Louie Burrows, from Riva, 15 September 1912. In his letter to David Garnett, dated 11 September 1912 , Lawrence says the '10 Italian words' he knew included *casa* for house and *d'affitare* for to let.

12. 'Evidently a quick learner': *Ma basta*! Lawrence wrote to Dorothy Brett from Spotorno in November 1925, '*Non usciamo mai fuori della bisogna dei soldi*' – 'But enough! We are never free of the need for money', and to Earl Brewster the following February: '*Corraggio! Bisogna farsi corraggio! E sempre pazienza*!' – 'Courage, we need to take courage, and always have patience!' DHL to Dorothy Brett, from Spotorno, 25 November 1925 and to Earl Brewster, from Spotorno 11 February 1926.

13. San Gaudenzio: Antonia Cyriax, a friend of the Garnetts (referred to in Lawrence's letters as 'Mrs Anthony'), was hiding at the farm from her crazed Swedish artist husband, and needed company. On the Capelli family see Colm Kerrigan, *Newsletter of the DH*

Lawrence Society No 92 Part 2. DHL on Mrs Anthony and the deserted lemon house: *Twilight in Italy*, in the collection *DH Lawrence in Italy*, Penguin edition, 1999, pp. 41ff.

14. Lawrence and Frieda meet Lady Cynthia Asquith: *Remember and Be Glad, Autobiography of Lady Cynthia Asquith*, 1952.

15. 'I walked all the way from Schaffhausen': DHL to Edward Garnett, from Lerici, 30 September 1913. See also *Italians In Exile* and *The Return Journey* in *Twilight in Italy*.

16. Lawrence and Frieda 'thinking of Lerici': DHL to Lady Cynthia Asquith, from Irschenhausen, 20 August 1913.

17. 'Jolly good food, wine, and all included': DHL to Edward Garnett, from Lerici, 30 September 1913. The hotel is now called the Hotel Shelley e Delle Palme.

18. 'Frieda *will* hire a piano': DHL to Lady Cynthia Asquith, from Fiascherino, 25 November 1913.

19. 'I am so happy with the place we have at last discovered': DHL to Edward Garnett from Lerici, 30 September 1913. 'We have got a tiny four-roomed cottage amongst the vines': DHL to the American publisher Mitchell Kennerley, from the Villino Ettore Gambrosier, Fiascherino, 5 October 1913. Lawrence used the spelling Gambrosier: locally the name is also spelt 'Gambroisier'.

20. 'If you can't be a real poet you'll drown like one, anyhow': Frieda Lawrence, *Not I, But the Wind*, p. 63.

21. 'The full moon shines on the sea': DHL to Sir Edward Marsh from Fiascherino, 14 October 1913.

22. 'I think Shelley a million thousand times more beautiful than Milton': DHL to Sir Edward Marsh, from Fiascherino, 17 December 1913.

23. DHL on the beauty of oranges and olives in the garden, DHL to Willie Hopkin: from Fiascherino, 18 December 1913. See also *La Baia di Lorenzo* by Silvio Vallero (Ezechiele Azzarini's grandson) and Pietro Ferrari.

The village wedding was interrupted by an unexpected visit from three of Marsh's Georgian poets – Robert Trevelyan, WW Gibson and Lascelles Abercrombie – who had come to see the Waterfields. Lina Waterfield was the granddaughter of Lucie Duff Gordon and the niece of Janet Ross, author of *Leaves from our Tuscan Kitchen* and chatelaine of the Poggio Gherardo estate near Florence, which the Waterfields eventually took over. See her memoir *Castle in Italy* and in *A Tuscan Childhood* by her daughter Kinta (Carinthia) Beevor.

24. The return to England: DHL to Arthur McLeod, from Fiascherino, 2 June 1914. Lawrence said he intended to return in September.

25. Lawrence's walk across Switzerland: he walked with AP Lewis, a Maxim-Vickers engineer he had met in Italy. DHL to Edward Garnett from Fiascherino, 5 June 1914. Nothing is known about Lewis; he may have been one of the men who accompanied DHL shortly afterwards in the Lake District, when Lawrence met the Ukrainian Jewish emigre SS Koteliansky, who became a lifelong friend. Catherine Carswell, *The Savage Pilgrimage*, 1932 pp. 23–4.

26. The wedding: Frieda Lawrence, *Not I, But the Wind*, p. 70. Her divorce absolute from Professor Weekley was published in *The Times* on 27 April 1914, while she and Lawrence were in Fiascherino. The witnesses at the ceremony on 13 July were Katherine Mansfield, John Middleton Murry and Gordon Campbell, an Irish lawyer Frieda and Lawrence had met at Broadstairs, and at whose South Kensington home they were staying. Lawrence bought the wedding ring on the way to the Register Office.

27. Lawrence's reaction to the First World War: *Remember and Be Glad, the autobiography of Lady Cynthia Asquith*, quoted in *DH Lawrence: Interviews and Recollections*, edited by Norman Page, 1981, Vol. 1, pp. 97ff: DHL to

Lady Cynthia Asquith, from Greatham, 31 January 1915.
See also Stephen Spender, *DH Lawrence, England and
the War* in Stephen Spender, op. cit., pp. 71–6; and Paul
Delany, *DH Lawrence's Nightmare: The Writer and His
Circle In the Years Of the Great War*, 1979.

28. 'I am very much flattered by your offer': DHL to Martin
    Secker, from Croydon, 12 June 1911.

29. Frieda and Lawrence at Chesham: Compton
    Mackenzie, *My Life and Times, Octave IV 1907–1914*,
    pp. 221–5. He gives another version in his collection
    of essays *On Moral Courage*, 1962, pp. 104ff. Oddly,
    Mackenzie does not mention Martin Secker in his
    account, writing only that he and his fellow novelist
    Gilbert Cannan went to visit Frieda and Lawrence at
    Chesham: Secker himself however is quite clear that he,
    Mackenzie and Cannan were all there. In the Foreword
    to his *Letters From A Publisher* Secker writes that he
    visited the Cannans several times, and on one occasion
    'during the hot, dry August of 1914' was accompanied
    by Compton Mackenzie, 'at that time staying with me in
    Iver … After lunch Gilbert suggested we should visit the
    Lawrences who were living not far off in a small modern
    workman's cottage, where we met Lawrence and Frieda
    for the first time.'

30. The move to Greatham: to repay Viola Meynell,
    Lawrence gave daily lessons to her niece to prepare
    her for St Paul's Girls School, which Barbara and Elsa
    Weekley also attended. The move to Hampstead:
    Catherine Carswell: *The Savage Pilgrimage*, pp. 34–5.
    Lawrence was unaware that Catherine had lost her
    job of reviewing for the *Glasgow Herald* after ten years
    because she had given *The Rainbow* a favourable notice,
    op. cit. p. 45.

31. 'Further influential friends and admirers': among
    others the philosopher Bertrand Russell, the novelists
    Aldous Huxley and EM Forster, the journalist

Catherine Carswell and her barrister husband Donald, and Michael Arlen of *The Green Hat* fame, on whom Michaelis in *Lady Chatterley's Lover* is said to be based.

32. The banning of *The Rainbow*: having divided the story of the Brangwen sisters, Ursula and Gudrun, into two parts, Lawrence called the first part *The Rainbow*. Viola Meynell typed the manuscript for him. The novel was published by Methuen but subsequently prosecuted for obscenity, and Methuen said they regretted having issued it in the first place. Some sources suggest the prosecution was instigated by a body called the National Purity League. This however derives from a remark made by DHL intended as a joke (see his letter to Thomas Dunlop, 16 December 1915):

33. The Lawrences in Cornwall suspected of spying: Catherine Carswell, op. cit. pp. 84–100, and Frieda Lawrence, *Not I, But the Wind*, pp. 77–86. Lawrence and Frieda lived first at Porthcothan near Padstow and then at Higher Tregerthen near Zennor, not far from Land's End. Frieda was, she wrote in her memoirs, regarded as a 'Hunwife in a foreign country'. Lawrence was furious with her when she started jumping and running while holding a white scarf aloft, shouting at her 'Can't you see they'll think you're signalling to the enemy?!' According to Compton Mackenzie, the coastguards' suspicions were reinforced by the fact that Lawrence had painted the cottage roof in bright colours.

34. 'For two years they survived': in London the Lawrences stayed with the poet Dollie Radford in Hampstead and then in a bed-sit at Mecklenburgh Square owned by Hilda Doolittle, the American poet HD, wife of the poet Richard Aldington. In Berkshire they stayed at Chapel Farm Cottage in the village of Hermitage, five miles from Newbury, lent to them by Dollie Radford. In the Midlands Lawrence, with help from Ada, found a bungalow on the edge of Middleton-by-Wirksworth

in Derbyshire, the home village of Lawrence's mother's family, the Beardsalls.

35. Lawrence's prediction of another war: from *The Flowers of the Forest* by David Garnett, 1955 p. 190

3: Capri to Sicily

1. Sir Walter Becker's hospital in Turin: it was transferred to the Royal Army Medical Corps in May 1918.

2. Italy 'does all her weeping in the press': DHL to Lady Cynthia Asquith, 8 November 1919.

3. 'A note from the writer Norman Douglas': Douglas, the brilliant author of the novel *South Wind* and whimsical but erudite travel books such as *Siren Land* and *Old Calabria*, was later angered by Lawrence's caricature of him as James Argyll in *Aaron's Rod*, published in 1922. However he was crucial in having *Lady Chatterley's Lover* published by Pino Orioli, the Florentine bookshop owner and publisher who was Douglas' close companion for years and who issued some of Douglas' own works when they ran into censorship problems in England.

4. The statue of David: in *Aaron's Rod*: Lawrence says David stands 'in the position Michelangelo chose for him'. The original was moved in to the Accademia Gallery in 1873 and replaced by a copy in 1910.

5. 'Here am I on my lonely-o, waiting for Frieda': DHL to Gertrude Cooper, a childhood friend who suffered from TB and lived with his sister Ada, from Florence, 20 November 1919.

6. Frieda's reaction to Florence: from *Not I, But the Wind*, p. 92.

7. Abruzzo 'a bit staggeringly primitive': DHL to Rosalind Baynes, from Picinisco, 16 December 1919. Rosalind Baynes, nee Thornycroft, lived at Hermitage near Newbury and was the sister of Joan Farjeon, an artist

and wife of the drama critic, theatre manager and playwright Herbert Farjeon, brother of the children's writer Eleanor Farjeon. Orazio Cervi is portrayed in *The Lost Girl* as Pancrazio, uncle of Ciccio, the novel's Italian hero. Rosalind's frequently absent husband was the psychologist and disciple of Carl Jung, Helton Godwin Baynes; they divorced in 1921, and she married the art historian Arthur (AE) Popham. She is assumed to be one of the models for the character of Lady Chatterley, whose father is described as a Royal Academician.

8. The journey south to Capri: DHL to WE and SA Hopkin, from Capri, 9 January 1920, and Catherine Carswell, op. cit., p. 128. 'Picinisco was too icy-mountainous': DHL to Martin Secker from Capri, 27 December 1919. Frieda and Lawrence in Capri, Compton Mackenzie, *My Life and Times, Octave Five, 1915–1923*, 1966, pp. 164–8. Mackenzie says Lawrence wrote *Fantasia of the Unconscious* on the typewriter, but in fact Lawrence wrote *Psychoanalysis and the Unconscious* on Capri in January 1920: he did not begin *Fantasia of the Unconscious* until June 1921, in Baden-Baden.

9. 'They also discussed an expedition to the South Sea islands': a recurring fantasy of Lawrence's. DHL continued to discuss it with Mackenzie by post after he had left Capri for Sicily: Compton Mackenzie, *My Life and Times Octave Five 1915–1923*, 1966, pp. 184–5.

10. 'Capri 'little more than a stewpot of semi-literary cats': DHL to Catherine Carswell, 5 February 1920. Elizabeth Gaskell's *Cranford*, published in 1851, was modelled on Knutsford in Cheshire.

11. Lawrence prefers Sicily to Capri: DHL to Fritz Krenkow, 20 March 1920. Also Compton Mackenzie, *My Life and Times Octave Five 1915–1923*, 1966, pp. 169–72 and pp. 177–9. *The Lost Girl* was a re-working of

an earlier 1913 story, *The Insurrection of Miss Houghton*, in which Alvina Houghton, a girl from a small town in the Midlands, marries an Italian, Ciccio, inspired by their landlord at Taormina, Francesco Cacopardo. The idea of Sicily had been planted in Lawrence's mind by one of Norman Douglas' friends in Florence, Maurice Magnus, a homosexual American poseur and former manager of the dancer Isadora Duncan. Lawrence was unaccountably indulgent toward Magnus, who committed suicide on Malta in November 1920. He appears in *The Lost Girl* as the impresario Mr May.

12. The Villa Fontana Vecchia and Sicily: DHL to Rosalind Baynes, 15 March 1920, to John Ellingham Brooks, 31 March 1920, to Jessica Brett Young, 31 March 1920, and to Lady Cynthia Asquith, 7 May 1920. Mount Etna 'witch-like under heaven': from *Sea and Sardinia*.

13. Lawrence and Frieda 'settled for a trip to Malta': they went with the actress Mary Cannan, a former neighbour at Chesham who had become one of the Capri expats following her divorce from the increasingly deranged novelist Gilbert Cannan. Mary had accompanied Lawrence and Frieda to Sicily, and had helped them to find the Villa Fontana Vecchia. Mary Cannan was the former wife of JM Barrie of *Peter Pan* fame, for whom her second husband Gilbert Cannan had worked as a secretary.

14. On Rosalind Baynes's affair with Lawrence, see the account by Brenda Maddox in her biography of Lawrence, *The Married Man*, pp. 278ff., of a memoir left by Rosalind Thornycroft (Rosalind Baynes) privately published in 1991; and *Among the Bohemians* by Virginia Nicholson, 2002. Rosalind had moved to Florence in January 1920. After sleeping with Rosalind, Lawrence wrote a series of highly erotic poems, ostensibly about fruit, most notably *Figs* and *Medlars and Sorb Apples*.

15. 'I expect Frieda here today': DHL to Compton Mackenzie, from Venice, 7 October 1920.

16. 'We got back here last week': DHL letters to Compton Mackenzie quoted in *My Life and Times Octave Five 1915–1923*, 1966, p. 191.

4: Sardinia to Spotorno

1. 'After another interlude in Germany': in March 1921 Frieda left for Baden Baden to visit her family when her sister Else sent a telegram saying their mother Anna had suffered a heart attack. Lawrence accused Frieda of fabricating the emergency and refused to go, but eventually joined her in April, admitting he was bored and lonely. Lawrence and Frieda spent the summer in the Black Forest and the Austrian Tyrol and returned to Taormina by way of Florence, where Mary Cannan and the Carswells were staying. According to Catherine Carswell Lawrence, now 37, was looking a more prosperous *signore* thanks to the sales of his stories in America. Catherine Carswell, *The Savage Pilgrimage*, 1932, pp. 157–8.

2. Lawrence and Frieda had separate bedrooms: at the Hotel Krone. See Janet Byrne, op cit pp. 249–50. 'The sex-idea burned out of one': from Lawrence's *Fantasia of the Unconscious*, 1922 'I give up knowing anything about love': DHL to Earl and Achsah Brewster, from Baden Baden, 15 May 1921.

3. 'If I hadn't my own stories to amuse myself with I should die': DHL to Earl Brewster, from Taormina, 2 November 1921. DHL 'done with Italy': Catherine Carswell, op. cit., p. 154. 'The country is sickening': DHL to Mary Cannan, from Taormina, 5 December 1921. The Villa Fontana Vecchia did not lose its literary connections: it was later occupied by Truman Capote.

4. Mabel Dodge Sterne: Mabel was married to Maurice Sterne, a Russian-born sculptor. She had previously

lived with her second husband, Edwin Dodge, an architect from Boston, in the magnificent Renaissance Villa Curonia at Arcetri, south of Florence, where she entertained among others André Gide, Gertrude Stein and Eleanora Duse.

5. Lawrence 'did not take to Ceylon': the passage was paid for by the award to *The Lost Girl* of the newly founded James Tait Black prize for fiction, worth 100 pounds. Lawrence passed the journey translating *Mastro don Gesualdo* by Giovanni Verga, the Sicilian writer, who died in 1922. According to an Italian scholar Lawrence made errors in translation but captured Verga's 'sensuality and melancholia'. Mary Corsani, *DH Lawrence e L'Italia*, 1965, pp. 88ff.

6. Frieda and Lawrence fall out in Mexico City: account by the American poet Witter Bynner, quoted in David Ellis, *DH Lawrence: Dying Game, 1922–1930*, 1998, p. 105. Bynner appears as Owen Rhys in *The Plumed Serpent*. 'I feel so cross with Lawrence': Frieda Lawrence to Adele Seltzer, wife of Lawrence's American publisher, quoted in David Ellis, op. cit., p. 124.

7. The Cafe Royal dinner: see Catherine Carswell's memoir of Lawrence, *The Savage Pilgrimage*, and *Lawrence and Brett: a Friendship*, by Dorothy Brett. The dinner was attended by Frieda, Catherine Carswell, her husband Donald, Dorothy Brett, John Middleton Murry, Mary Cannan, SS Koteliansky and the Polish-Jewish artist Mark Gertler, the model for the character of Loerke in *Women in Love*. The Cafe Royal closed in 2008 but reopened in December 2012 as part of a luxury hotel.

8. Rina 's mysterious haemorrhage: 'I am so sorry you aren't well!' Frieda Lawrence to Rina at Bridgefoot, from 110 Heath Street, Hampstead NW3, 20 December 1923, 3.30 pm. Bridgefoot Archive. 'We have worked so hard on the ranch': Frieda Lawrence to Rina

Secker at Bridgefoot, from Taos, dated 18 June 1924 but postmarked New York 26 June 1924. Bridgefoot Archive. 'We have left the ranch for the winter': Frieda Lawrence to Rina Secker at Bridgefoot, from the Hotel Monte Carlo, Mexico City, dated 1 November but postmarked 31 October 1924. Bridgefoot Archive.

9. Frieda Lawrence's 1924 letters to Rina Secker from New Mexico and Mexico City: Bridgefoot Archive. Lawrence homesick for Europe: letter to Nancy Pearn of Curtis Brown, from Spotorno, 21 November 1925.

10. Lawrence at Bridgefoot: DHL to Alfred Decker Hawk and Lucy Hawk, 7 October 1925, from Garland's Hotel, Suffolk St, Pall Mall, London SW1. 'Of course I'm in bed with a cold': DHL to Martin Secker, from his sister Emily's house, c/o Mrs. S. King, 16 Brooklands Road, Sneinton Hill, Nottingham, not dated but October 1925. William Gerhardie said of Lawrence at this time that 'In the sunlight his red-bearded face looked harrowed': William Gerhardie, *Memoirs of a Polyglot*, quoted in Norman Page, op. cit., Vol. 2, p. 225. The surname is sometimes spelt Gerhardi.

11. Barbara Weekley Barr on DHL, and his views on her fiancé: from her *Memoir of DH Lawrence*, in *DH Lawrence: Novelist, Poet, Prophet*, edited by Stephen Spender, 1973, pp. 10–19.

12. 'We may stay on the Italian Riviera for a while': DHL to Dorothy Brett, 28 October 1925.

5: The Lure of the Italian Riviera

1. 'Italy was seen as the land of spontaneity and escape': Alessandro Bartoli, *The British Colonies in the Italian Riviera in '800 and '900*, Savona, 2008.'A polite invasion by elite tourism': Giovanni Assereto, lecturer in modern history, Genoa University, preface to Alessandro Bartoli op. Cit.

2. 'The Riviera had been a backwater': Michael Nelson, *Queen Victoria and the Discovery of the Riviera*, 2001, p. 8.

3. The 1929 Alassio guide: it cited the medical opinion of Dr Giuseppe Schneer, author of a pamphlet entitled 'Alassio and its Climate compared to that of San Remo, Menton, Nice and Cannes.'

4. 'An illusion of visitors from the north': Cecil Roberts, *Portal to Paradise*, 1955, pp. 49–55.

5. 'A carefree world of winter expatriate colonies': Lee Marshall, *Daily Telegraph*, 20 July 2010.

6. 'A high degree of respect for the natural and human landscape': Giovanni Assereto, preface to Alessandro Bartoli, op. cit.

7. The arrival of the English a boon to the local economy: Maura Muratorio, *Daniel Hanbury and the British colony of Alassio*, 2004, p. 34 and p. 124. On Edward Elgar in Alassio, see Michael Kennedy, *The Life of Elgar*, 2004, p. 94.

8. 'But the stuccoed, turreted villas are still there': Thomas Hanbury died in 1907 and his son Daniel in1948. La Mortola is now run by Genoa University. Thomas Hanbury also developed gardens in Britain: he donated the garden at Wisley in Surrey to the Royal Horticultural Society, which still owns it. See *La Mortola: In the Footsteps of Thomas Hanbury* by Alasdair Moore, 2004.

9. 'The Villa della Pergola survives as an exclusive hotel': Daniel Hanbury's second wife Ruth, Lady Hanbury, lived there until her death in 1982. It was saved from developers by a consortium headed by locally-born Antonio Ricci, a well-known Italian television producer, whose wife Silvia Arnaud Ricci oversees the restoration and management of the historic villa and its gardens. The villa and gardens are opened to the public each year by arrangement with FAI, the Italian version of the National Trust or English Heritage.

10. 'Much of the English Library has survived': many
    though not all of the books were saved from dispersal
    by volunteers including the present librarian, Jacqueline
    Rosadoni, née Poole, a longtime British resident of
    Alassio. They have since been re-housed in the Richard
    West Gallery on Viale Hanbury, the former premises of
    the Alassio civic library.

11. 'Went to Alassio yesterday to see F's daughter, Barby';
    DHL to Dorothy Brett, from Spotorno, 5 December
    1925.

6: Rina and Martin

1. Rina 'the inspiration for Lady Chatterley': Adrian
   Secker to Professor James T. Boulton of Birmingham
   University, 28 November 1985, and to Adrienne Dion, 5
   January 1990. Bridgefoot Archive.

2. Siebenhaar hopes to make a good film': Frieda Lawrence
   to Rina Secker, from London NW1, 19 March 1933,
   Bridgefoot Archive.

3. They were obviously very close': Adrian Secker to
   Adrienne Dion, 5 January 1990. 'The film was never
   made': according to Barby, because Siebenhaar ran out
   of funds. See Chapter 13.

4. Rina 'might do well as a society columnist': DHL to
   Rina Secker, from Florence 1 July 1927, Bridgefoot
   archive. Iris Tree was painted in the nude by Modigliani
   and sculpted by Jacob Epstein. She later played herself
   in a cameo role in Federico Fellini's 1960 film *La Dolce
   Vita*, and died in 1968. 'Why don't you write?' Frieda
   Lawrence to Rina Secker, from Florence, 13 May 1926.
   Bridgefoot Archive.

5. Rina a 'living block of discontent': DHL to Dorothy
   Brett, from Spotorno, 19 December 1925. Also DHL
   to Martin Secker, 30 November 1925: Rina 'was very
   nervosa at first'.

6. 'But she was also vibrant', author interview with Anthea Secker, at Bridgefoot, 9 February 2011. Rina's family background: author interviews with Sergio Gazzera, Rina's cousin, and Michelangelo Fessia, Luigi Capellero's great nephew, Bene Vagienna, Piedmont, 17 January 2012. Bene Vagienna boasts Baroque churches and a statue of the Renaissance poet and diplomat Giovanni Botero.

7. 'A family higher up the social scale': the Gazzeras' status was later reinforced by the rise of General Pietro Gazzera, Rina's uncle, Minister of War under Mussolini from 1928 to 1933. He resisted Mussolini's overseas adventure and was, the Turin paper *La Stampa* wrote in its obituary, 'an upright and honest military man' and not himself a Fascist. *La Stampa*, 1 July 1953.

8. 'They were married at Bene Vagienna': marriage certificate dated 10 June 1895, Stato Civile office, Bene Vagienna, Province of Cuneo.

9. Rina's birth certificate: archives of the Etat Civil, Monaco, for 1896. Anna Marie was born in Gerrard St on 26 April 1897: birth certificate, County of Westminster, sub district of St Anne, Soho 1897. There was a third child, Giovanni, born in 1898, who died young: author interview with Sergio Gazzera, Bene Vagienna, 17 January 2012.

10. Luigi Capellero 'tried his luck in the hotel business': the four-storey London House in Rue Albert had a restaurant at street level, the Cafe Suisse, now called 'La Villa'; Rue Albert has been re-named Rue Suffren Reymond. Author visit to Monte Carlo, 19 January 2012. See also Pierre Laplace, *Les Hotels d'Hier et Aujourd'hui à Monaco*, Vol. 1, 2008, and *Journal de Monaco*, 5 May 1896. Rina was baptised on 12 April 1896, at the church of Ste Devote, the patron saint of Monaco. In February 1955 she went back there and made enquiries about citizenship, but was told it was only

granted to those who were born there before 1820 or were the third generation in the Principality.

11. Soho: the Cappelleros were at 58A Old Compton St. The Italian Society of Mutual Aid for Hotel and Restaurant Employees was established in Gerrard St in 1886.

12. 'A studio photograph taken at this period'; the photographer's studio was JW Gorsuch at 48 Junction Road, Upper Holloway. The photograph is dated June 1905 by Rina.

13. 'Attending a convent school on Haverstock Hill': run by the Sisters of Providence of the Immaculate Conception – today a womens' hostel run by the same order. Adrian recalled that his mother had had 'an ordinary well to do upbringing in Highgate' and despite her birth in Monaco was 'to all intents and purposes English'. Bridgefoot Archive.

14. The Crichton restaurant: at 6 St John's Hill. It hosted annual professional conferences of groups such as doctors, engineers, printers and midwives. The move to Wandsworth: to 15, Trefoil Rd SW11.

15. Rina 'attended the Slade School of Art': University College London, which keeps the Slade archives, has no record of her. Possibly she attended a summer school or evening classes. 'Love, that releases no beloved from loving' is from Canto V of the Inferno in Dante's *Divine Comedy*: '*Amor, ch'a nullo amato perdona, mi prese del costui piacer sì forte, che, come vedi, ancor non m'abbandona*'.

16. Rina and Annie taken back to Bene Vagienna in WW1: author interview with Sergio Gazzera, 17 January 2012. Anna Marie is listed as an assistant in the office of Captain Edward Frysinger at the Red Cross in Turin 1918–19 in an appendix to *The Story of the American Red Cross in Italy* by Charles Montague Bakewell, 1920. She emigrated to the US, married Frysinger and became an

American citizen in 1925. See Dramatis Personae.

17. Rina 'seems to have worked for the American YMCA': in a letter to Martin Secker from Turin dated 18 January 1932, Rina writes that 'Turin is the same as ever – I am having a very social time' and adds: 'Tomorrow morning I shall make a jaunt to the YMCA to see what's happened to it', Bridgefoot Archive. Her (well-thumbed) English-Italian dictionary, issued in 1918, bears the inscription 'N. Flaten, Jan 8 1919, Turin, Italy, YMCA'. Nils Flaten, an American of Norwegian origin, served with the YMCA in Turin and Novara between 1 November 1918 and 3 July 1919.

18. *A Farewell to Arms* 'rather gruesome and not too true to things as they were': Rina Secker to Martin Secker from Alassio, Bridgefoot Archive. The letter is dated by Rina 23 January 1930, but the envelope is postmarked 24 January 1931, so she may have mistaken the year. *A Farewell to Arms* was published in 1929.

19. 'Pack up in London': the Crichton was owned by the Capelleros in a partnership with a Swiss Italian, Peter Sasselli, dissolved in 1920. *The London Gazette*, 29 October 1920, and *The Times* Law Notices, 6 October and 30 October 1920, on 'Capellero v Sasselli' in the Lord Chief Justice's Court.

20. 'For a while Luigi lived and worked at Pegli': Anna Marie left for the US with Edward Frysinger on April 1919 on the SS *Dante Alighieri* from Genoa, giving her father Luigi as a reference and his place of residence as Pegli. This suggests Luigi had already moved to the Riviera before his partnership in the Crichton restaurant was formally dissolved. US Customs immigration and passenger records, National Archives, Washington DC.

21. The name Klingender dropped by deed poll: British anti-German feeling deepened during the Boer war and reached near-hysteria levels after William Le Queux

published *The Invasion of 1910* in instalments in the *Daily Mail* in 1906. However John Worthen suggests Secker's name change was simply 'a brilliant piece of Anglicisation and potential niche-marketing'. Letter to the author, 20 February 2013.

22. Martin Secker 'born into a long established German immigrant family': on 6 April 1882. The Klingenders were originally from Hesse. Secker's grandfather, William Klingender, became a cotton merchant and ship owner in Lancashire, where Secker's father, Edward Henry Klingender, was born in 1853. He married Julia Clark, and they lived first at Carshalton and then at Beckenham in Kent with their two children, Percy (Martin) and Kathleen (born 1891), before Julia moved to Iver, apparently without her husband.

23. 'Set himself up as a publisher': at 5 John Street, Adelphi. The publisher he worked for as a reader from 1908 to 1910 was James Eveleigh Nash: see Secker's brief memoir, *Publisher's Progress: From My Unpublished Memoirs* in *The Cornhill Magazine* No. 1076, Summer 1973. Manuscripts and Special Collections, University of Nottingham.

24. 'Martin went into business partly thanks to a legacy': it is likely that Mrs Lamont also provided much of the financial support.

25. 'My dear, you cannot ask a woman to share her home': Rina Secker to Martin Secker, from Alassio, 23 May 1932, Bridgefoot Archive. 'Lucy Lamont and her unmarried sister Mercy Smart were still around when I was a boy, until my mother could not stand it and turned them out,' Adrian recalled. 'She thought they were a pair of old tabby cats and used to get quite vehement about LL's influence here when she was a young bride. But Lammy, as I knew her, remained firmly in our lives.' Adrian Secker, letter to Professor James T Boulton, 28 November 1985. Bridgefoot Archive.

26. Mrs Lamont 'head of the household': born in Stoke Newington, she had previously lived with her famous painter husband (she was his third wife) in St John's Wood and later as a widow in Bloomsbury. TR Lamont, the model for the Laird in George du Maurier's *Trilby*, died in 1898. Lucy Lamont edited works by Oscar Wilde, Swinburne and Algernon Blackwood for Secker as well as the memoirs of the painter Thomas Armstrong.

27. 'They moved down the hill': the former Dower House to a nearby mansion, Huntsmoor Park, Bridgefoot was owned from 1700 onwards by the Tower family. Martin Secker bought it from Christopher John Hume Tower in October 1922. Stella Rowlands, *Bridgefoot: A History of Bridgefoot House*, Iver Local History Booklet No. 6, 2001.

28. 'Neither of us had been swept into the Army': Frank Swinnerton, *Swinnerton: an Autobiography*, 1937, p. 216. Christopher Stone, brother in law of Compton Mackenzie and later editor of *The Gramophone*, urged Secker to 'Get into khaki and forget your nerves. The office boy will run the show in the meanwhile. Or put Mrs Lamont in charge!' Christopher Stone to Martin Secker, 2 March 1917, Bridgefoot Archive.

29. Secker never looked back: in an interview with *The Times* at the age of 86 in August 1968 – shortly before Rina's death – he was still proud of his gamble in issuing a novel others had turned down, observing that the gold lettering he had boldly put on the cover was 'as bright now as it was in 1911'. *The Times* Saturday Review, 24 August 1968.

30. 'Rina met Martin Secker on a train': Notes by Adrian Secker, Bridgefoot Archive. This may have been in September 1919, when Secker went to Capri to see not only Compton Mackenzie but also Francis Brett Young, another of his authors. Brett Young papers, Birmingham

University. Mackenzie lived on Capri from 1913–20 with his wife Faith, whose lesbian and heterosexual affairs (they had an 'open marriage') form the background to Mackenzie's novel *Extraordinary Women*, in which Capri is called Sirene.

31. 'Martin Secker came to spend a week on Herm with Rina', Compton Mackenzie, *My Life and Times Octave Five, 1915–1923*, 1966, p. 205.

32. The 'Dear Miss Capellero' letters 1920–21, Bridgefoot Archive. The Cafe Monico was a fashionable Italian restaurant and bar.

33. *Tre Croci*: the tale of three brothers disgraced when they forge a cheque to save their failing bookshop in Siena, a scandal which leads one of them to hang himself while the other two die of apoplexy and gout respectively. Tozzi died of pneumonia on 21 March 1920, praised by Italo Calvino and Alberto Moravia as one of the finest Italian authors of the early 20th century.

34. 'Rina and Martin were married': the witnesses at Eton Register Office on 30 August 1921 were Frank Swinnerton and Mrs Lamont. Both Rina and Martin give their address as Bridgefoot, though the marriage announcement in *The Times* described Martin as 'of Bridgefoot, Iver, Bucks' and Rina as 'of Bene Vagienna, Cuneo, Italy'. The honeymoon was a motoring tour of the West Country. Rina took photographs which are still at Bridgefoot: no doubt she used the 'tiny camera' Lawrence was later to praise her for taking 'good snapshots' with at Spotorno. DHL to Dorothy Brett, from Spotorno, 2 February 1926.

35. 'Dear Martin, I am so glad you've got a charming wife': Faith Mackenzie to Martin Secker, from Southampton, 13 September 1921, Bridgefoot Archive.

36. 'The house was crowded with doctors': Martin Secker to Rina Secker, 11 March 1937, Bridgefoot Archive. Secker said the birth was 'like a scene from *The Doctor's*

Dilemma', a reference to George Bernard Shaw's 1906 play.

37. 'What women go through to put a man into the world': Rina Lovioz to Carlo Lovioz, from Pixton Park, Dulverton, Somerset, 10 March 1953, Bridgefoot Archive.

38. Rina's note in red ink: written on the typescript of Lawrence's 1925 letter and two postcards to Martin Secker from Baden-Baden just before his journey to Spotorno, held at Manuscripts and Special Collections, University of Nottingham.

7: Down There By The Sea

1. 'I received a letter from Lawrence': Rina Secker to Martin Secker from Spotorno, 7 November 1925. Bridgefoot Archive. DHL and Rina's hat box: DHL to Martin Secker, from Baden-Baden, not dated but October 1925.

2. 'Perhaps you will be at home by the time this arrives', DHL to Rina Secker, 3 November 1925, Bridgefoot Archive. He made similar remarks about his German in-laws to Dorothy Brett the following day: 'Here I am stunned with hearing old ladies talk German, and having to talk back, and having to play whist with ancient Baronesses, Countesses and Excellencies'. DHL to Dorothy Brett, from Baden-Baden, 4 November 1925.

3. Frieda's account of their arrival in Spotorno, and DHL's letters to his mother in law, Anna von Richthofen: from *Not I, But the Wind*, p. 167ff.

4. Rina's reaction to the Hotel Miramare, the attack on Mussolini and the Lawrences' arrival in Spotorno: letters to Martin Secker from Spotorno, 27 April 1922, 29 April 1922, 30 April 1922, 4 May 1922, 6 May 1922, 3 July 1923, 6 July 1923, and from the Grand Hotel Baglioni, Florence, 29 June 1923; from Spotorno 7

November 1925, 10 November 1925, 15 November 1925, Bridgefoot Archive. Reggie Turner in Florence 'a funny old thing': Lawrence caricatured Turner as 'Algy Constable' in *Aaron's Rod*.

5. 'Today has been very exciting': Rina Secker to Martin Secker, from Spotorno, 16 November 1925, Bridgefoot Archive.

6. 'We got here yesterday': DHL to Curtis Brown, from Spotorno, 16 November 1925.

7. The Hotel Miramare: Alberto Bevilacqua, *Attraverso Il Tuo Corpo*, 2002, pp. 47 and 93. Rina is quite clear that the Lawrences were lodged at the Hotel Ligure on arrival: presumably they moved into the Villa Maria after a few days. Before arriving in Spotorno Lawrence gave the Miramare as their address 'for the time being' (letter to Dorothy Brett, 11 November 1925) and after arrival wrote 'c/o Signor Capellero, Villa Maria, Spotorno'.

8: The Villa Bernarda

1. 'Met Ls on beach': Rina Secker's travel diary, Bridgefoot Archive.

2. 'Here it's sunny': DHL to Vere Collins of the Oxford University Press, 17 November 1925. The textbook was called *Movements in European History*.

3. 'So the L's have really come': Martin Secker to Rina Secker, 18 November 1925, Bridgefoot Archive.

4. 'The Villa Bernarda was 'a three decker': DHL to John Middleton Murry, from Spotorno, 19 November 1925.

5. 'The Villa Bernarda 'typically Ligurian in construction': author interview with Alberto Bevilacqua, Rome, 7 September 2010.

6. 'We've taken this villa': DHL to Martin Secker, from Spotorno, undated but November 1925.

7. 'We've taken the Villa Bernarda till March': DHL to

Dorothy Brett, from Spotorno, 19 November 1925.

8. 'You must come and look at him he is so smart': from
    Frieda Lawrence, *Not I, But the Wind*, p. 167. Ravagli 5ft
    9ins: according to US immigration papers, 4 April 1935.

9. Ravagli showed Frieda round the villa: Alberto Bevilacqua,
    Attraverso Il Tuo Corpo, 2002, pp. 28ff. John Worthen
    argues that if Frieda consummated her affair with
    Ravagli at Spotorno in February or March 1926 'she would
    have had to have been incredibly discreet about it', and
    it is more likely that a fully-fledged affair did not begin
    until the following year. Letter from John Worthen to the
    author, 2 February 2013. 'A woman writer': Martha Gordon
    Crotch, *Memories of Frieda Lawrence*, published by the
    Tregarda Press, Edinburgh in 1975, held at Manuscripts
    and Special Collections, University of Nottingham.

10. 'The rooms at the Villa Bernarda smallish but quite
    convenient': Rina Secker to Martin Secker, from
    Spotorno, 19 November 1925, Bridgefoot Archive.

11. 'It's on the sea on the Riviera': DHL to William Hawk,
    from Spotorno, 18 December 1925.

12. 'We are settled in our cottage': DHL to Martin Secker,
    from Spotorno, 30 November 1925.

13. 'Frieda tells me that I am not the same person that I
    was': Rina Secker to Martin Secker, from Spotorno, 19
    November 1925, Bridgefoot Archive.

14. 'I will let you decide by yourself': Rina Secker to Martin
    Secker, from Spotorno, 5 November 1925, Bridgefoot
    Archive.

15. 'Adrian is getting quite attached': Rina Secker to Martin
    Secker, from Spotorno, 3 December 1925, Bridgefoot
    Archive.

16. 'We ought to manage on five shillings a day': DHL to
    Dorothy Brett, from Spotorno, 25 November 1925.

17. *The Ghost Book*: it appeared in 1926. Other authors
    in Lady Cynthia Asquith's first collection of ghost
    stories included Walter De La Mare, Enid Bagnold and

LP Hartley. Lawrence wrote *The Rocking Horse Winner* in February 1926 and it was first published in July 1926 in *Harper's Bazaar*.

18. Ravagli and the smoking chimney: quoted in Paul Poplawski, *DH Lawrence: A Reference Companion*, 1966.

9: Naked in the Sun

1. Martin Secker's sense of the ridiculous: Compton Mackenzie, *My Life and Times, Octave Four, 1907– 1914*, p. 124, and *Octave Five 1915–1923*, pp. 163–4; Swinnerton, op. cit., p. 217.

2. 'Your description of life at Spotorno': Frank Swinnerton to Martin Secker, from Cookham Dean, 7 January 1926, Bridgefoot Archive.

3. 'He's a nice gentle soul': DHL to Dorothy Brett, from Spotorno, 19 December 1925.

4. 'I have on the table here four tumblers', Rina Secker to Martin Secker, from Spotorno, 28 February 1926, Bridgefoot Archive. See Keith Sagar, *The Life of DH Lawrence, An Illustrated Biography*, p. 197: '*Sun* was clearly suggested to Lawrence by the situation of the Seckers – Rina and her little boy of twenty months, Adrian, sunbathing in the lemon groves at Spotorno, and Martin coming to visit them when he could'. See also John Worthen, *DH Lawrence: The Life of An Outsider*, p. 335.

5. 'I can't bear really to be away from home': Rina Secker to Martin Secker, from Spotorno, 21 February 1926, Bridgefoot Archive.

6. 'I wish I could post you some of the warmth and sun': Rina Secker to Martin Secker, from Spotorno, 8 March 1926 and 21 January 1927, and from Alassio 19 October 1931, Bridgefoot Archive.

7. 'A friend in Paris, Harry Crosby': DHL to Martin Secker, from Gstaad, 14 August 1928. The first version of *Sun* was included in *The Woman Who Rode Away And*

Other Stories, published in 1928 by Secker in the UK and Knopf in the US. Lawrence maintained at times that the differences between the two versions of *Sun* were 'only very slight', and at other times that the first version had been expurgated because the general public was not ready. But as Neil Reeve has observed, Lawrence needed to show Harry Crosby he had bought something with added value, not just a re-working of an extant story. See *Liberty In a Tantrum: DH Lawrence's 'Sun'* in *The Cambridge Quarterly*, 24:3, 1995. *Coterie* magazine, edited by Russell Green, was issued from 1919 onwards at a bookshop in the Charing Cross Road.

8. 'Bandol dull – a bit like Spotorno – Frieda gets rather bored without a house': DHL to Martin Secker, from Bandol, 3 December 1928.

9. 'Sorry Bridgefoot is rather a trial': DHL to Martin Secker, from Bandol, 13 November 1929.

10. 'I am glad Rina is in Alassio': DHL to Martin Secker, from Bandol, 28 December 1929.

10: The Virgin and the Gipsy

1. 'Secker is here – with wife and child': DHL to John Middleton Murry, from Spotorno, 12 December 1925.

2. 'Now it is evening': DHL to Anna von Richthofen from Spotorno, 16 December 1925, translated from German and quoted by Frieda Lawrence in *Not I, But the Wind*, p. 170.

3. 'Absolutely nothing to buy here': DHL to Dorothy Brett from Spotorno, 17 December 1925. Strega (meaning Witch) is in fact a herbal liqueur which originated as a supposed love potion at Benevento in southern Italy; the yellow colour comes from saffron.

4. 'In the daytime we live in the sitting-room': DHL to Earl and Achsah Brewster, from Spotorno, 18 December 1925.

5. 'We had a very mild Christmas Day': DHL to Dorothy Brett, from Spotorno, 29 December 1925.

6. 'I can't stand Frieda's children': DHL to Dorothy Brett, from Spotorno, 4 November 1925 and 17 December 1925.

7. Barbara Weekley in Alassio and relationship with DHL: from her *Memoir of DH Lawrence*, in Stephen Spender, op. cit., p. 20ff.

8. 'Barby Weekley is here since Christmas Day': DHL to Dorothy Brett, from Spotorno, 29 December 1925. The incident in which Lawrence flung wine in Frieda's face is in Barby's *Memoir of DH Lawrence*, in Stephen Spender, op. cit., p. 20ff., and also in Frieda's memoirs: see Frieda Lawrence, *Not I, But the Wind*, pp. 167–9.

9. 'Barby was here for a few days': DHL to Dorothy Brett, from Spotorno, 6 January 1926.

10. 'Went for a long walk today with L and Barby': Rina Secker to Martin Secker, postcard from Spotorno, 27 January 1926, Bridgefoot Archive.

11. 'The sea is most tempting': DHL to Dorothy Brett, from Spotorno, 6 January 1926. His idea of going to Russia: DHL to SS Koteliansky, from Spotorno, 4 January 1926.

12. 'My sister arrives on Feb 9th': DHL to Dorothy Brett, from Spotorno, 25 January 1926.

13. 'I spent yesterday afternoon with the L's': Rina Secker to Martin Secker, from Spotorno, postmarked 25 January 1926. Bridgefoot Archive. Rina uses the correct Oriental word for persimmons, 'Kaki', rather than the Italian transliteration, 'cachi'. Lawrence had been much taken with persimmons at Gargnano in 1912: see Chapter 2.

14. 'The Lawrence menage sounds rather a strain': Martin Secker to Rina Secker, from Bridgefoot, 27 January 1926, Bridgefoot Archive.

15. 'Barby 'surprised that Frieda takes all his tempers so quietly': Rina Secker to Martin Secker, from Spotorno, 31 January 1926, Bridgefoot Archive.

16. Frieda's sanity: on 19 January 1932 Martin wrote to Rina from Bridgefoot: 'Frieda Lawrence has appeared in town and I am lunching with her next Friday. I shall never regard her as perfectly sane', Bridgefoot Archive.

17. 'Barbara has been here a week': DHL to Martin Secker, from Spotorno, 20 January 1926.

18. 'Here is the rest of the gipsy story': DHL to Martin Secker, from Spotorno, 21 January 1926.

19. 'No point in killing oneself like Keats': DHL to John Middleton Murry, from Spotorno, 4 January 1926.

20. 'A bit of friction down at the Villa Maria': DHL to Martin Secker, from Spotorno, 1 February 1926.

21. 'Beastly weather' in Spotorno and Rina's snapshots 'rather good': DHL to Dorothy Brett, from Spotorno, 2 February 1926.

22. Lawrence ill with 'flu: DHL to Dorothy Brett, from Spotorno, 11 February 1926.

23. 'I've been in bed six days with 'flu': DHL to Martin Secker, from Spotorno, undated but February 1926.

24. The English colony 'about to spread': Rina Secker to Martin Secker, from Spotorno, 1 February 1926, Bridgefoot Archive. Elsa was engaged to Bernal Edward de Martelly Seaman, known as Teddy, a Royal Navy officer. They were married in 1929. He was the nephew of Lady Becker, wife of Sir Walter Becker the Italian-based shipowner and philanthropist with whom DHL briefly stayed in Turin in 1919.

25. 'Life at the Villa B sounds hectic': Martin Secker to Rina Secker, from Iver, 7 February 1926, Bridgefoot Archive.

26. 'My sister is here with a friend': DHL to Earl Brewster, from Spotorno, 11 February 1926.

27. Rina translating *The Captain's Doll*: Rina Secker to Martin Secker, from Spotorno, 3 February 1926, Bridgefoot Archive.

28. Frieda 'becoming very agitated': Rina Secker to Martin Secker, from Spotorno, 3 February 1926, Bridgefoot Archive.

29. Lawrence and Frieda having 'furious rows': Barbara Weekley Barr, *Memoir of DH Lawrence* in Stephen Spender, op. cit., p. 21.

11: 'Such Combustible People!'

1. 'I wouldn't marry you Barby': Barbara Weekley Barr, *Memoir of DH Lawrence* in Stephen Spender, op. cit., p. 23.

2. 'I left poor Grandmother unconscious': Rina Secker to Martin Secker, from Spotorno, 8 February 1926, Bridgefoot Archive.

3. 'A bad cold caught in the snows': Rina Secker to Martin Secker, postcard from Spotorno, 11 February 1928, Bridgefoot Archive.

4. 'Terrific happenings at the Villa Bernarda': Rina Secker to Martin Secker, from Spotorno, 15 February 1926, Bridgefoot Archive.

5. Barby's account under-stated: Barbara Weekley Barr, in Stephen Spender, op. cit., p. 24.

6. 'My sister's coming was occasion for another rumpus': DHL to Dorothy Brett, from Spotorno, 16 February 1926.

7. 'I feel absolutely swamped out': DHL to William Hawk, from Spotorno, 19 February 1926.

8. 'A real risk of Frieda and Lawrence parting company': Rina Secker to Martin Secker, from Spotorno, 17 February 1926, Bridgefoot Archive.

9. 'The Villa Bernarda "in possession of a feminine colony"': Rina Secker to Martin Secker, from Spotorno, 24 February 1926, Bridgefoot Archive.

10. Frieda puts the blame on Ada: Frieda Lawrence, *Not I, But the Wind*, pp. 167–9.

11. 'You were right about the Riviera': DHL to Martin Secker, from Monte Carlo, postcard dated 24 February 1926.

12. 'I still go up to the Villa B': Rina Secker to Martin

Secker, from Spotorno, 4 March 1926, Bridgefoot Archive.

13. 'I am in Capri with the Brewsters for a few days': DHL to Martin Secker, from Capri, 4 March 1926. Lawrence was met at the port of Capri by Brett, accompanied by Harwood, the teenage daughter of the Brewsters. He stayed at the Brewsters' home on Capri, the Villa Torre dei Quattro Venti. He also met Faith Mackenzie, who recorded that Lawrence had fled to Capri because the women in his life had been 'more than usually breath-taking and exasperating just lately'. *More Than I Should*, 1940, p. 32.

14. 'I had so wanted you to have a nice time': DHL to Ada Clarke, from Capri, 2 March 1926.

15. Lawrence 'worn out by constant battles with Frieda', and his abortive attempt to make love to Brett: Dorothy Brett, *Lawrence and Brett: A Friendship*, 1933.

16. 'A muddled, unsatisfactory sort of winter'; DHL to Catherine Carswell, from Capri, 4 March 1926.

17. 'I can't stand it when she clings too tight': DHL to Earl and Achsah Brewster, from Spotorno, 11 April 1926.

18. 'I have been moving around a bit': DHL to Mabel Luhan, from Ravello, 18 March 1926.

19. 'The weather isn't worthy the name': DHL postcard to Martin Secker at the Villa Maria, Spotorno, from Ravello, 21 March 1926, also postmarked 22 March 1926 at Spotorno on arrival, Bridgefoot Archive.

20. DHL greeted by Frieda, Barby and Elsa at Spotorno, Frieda Lawrence, *Not I, But the Wind*, p. 169. Martin Secker had evidently returned to Iver by the time Lawrence got back to Spotorno.

21. 'Everybody 'very nice and pleased to see me': DHL to Martin Secker from Spotorno, 4 April 1926.

22. Frieda 'caught more than she bargained for': DHL to Dorothy Brett, from Spotorno, 11 April 1926.

23. 'They say an Englishman at forty is almost always

bronchial': DHL to his German mother-in-law, Anna von Richthofen, from Spotorno, 4 April 1926.

24. Frieda 'undoubtedly loved Lawrence': Janet Byrne, *A Genius for Living, A Biography of Frieda Lawrence*, 1996, p. 316. Byrne writes that Frieda and Ravagli 'began an affair sometime after their first meeting alone, either almost immediately or about two years later, in 1928', Byrne, op. cit. p. 311. See also Jeffrey Meyers, *DH Lawrence and the Experience of Italy*, p. 157: 'After Lawrence's death Frieda, who never valued fidelity, revealed that Lawrence had become sexually impotent toward the end of 1926 and that she had slept with Lieutenant Angelo Ravagli, who had been their landlord in Spotorno, while Lawrence was in France in October 1928'.

25. 'Just as I want to travel': quoted in John Worthen, *DH Lawrence: The Life of An Outsider*, 2005, p. 337 and p. 375. On whether Lawrence was impotent, see op. cit. p. 338. See also Catherine Carswell, *The Savage Pilgrimage*, 1932, p. 75: Carswell strongly took issue with those who suggested that because Lawrence's marriage to Frieda was 'without issue' he may have been impotent from the outset. Carswell also denied Lawrence had ever been homosexual, even though Compton Mackenzie claimed that Lawrence once told him that 'the nearest I've ever come to perfect love was with a young coal-miner when I was about sixteen'. Compton Mackenzie, *My Life and Times: Octave Five 1915–1923*, pp. 167–8.

12: The Villa Mirenda

1. 'Italy is still very nice': DHL to SS Koteliansky, from Spotorno, 10 April 1926.

2. 'We shall leave this house on the 20th': DHL to Dorothy Brett, from Spotorno, 10 April and 17 April 1926.

3. Lawrence shows Elsa and Barby round the Uffizi gallery:
    Barbara Weekley Barr, in Stephen Spender, op. Cit.
    On Lawrence's reaction to Florence see Simonetta de
    Filippis' essay 'DH Lawrence and Tuscany' in *Il Corpo,
    La Fiamma, Il Desiderio*, edited by Serena Cenni and
    Nick Ceramella, a collection of papers presented at a
    conference in Florence in 2008.

4. 'We came here ten days ago': DHL to Martin Secker,
    from the Pension Lucchesi, 28 April 1926.

5. 'It was April': Frieda Lawrence: *Not I, But the Wind*, p.
    174.

6. *Adventures of a Bookseller*: published in a limited
    edition in Florence but then re-published for a general
    readership by Chatto and Windus in 1938. Orioli had
    previously had a bookshop in London.

7. 'Arthur Wilkinson seems nice': DHL to Martin Secker,
    from Scandicci, Florence, 28 April 1926.

8. 'I love this place in easy reach of Florence': Frieda
    Lawrence to Rina Secker, from the Villa Mirenda,
    13 May 1926, Bridgefoot Archive. The villa is private
    property and today can only be visited by arrangement.

9. Barby finds the Villa Mirenda 'a house of magic':
    Barbara Weekley Barr, in Stephen Spender, op. cit., p. 27.

10. 'Pity one has to write at all': DHL to Dorothy Brett,
    from Baden-Baden, 29 July 1926.

11. Frieda and DHL visit the Sitwells, Frieda Lawrence
    to Rina Secker, from Florence, no date, but June 1926,
    Bridgefoot Archive; Edith Sitwell in *The Observer*, 13
    November 1960; Osbert Sitwell, *Penny Foolish*, 1935,
    quoted in Norman Page op. cit., Vol 2, pp. 244–5; and
    DHL to Martin Secker, from Florence, 8 June 1926.
    Edith Sitwell writes that her visit with Osbert to see
    Frieda and Lawrence for tea was 'a few days later'; in fact
    it was nearly a year later, in May 1927. The Sitwell family
    sold the Castello di Montegufoni in 1972; it is now a
    residential hotel.

12. Visit to the Villa Mirenda by Lord Berners and DHL on Rina's hairstyle: Frieda Lawrence to Rina Secker, from Scandicci, Florence, no date, but June 1926, Bridgefoot Archive.

13. 'In the hot weather, the days slip by': DHL to Martin Secker, from Scandicci, Florence, 5 July 1926.

14. 'I have painted window frames by the mile': quoted in David Ellis, *DH Lawrence: Dying Game, 1922–1930*, p. 674.

15. 'We got back here just a week ago': DHL to Martin Secker, from Scandicci, Florence, 12 October 1926.

16. Frieda asks Rina and Martin to stay with them in Florence: Frieda Lawrence to Rina Secker, from Scandicci, Florence, 28 November 1926, Bridgefoot Archive. The painting 'Boccaccio Story' depicts the *Decameron* tale of a young gardener in a convent who pretends to be dumb so that the nuns will have sex with him, thinking he is unable to reveal their secret. It shows the gardener lying naked on his back.

13: Florence and *Lady Chatterley*

1. Lawrence begins the first version of *Lady Chatterley's Lover*: Frieda Lawrence to Rina Secker, from Scandicci, Florence, 9 November 1926, Bridgefoot Archive; Frieda Lawrence, *Not I, But the Wind*; DHL to Martin Secker, from Scandicci, Florence, 15 November 1926, and 23 November 1926. John Worthen dates the start of the novel to around 22 October 1926: Worthen, op. cit., pp. 348–9.

2. 'I'm getting on with the novel': DHL to Martin Secker, from Scandicci, Florence, 8 January 1927.

3. 'It won't take me very long, I think': DHL to Martin Secker, from Scandicci, Florence, 8 February 1927.

4. 'Is Rina in Italy?': DHL to Martin Secker, from Scandicci, Florence, 12 January 1927.

5. 'We heard from Rina': DHL to Martin Secker, from
   Scandicci, Florence, 8 February 1927.

6. DHL going to Ravello to stay with the Brewsters: DHL
   to Martin Secker, from Scandicci, Florence, 15 March
   1927.

7. 'Had a letter from DHL the other day': Rina Secker
   to Martin Secker, from Spotorno, 14 February 1927,
   Bridgefoot Archive.

8. 'I've finished my novel': DHL to Martin Secker,
   from Scandicci, Florence, 15 March 1927. The second
   version is now known as *John Thomas and Lady Jane*,
   to distinguish it from *The First Lady Chatterley* and
   the third and final version, *Lady Chatterley's Lover*.
   See the Introduction to the 1972 Penguin edition of
   John Thomas and Lady Jane by Roland Gant, the then
   Editorial Director of Heinemann.

9. 'A man dare possibly possess a penis': DHL to Martin
   Secker, from Scandicci, Florence, 29 April 1927.
   Catherine Carswell maintained that far from being
   pornographic, Lawrence had the 'working class trait'
   of having 'extreme distaste of anything that could be
   regarded as indecent. It would indeed be easy to call him
   prudish'. Catherine Carswell, op. cit., p. 68.

10. Ravagli at the Villa Mirenda: DHL to Martin Secker
    from Scandicci, Florence, 15 November 1926. The
    court martial visit: Ravagli's account to Edward Nehls,
    quoted in David Ellis, op. cit., p. 348. The Ravaglis
    remained married under Italian law: the Capitano's
    divorce from Serafina in the US was not recognised in
    Italy. Their third child, Federico (whose godmother was
    Frieda), died in a diving accident at Alassio at the age
    of 35.

11. 'Frieda rejoined Lawrence ... he was ill again': but not
    inactive. Quite apart from the *Lady Chatterley* re-writes,
    in the Spring of 1927 his play *David* was performed in
    London, and he wrote *None of That!* in which the power

struggle between an American woman and a bullfighter in Mexico City recalls the theme of *Lady Chatterley*.

12. 'Women will have it that I am a peculiarly unattractive female ... I get such fun out of the peasants': Frieda Lawrence to Rina Secker at Bridgefoot, from Scandicci, Florence, 25 May 1927, Bridgefoot Archive.

13. Lawrence's collapse on a hot afternoon: Frieda Lawrence: *Not I, But the Wind*, p. 182.

14. 'It's a relief to be here after the friction and bossiness of Italy': DHL to Martin Secker, from the Hotel Fischer, Villach, Carinthia, Austria, 17 August 1927.

15. Michaelis, or Mick: based on the Armenian author Michael Arlen (real name Dikran Kouyoumdjian), whose best known story, *The Green Hat*, was made into a film starring Greta Garbo under the tile *A Woman of Affairs*.

16. 'Mellors has evolved': towards the end of his life Ravagli told Ruth Hall of *The Observer* that he preferred magazines to books and had tried to read *Sons and Lovers* but found it 'too heavy – *much* too heavy. We don't need literature to know what to do'. On the other hand he was not an uneducated manual labourer but a figure of some status and distinction in Spotorno. In a 2001 book entitled *Lady Chatterley e Il Mulattiere* an Italian author, Gaetano Saglimbeni, claimed a rival model for Mellors: a 24-year-old Sicilian mule driver named Peppino D'Allura with whom Frieda had an affair during the Lawrences' stay at Taormina in the summer of 1922.

17. Lawrence was 'all the characters': John Worthen, *DH Lawrence, The Life of An Outsider*, Penguin edition p. 374. Enid Hopkin on Frieda and Lorenzo: Enid Hilton Hopkin, *More than One Life: a Nottinghamshire Childhood with DH Lawrence*, 1993, quoted in David Ellis, *Dying Game*, p. 412. Also in Worthen op. cit., p. 352.

18. 'It is frankly a novel about sex': DHL to Martin Secker,

from Les Diablerets, 18 February 1928.

19. The Warren Gallery exhibition: DHL to Dorothy
Warren from Scandicci, 27 March 1928.

20. Frieda again invites Rina to Florence: Frieda Lawrence
to Rina Secker, from Scandicci, Florence, 21 March 1928,
Bridgefoot Archive. Lawrence asked Martin to tell Rina
she should take the No 16 tram from the Duomo.

21. 'Frieda was away a week with Barby in Alassio': DHL to
Martin Secker, from Scandicci, Florence, 24 April 1928.

22. 'I think we must go away sooner than I said': Frieda
Lawrence to Rina Secker, from Scandicci, Florence,
2 April 1928, Bridgefoot Archive. Before they left
Tuscany the Lawrences paid a visit to Lina and Aubrey
Waterfield, the couple they had met at Lerici on the eve
of the First World War and who were now at Poggio
Gherardo, the villa near Florence left to their family by
Lina's aunt, the writer Janet Ross. Also there was the
socialite and interior decorator Sybil Colefax. Lawrence
was looking 'far more ill than we had ever seen him, and
had lost much of his former vitality and sparkle, while
Frieda was so full of vigour that she interrupted his
talk all the time in order to tell his stories herself'. Lina
Waterfield, *Castle in Italy*, p. 143.

23. Film rights to *Lady Chatterley's Lover*: letter to Rina
Secker from JE Siebenhaar, Paris, 11 August 1933,
Bridgefoot Archive. See also Chapter 6. The film
contract is in the Nottingham University archives.
Barby records that she went round the Midlands with
the Swiss film team to find locations, came across the
Sitwells' house, Renishaw, and sent a telegram to Osbert
Sitwell asking him if it might be used for Wragby Hall.
He replied that the idea was as 'gross as it is libellous'.
Siebenhaar 'was later obliged to abandon the project
through lack of funds': Barbara Weekley Barr in Stephen
Spender, op. cit., p. 29.

14: Death in Vence

1. The Île de Port-Cros: Lawrence told Secker 'We are here with Richard and Dorothy Aldington – and Brigit Patmore – known them a long while', but in fact Aldington was still married to the American poet Hilda Doolittle (HD), and they only divorced in 1938. He and Dorothy (Arabella) Yorke were regarded as a couple, but never married. Brigit Patmore, 'Conversations with Lawrence', *The London Magazine*, June 1957, in Norman Page, op. cit., pp. 248–53; DHL to Martin Secker from La Vigie, Île de Port-Cros, not dated but December 1928; DHL to Laurence Pollinger of Curtis Brown, 30 October 1928; and DHL to Lady Ottoline Morrell, 28 December 1928; Brenda Maddox, *The Married Man, A Life of DH Lawrence*, 1994, pp. 464–5. Brigit Patmore, an aspiring writer and literary hostess, was the model for Clariss Browning in *Aaron's Rod*.

2. Paris 'terribly noisy': DHL to Martin Secker from the Hotel de Versailles, Bvd Montparnasse, Paris, 3 April 1929. On Lawrence in Paris, see *Print of a Hare's Foot: An Autobiographical Beginning* by Rhys Davies, 1969.

3. 'We are enjoying it here, right on the sea': Frieda Lawrence to Rina Secker, from Palma de Mallorca, 8 May 1929, Bridgefoot Archive.

4. Lawrence finds his mother-in-law a 'terrible old woman': DHL to Pino Orioli, from Baden-Baden, 2 August 1929.

5. 'We've got a commonplace little house on the sea': DHL to Martin Secker, from Bandol, 3 November 1929.

6. The Lawrence's at the Villa Beau Soleil and the transfer to the Ad Astra Sanatorium: Frieda Lawrence, *Not I, But the Wind*, p. 267ff.

7. Have you had any communication from the Lawrences at Bandol?'; Martin Secker to Rina Secker in Alassio, 10 January 1930, Bridgefoot Archive.

8. Aldous Huxley on Lawrence's final days: Introduction to *Selected Letters of DH Lawrence*, 1950, pp. 28–9.

9. 'Yes, it was better for Lawrence to come here': Frieda
   Lawrence to Martin Secker, at Bridgefoot from the
   Ad Astra Sanatorium, undated but February 1928.
   Bridgefoot Archive. DHL moved in to the Ad Astra
   sanatorium on 6 February 1930, and to the Villa
   Robermond on 1 March.

10. 'This winter makes me know I shall just die': DHL
    to Dorothy Brett, from Villa Beau Soleil, Bandol, 8
    January 1930.

11. Jessie Chambers's vision of Lawrence on the day of his
    death: Jessie Chambers, in Stephen Spender, op. cit.,
    Vol. 2, pp. 298–9.

12. Lawrence appears to Rina in a dream: Martin Secker
    to Rina Secker, not dated, but almost certainly 8
    March 1930, Bridgefoot Archive. The letter is headed
    'Saturday evening': 8 March was the Saturday following
    Lawrence's death on Sunday, 2 March. 'Poor DHL'
    Secker wrote. 'He must have collapsed at the end, for
    here is a pathetic letter from Frieda, written three days
    before the end, which reached me last Monday'. Secker
    said that according to press reports, Lawrence's 'last,
    whispered words' were 'I have several Waterloos to fight
    tonight'.

13. 'I saw Frieda on her last visit to England': Martin Secker
    from Bridgefoot to Rina in Cannes, New Year's Eve,
    1963, Bridgefoot Archive. Secker's tribute to Frieda: in
    the foreword to *Letters from a Publisher, Martin Secker
    to DH Lawrence and Others, 1911–1929*, 1970.

14. Ravagli and Lawrence's ashes: see Jeffrey Robinson,
    'The DH Lawrence Tombstone Mystery', *International
    Herald Tribune*, 12 November 1976.

15. Rina on hopes of an English colony at Spotorno: Rina
    Secker to Martin Secker, from Spotorno, 21 February
    1926, 8 March 1926 and 121 January 1927, Bridgefoot
    Archive.

16. 'No I haven't had any news from the Lawrences': Rina

Secker to Martin Secker, from Alassio, 14 January
1930. Rina 'sorry to hear about poor DH': Rina Secker
to Martin Secker, from Alassio, 27 January 1930,
Bridgefoot Archive. On his last trip to England in 1926
Lawrence told Secker that he intended to see him 'and
Rina too, I hope' in London, but if he did there is no
record of it. He may have made a last visit to Bridgefoot
– he certainly went to see Richard Aldington and
Arabella Yorke at Padworth near Reading, which as he
reminded Rina on 26 April 1926 was 'not so very far
from you' – but again I find no record of it.

17. 'I always think of poor DHL when I am in Spot':
    Rina Secker to Martin Secker, from the Villa Maria,
    Spotorno, 29 April 1931, Bridgefoot Archive.

18. 'Amusing, *nicht wahr*?' Rina Secker to Martin Secker,
    from Zurich, 21 November 1950, Bridgefoot Archive.

19. 'I suppose I had better pack all the household things':
    Rina Secker to Martin Secker from Alassio, 23 March
    1931, Bridgefoot Archive.

20. 'When I think of all my disillusions': Rina Secker
    to Martin Secker from Blair Atholl, 23 August 1933,
    Bridgefoot Archive. It appears Martin had had an affair.
    Mrs Lamont sent him a letter of rebuke on 9 November
    1930, which he tore up but kept. In a letter to Rina in
    Alassio on the Mrs Coltman affair postmarked 27 April
    1932, Martin said he was 'ashamed' of his past behaviour
    and 'deeply sorry that nothing can be done to efface it'.
    In a note in red ink attached to the letter – presumably
    written when she was putting her archive in order
    in 1962 – Rina tartly comments that at the time her
    husband was writing he was still keeping his mistress,
    who she named only as Lily Ann, 'in a flat in Maida Vale
    at 5 guineas a week, plus!'

21. Rina loath to leave Alassio: letter to Martin Secker, 24
    March 1930, Bridgefoot Archive.

22. Rina's reaction to her mother's death and her return to

Alassio: Rina Secker to Martin Secker from Alassio, 31 January 1937, 4 February 1937, 10 February 1937, 17 February 1937, 28 February 1937, 10 March 1937, 17 March 1937 and 24 March 1937, Bridgefoot Archive.

23. England 'an impossible place to live in': Rina Secker to Martin Secker, from Spotorno, 12 May 1931. Bridgefoot Archive.

24. The PNEU school: the villa, in Via Garibaldi in Alassio, was bought in 1905 by the father of the present owner, Vittoria Prato-Previde, and leased to the school.

25. 'I wish somebody would be brave enough to shoot Mussolini': Rina Secker to Adrian Secker, from Bridgefoot, 9 October 1935, Bridgefoot Archive.

26. 'In 1935 his firm went into receivership': *Martin Secker and Warburg, The First Fifty Years: A Memoir* by George Malcolm Thomson, 1986. Thomson says that although Martin Secker was a 'brilliant publisher', he was in the end 'a commercial failure'. Warburg put this down to 'lack of capital' and the fact that 'as a Tory' Secker found the politics of his successors too far to the Left.

27. 'It is very lovely out here': Rina Secker to Martin Secker, from Alassio, 22 February 1937, Bridgefoot Archive.

28. Rina's relationship with Carlo Lovioz: Rina to her sister Anna Marie Frysinger from London, 17 November 1937 and 1 October 1938. Rina remained on good terms with Martin, who in January 1952 sent her his privately published edition of Lawrence's letters. 'I am sending you the DHL Letters, which I am sorry not to have done earlier: it has been sitting on the small bookcase in the Garden Room since you first mentioned it': Martin Secker to Rina Lovioz, 25 January 1952, Bridgefoot Archive.

29. 'There are too many indelible memories': Rina Lovioz to Carlo Lovioz, from Pixton Park, Dulverton, Somerset, 5 June 1952, Bridgefoot Archive. Pixton Park was the estate of the Herbert and Waugh families: Adrian had

been at Ampleforth with Auberon Herbert, whose sister Laura married the writer Evelyn Waugh. Rina also wrote from the Cowdray Club for nurses and professional women, founded in 1922 and disbanded in 1974, although the club's archives, kept at the London Metropolitan Archives, do not record her as a member.

30. Rina on *Sinister Street* and the death of Shaw: Rina Lovioz to Adrian Secker from Hotel Quisisana, Locarno 7 January 1950, and from the Hirslanden Klinik, Zurich, 2 November 1950, Bridgefoot Archive.

31. Rina's death: death certificate issued at Eton, sub-district of Slough, county of Buckingham. The main cause of death was given as bronchial pneumonia.

15: DHL the Italian

1. 'It is extraordinary the change, when one crosses the Alps': DHL to SS Koteliansky, from Spotorno, 4 January 1926.

2. Italy meant 'above all, the sun' for Lawrence: author interview with Alberto Bevilacqua, Rome, 7 September 2010.

3. Lawrence had 'a real understanding and liking for the Italian people': Lina Waterfield, *Castle in Italy*, p. 141.

4. Lawrence caricatured the English upper classes: Compton Mackenzie, *On Moral Courage*, 1962, p. 124.

5. 'When I drive across this country, with the autumn falling': DHL to Lady Cynthia Asquith, November 1915 – no date but probably 9 November.

6. 'Travel was for Lawrence not just a search for warm climate': Jeffrey Meyers, *DH Lawrence: A Biography*, 1990, p. 103.

7. Italy meant different things to Lawrence at different times: Simonetta de Filippis, 'Lawrence of Etruria', in *DH Lawrence In the Modern World*, edited by Peter Preston and Peter Hoare, 1989, p. 104ff, and Jeffrey

Meyers, *DH Lawrence and the Experience of Italy*, 1982, pp. 2–11 and 12–28.

8. Lawrence finds Verga quite modern and Homeric: DHL to Edward Garnett, from Taormina, 10 November 1921.

9. Lawrence felt that Italy offered 'a kind of natural magic': Leo Hamalian, Introduction to *DH Lawrence in Italy*, 1982.

10. Lawrence drawn to Catholic countries: Alan Sillitoe, *DH Lawrence and His District*, in Stephen Spender, op. cit., p. 45.

11. The Bersaglieri at a performance of Hamlet: from Twilight *in Italy*, in *DH Lawrence and Italy*, Penguin edition, 2007, pp. 64–5.

12. Stendhal's envy of the Italians on the Riviera: quoted in Jonathan Keates, *Stendhal*, 1995, pp. 168–9.

13. 'Yesterday Italy was at her best': DHL to Cecily Lambert Minchin, from the Albergo delle Palme, Lerici, 18 November 1919.

14. In the Mediterranean 'one sheds one's avatars': DHL to Lady Cynthia Asquith, from Capri, 25 January 1920.

15. Lawrence had a sharp eye: Anthony Burgess, introduction to the 1972 Viking edition of Lawrence's Italian travel writing, *DH Lawrence and Italy*.

16. 'Hideous rawness of the world of men': from *The Return Journey* in *Twilight in Italy*.

17. Lawrence alarmed over Italian emigration to America: DHL to May Chambers Holbrook, the sister of Jessie Chambers, from Lucerne, Switzerland, 22 September 1913.

18. 'It is still lovely to see the meadows lush green': DHL to Martin Secker, from Villach, Austria, 17 August 1927.

19. 'I'm not eager to go back to Italy': DHL to Martin Secker, from Irschenhausen, near Munich, 17 September 1927.

20. Lawrence finds Tuscany 'warm and cloudy with bits of sun': DHL to Martin Secker, from the Villa Mirenda, 21 October 1927.

21. 'I was at Forte dei Marmi two weeks': DHL to Martin Secker, from Florence, c/o Orioli, 9 July 1929.

22. DHL on the Etruscans: see *Sketches of Etruscan Places*, first published posthumously in 1932, and 'Lawrence of Etruria' by Simonetta de Filippis of Naples University, in *DH Lawrence In the Modern World*, edited by Peter Preston and Peter Hoare, 1989, pp. 104–20.

23. 'To be with Lawrence 'was a kind of adventure': from Aldous Huxley's introduction to Lawrence's *Selected Letters*, p. 26.

24. 'In the sunshine, even death is sunny', from Lawrence's essay *Flowery Tuscany*, written in 1927 but published posthumously in *Sketches of Etruscan Places and other Italian Essays*. Also in *DH Lawrence, Selected Essays*, Penguin edition 1981, pp. 153–4.

Dramatis Personae

1. Anna Marie and Edward Frysinger in the US: immigration and census records, US National Archive, Washington DC.

2. Frieda and Angelo Ravagli in the US: immigration and census records, US National Archive, Washington DC.

3. Ravagli's last days in Spotorno: *La Stampa*, 14 February 1976.

4. Adrian and Rina in Rome at the outbreak of war and his subsequent internment in Merano and Kreuzburg: taken from Adrian Secker's prison camp diary and Rina Lovioz's war time diary in Merano, Bridgefoot Archive. Obituary of Adrian Secker: in *The Times*, 17 September 1998.

5. 'I am delighted to hear of your marriage': Faith Mackenzie to Martin Secker, from 13c Sheffield Terrace, Campden Hill, London W8, 2 March 1955, Bridgefoot Archive.

6. Barby's breakdown and subsequent marriage, see Brenda

Maddox, *The Married Man*, pp. 515–16. Barby and her husband of a year, Stuart Barr, attended Lawrence's funeral at Taos: Barr delivered the oration because a local judge who was due to do so failed to turn up. Barbara Weekley Barr in Stephen Spender, op. cit., p. 36.

Bibliography

Aldington, Richard: *Portrait of a Genius, But ... The Life of DH Lawrence 1885 to 1930*, Heinemann, London 1951.

Aldington, Richard (ed): *Selected Letters of DH Lawrence*, with an Introduction by Aldous Huxley, Penguin Books, London 1950.

Astengo, Domenico, Duretto, Emanuela & Quaini, Massimo (eds): *La Scoperta della Riviera*, Sagep Editrice, Genoa 1982.

Asquith, Lady Cynthia: *Remember and Be Glad*, James Barrie, London 1952.

Baedeker, Karl: *The Riviera, A Handbook for Travellers*, Leipzig 1931.

Baring-Gould, Sabine: *A Book of the Riviera*, Methuen, London 1905.

Bartoli, Alessandro: *The British Colonies in the Italian Riviera in '800 and '900*, Daner Elio Ferraris Editore, Savona 2008.

Bevilacqua, Alberto: *Attraverso Il Tuo Corpo*, Mondadori Editore, Milan 2002.

Boulton, James T (ed): *DH Lawrence, Selected Letters of DH Lawrence*, Cambridge University Press, 1997.

Burgess, Anthony: *Flame Into Being, The Life and Work of DH Lawrence*, Heinemann, 1985.

Byatt, AS: *The Shadow of the Sun*, Chatto and Windus, London 1964.

Byrne, Janet: *A Genius For Living, A Biography of Frieda Lawrence*, Bloomsbury, London 1996.

Calvino, Italo: *Hermit in Paris, Autobiographical Writings*, translated by Martin McLaughlin, Jonathan Cape, London 2003.

Carswell, Catherine: *The Savage Pilgrimage, A Narrative of DH Lawrence*, Martin Secker, London 1932.

Cenni, Serena and Ceramella, Nick (eds): *Il Corpo, La Fiamma, Il Desiderio: DH Lawrence, Firenze e la Sfida di Lady Chatterley*, Edizioni dell'Assemblea, Florence 2008.

Cerutti, Giuliano: *Vacanze a Spotorno, Storia dell'Ospitalita 1700–1960*, Albenga 2002.

Corsani, Mary: *DH Lawrence e L'Italia*, Mursia, Milan 1965.

Delaney, Paul: *DH Lawrence's Nightmare, The Writer and His Circle in the Years of the Great War*, The Harvester Press, Sussex, 1979.

Douglas, Norman: *South Wind*, Martin Secker, London 1917.

Dyer, Geoff: *Out of Sheer Rage, In The Shadow of DH Lawrence*, Little, Brown and Company, London 1997.

Eguez, Maria Luisa, Guglielmi, Laura and Sanguineti, Carla: *Qui e Bello Come Non Mai: In Viaggio con gli Scrittori da San Terenzo a Tellaro*, Agora Edizioni, La Spezia 2000.

Ellis, David: *DH Lawrence, Dying Game 1922–1930*, Cambridge University Press 1998.

Franks, Jill, *Revisionist Resurrection Mythologies: A Study of DH Lawrence's Italian Works*, Peter Lang, New York 1995.

Graves, Charles: *The Big Gamble, The Story of Monte Carlo*, Hutchinson, London 1951.

Hamalian, Leo: *DH Lawrence in Italy*, Taplinger Publishing Company, New York 1982.

Home, Gordon: *Along the Rivieras of France and Italy*, JM Dent, London 1926.

Hough, Graham: *The Dark Sun, A Study of DH Lawrence*, Duckworth, London 1956.

Huxley, Aldous (ed): *The Letters of DH Lawrence*, Heinemann, London 1932.

Kermode, Frank: *Lawrence*, Fontana Modern Masters, 1973.

Kinkead-Weekes, Mark: *DH Lawrence, Triumph to Exile, 1912–1922*, Cambridge University Press 1996.

Lawrence, DH: *DH Lawrence and Italy* (*Twilight in Italy, Sea and Sardinia, Sketches of Etruscan Places*), edited by Simonetta de Filippis, Paul Eggert and Mara Kalnins, with an Introduction by Tim Parks, Penguin Classics, London 2007.

Lawrence, DH: *Lady Chatterley's Lover*, Introduction by Richard Hoggart, Penguin, London 1960.

Lawrence, DH: *The First Lady Chatterley*, Foreword by Frieda Lawrence, Penguin, London 1973.

Lawrence, DH: *John Thomas and Lady Jane, The Second Version of Lady Chatterley's Lover*, Penguin, London 1973.

Lawrence, DH: *The Lost Girl*, Introduction by Richard Aldington, Penguin, London 1950.

Lawrence, DH: *Aaron's Rod*, Introduction by Richard Aldington, Penguin 1950.

Lawrence, DH: *St Mawr & The Virgin and the Gipsy*, Penguin, London 1950.

Lawrence, DH: *The Princess And Other Stories*, Penguin, London 1971.

Lawrence, DH: *The Woman Who Rode Away and Other Stories*, Penguin, London 1950.

Lawrence, DH: *Mr Noon*, edited by Lindeth Vasey with an Introduction by Melvyn Bragg, Grafton Books, London 1985.

Lawrence, DH: *Selected Essays*, Penguin Books, London 1950.

Lawrence, DH: *Selected Poems*, edited by Keith Sagar, Penguin Books, London 1972.

Lawrence, Frieda: *Not I, But the Wind*, Heinemann, London 1935.

Mackenzie, Compton: *My Life and Times*, ten volumes (Octaves One to Ten), Chatto and Windus, London 1963–71.

Mackenzie, Compton: *On Moral Courage*, Collins, London 1962.

Mackenzie, Faith: *More Than I Should*, Collins, London 1940.

Maddox, Brenda: *The Married Man, A Life of DH Lawrence*, Sinclair–Stevenson, London 1994.

Meyers, Jeffrey: *DH Lawrence and the Experience of Italy*, University of Pennsylvania Press, Philadelphia 1982.

Meyers, Jeffrey: *DH Lawrence, A Biography*, Macmillian, London 1990.

Michelucci, Stefania: *Space and Place in the Works of DH Lawrence*, McFarland, US, 2002.

Moore, Harry T: *The Priest of Love, A Life of DH Lawrence*, Penguin Books, London 1962.

Moore, Harry T and Warren Roberts: *DH Lawrence*, Thames and Hudson, London 1988.

Muratorio, Maura: *Daniel Hanbury e la Colonia Inglese di Alassio*, Marco Sabatelli Editore, Savona 2004.

Murray, John: *A Handbook for Travellers in Northern Italy*, London 1843.

Murry, John Middleton: *Reminiscences of DH Lawrence*, Cape, London 1933.

Page, Norman (ed): *DH Lawrence, Interviews and Recollections*, 2 volumes, Macmillan, London 1981.

Preston, Peter & Hoare, Peter: *DH Lawrence in the Modern World*, Macmillan/Cambridge University Press 1989.

Roberts, Cecil: *Portal to Paradise, An Italian Excursion*, Hodder and Stoughton, London 1955.

Roberts, Neil, *DH Lawrence, Travel and Cultural Difference*, Palgrave Macmillan, London 2004.

Rolph, CH (ed): *The Trial of Lady Chatterley*, Penguin Books, London 1961 (re-issued 1990).

Sagar, Keith: *The Life of DH Lawrence, An Illustrated Biography*, Methuen 1980.

Sagar, Keith: *DH Lawrence, A Calendar of His Works*, Manchester University Press 1979.

Secker, Martin: *Letters From a Publisher 1911–1929 to DH Lawrence and Others*, Enitharmon Press, limited edition of 350 copies, 1970.

Secker, Martin (ed): *Letters From DH Lawrence to Martin Secker 1911–1930*, privately published limited edition of 500 copies, 1970.

Spender, Stephen (ed): *DH Lawrence, Novelist, Poet, Prophet*, Weidenfeld and Nicholson, London 1973.

Squires, Michael: *Lawrence and Frieda, A Portrait of Love and Loyalty*, Andre Deutsch, London 2008.

Squires, Michael & Talbot, Lynn K: *Living at the Edge, A Biography of DH Lawrence and Frieda von Richthofen*, University of Wisconsin 2002.

Swinnerton, Frank: *Swinnerton, An Autobiography*, Hutchinson, London 1937.

Thomson, George Malcolm: *Martin Secker and Warburg, The First Fifty Years*, Secker and Warburg, London 1986.

Tomalin, Claire: *Katherine Mansfield, A Secret Life*, Penguin, London 1988.

Vallero, Silvio and Ferrari, Pietro: *La Baia di Lorenzo*, Edizioni Cinque Terre, 2012.

Waterfield, Lina: *Castle in Italy*, John Murray, London 1962.

Worthen, John: *DH Lawrence, The Life of an Outsider*, Penguin Books, London 2005.

Worthen, John: *DH Lawrence, The Early Years 1885–1912*, Cambridge University Press 1991.

RICHARD OWEN was the Rome correspondent of *The Times* for 15 years. He was previously the paper's correspondent in Moscow, Brussels and Jerusalem, and also served as Foreign Editor. Owen has written several works of non-fiction including *Crisis in the Kremlin: Soviet Succession and the Rise of Gorbachov*, and *Letters from Moscow*.

ISBN 978-1-907973-98-7

NORTHERN

ITALY